D1106798

Twayne's Theatrical Arts Series

Warren French
EDITOR

Luis Buñuel

Luis Buñuel directing *Tristana* (1970).

Luis Buñuel

VIRGINIA HIGGINBOTHAM

University of Texas

BOSTON

Twayne Publishers

1979

Luis Buñuel
is first published in 1979 by Twayne Publishers,
A Division of G. K. Hall & Co.

Printed on permanent/durable acid-free paper and bound
in the United States of America

First printing, June 1979

Library of Congress Cataloging in Publication Data

Higginbotham, Virginia, 1935–
Luis Buñuel.

(Twayne's theatrical arts series)
Bibliography: p. 203–205
Filmography: p. 206–19
Includes index.
1. Luis Buñuel, 1900– 2. Moving-picture
producers and directors—Spain—Biography.
3. Moving-pictures—Spain—Catalogs.
PN1998.A3L86 791.43'0233'0924 [B]
78-24229
ISBN 0-8057-9261-9

Contents

About the Author

VIRGINIA HIGGINBOTHAM was born in Dallas, Texas, and is a graduate of Southern Methodist University. Her doctorate in Spanish is from Tulane University. She has been a member of the Spanish and Portuguese Department at the University of Texas for the past twelve years. She has taught courses in Hispanic Film as well as in Spanish Literature and Surrealism. She is the author of numerous essays on literature and film topics, as well as of *The Comic Spirit of Federico García Lorca* (1976).

Editor's Foreword

THE FIRST OF LUIS BUÑUEL'S FEATURE FILMS that I saw was *Viridiana* during its opening run in New York in 1962. I had heard, of course, the fabulous story of the distinguished exile's being invited after a quarter century back to his native Spain where a gradually relaxing Franco dictatorship was striving to make its cultural peace with a long-alienated world by subsidizing some of the nation's outcast artists. Then there was the story of Buñuel's shooting the film off the cuff and smuggling the reels across the border to be edited in France into a savage satire that would outrage his patrons and result in the Spanish government's refusal to allow the film it had paid for to be shown in the country where it had been made. I knew from the excited talk of others that the ruling Fascist upper class and its principal props, the reactionary Catholic church and the ubiquitous police in their medieval garb, and even its victims, Spain's rural paupers, took a tremendous drubbing.

Still I was unprepared for what happened on the screen—in the way that one can never be quite prepared for Buñuel when he is at his most demonically inspired. *The Miracle* decision was already ten years in the past and the uproar over Otto Preminger's innocuous *The Moon Is Blue* and Elia Kazan's less innocent but hardly less campy *Baby Doll* were some years behind us, but still the American cinema was timorous about those subjects supposedly never discussed in polite society—sex, religion, and politics. To see *not* the noisy but emptily banal lampoonings of such sacred cows in Richard Brooks's *Elmer Gantry* (1960, cautiously based on a Sinclair Lewis novel from the 1920s), but a deadly serious picture that unremittingly and unflinchingly placed before us the sociologically and psychologically disastrous consequences of prurient sexual attitudes and anachronistic religious and political institutions—and that at the same time was both outrageously funny and artistically masterful—was to have an experience that reawakened one's concept of the power and possibilities of the screen.

Luis Buñuel has been providing this kind of artistic shock treatment for half a century, whenever he has had the opportunity, which is not nearly so frequently as he should have.

Already a legendary figure in 1930 at the age of thirty, this inspiriting genius of the twentieth century's distinctive medium would deserve a place in this series solely on the basis of the three short noncommercial films he was by then responsible for—*Un Chien andalou*, *L'Age d'or*, and *Las Hurdes* (*Land without Bread*); yet he was not able to sign another film as distinctively his own until 1947 when he at last found a refuge in Mexico. There he turned out seventeen pictures by 1960. Although lamented by some aficionados as of an uneven merit that represent a waste of genius, this Mexican group includes at least one film, *Los olvidados* (*The Young and Damned*, 1950) that, although unsparingly grim, is a timeless work of art, one of the greatest masterpieces in its medium; and, as we are gradually beginning to get acquainted with the others, we are discovering that each bears some distinctive stamp of Buñuel's genius.

What not even the most optimistic prophet or devoted admirer would have dared to predict as he wandered dazed from his first exposure to *Viridiana*—which was looked upon by most critics as a kind of twilight triumph and vindication by a sadly neglected genius—is that beginning at age sixty, Buñuel would turn out a series of films that would eclipse the work of many of his contemporaries and earn him his deserved place as one of the century's greatest creative figures. (By the time they are sixty—if they have survived—the work of many of the most outstanding artists has begun to deteriorate. In film alone, some critics think that D. W. Griffith did his last important work at forty-nine; Chaplin, at fifty-eight; even the still very active Alfred Hitchcock, at sixty-one.) Anyone who had speculated that there lie ahead *The Exterminating Angel*, *Tristana*, *The Phantom of Liberty*, *That Obscure Object of Desire*, and what deserve to be called the two greatest masterpieces of surrealism in any medium—*Belle de jour* and *The Discreet Charm of the Bourgeoisie*—would have been thought mad.

As has been observed with wonder, there is nothing else quite like this accomplishment in the history of cinema; I am not sure that there is anything remotely comparable in any art. Has ever an artist moved after age sixty from working in comparative obscurity with limited resources in a country out of the mainstream to claim at last his place beside the giants?

I can still recall the incommunicable pleasure of continuing to "discover" Buñuel—*El* in one of the revival houses that made Berkeley a unique oasis in the 1960s, *Belle de jour*, with an audience stunned to silence in a middle-class suburb of Kansas City, *The Discreet Charm* in a packed and wildly enthusiastic holiday season house in New York's Little Carnegie, *Los olvidados*, with a classroom full of deeply moved students, *Las Hurdes* at last in my own living room, since this grotesque classic has joined a library of landmark films that it is possible to collect. Somehow I remember much more vividly than with other pictures just where I first saw a Buñuel film, for there is something about the experience that makes it special and that charges with significance the place where it occurs, like the narrator's placement of the ordering jar in slovenly Tennessee in Wallace Stevens's poem "The Anecdote of the Jar." There is no need to explain why Buñuel must be represented in a series of books like this one devoted to the great creative forces in the performing arts; he is rather one of those who has made such a series possible and justified.

To do justice to such a figure is a challenging assignment to which Virginia Higginbotham has proved equal. I have found her study completely absorbing. Buñuel might be approached in many ways; but she has wisely observed that *one* of his great distinctions is providing the outstanding and perhaps the only substantial body of work in any art that has remained consistently surrealist. Andrew Sarris in *The American Cinema* calls *Belle de jour* "the purest expression of surrealism in the history of cinema"; this claim can be extended to the statement that Buñuel's films constitute the purest expression of the surrealist vision in any form. Virginia Higginbotham thus makes a valuable and necessary contribution to understanding his work by concentrating on the intellectual backgrounds out of which it springs and the usually misunderstood nature of the surrealism that it expresses.

Focusing on the masterpieces of recent years, she explores the ends toward which Buñuel has employed his means to arrive at this well-considered tribute, "It may be for the first time, one of the great moralists of the century happens to be a filmmaker." If there is anything that this century of indifference and alienation on the part of sensitive persons and clamorous fatuousness on the part of self-proclaimed messiahs has needed, it is a moralist with a fresh vision, unyielding tenacity, and uncompromising integrity. How a person with this extraordinary combination of qualities has, despite obstacles that would have defeated a lesser person and destroyed nearly anyone's sense of humor, maintained his composure and ironic detachment and embodied his rare qualities in a unique group of films that are fully as entertaining as they are thought-provoking is the story that this book has to tell.

W. F.

Preface

LUIS BUÑUEL is among the three or four most universally recognized Spanish artists of the twentieth century, along with Pablo Picasso, Pablo Casals, and Federico García Lorca. His generation, which came to maturity only to fall victim to the Spanish Civil War, included the poets Lorca and Rafael Alberti, Jean Miró, Salvador Dalí, and a host of lesser-known artists, writers, and scholars considered the most gifted in Spain since the seventeenth century. Yet the genius of contemporary Spain may prove to be none of the artists of this glittering array of talent, but the man who helped initiate an art form, the filmmaker Luis Buñuel.

This book serves not only to introduce the films of Buñuel to those unfamiliar with them, but also seeks to discuss the director's major themes and cinematic techniques. Going beyond the summary of movie plots, this study analyzes the visual style of the films and the preoccupations which lie beneath their narrative surface.

A discussion of literary and artistic movements might seem ornamental in a study of most film directors. Yet Buñuel's origins are so deeply rooted in the literary and artistic activity of his day, and his vision is so typically Spanish, that full appreciation of his mind and art is incomplete without delving to some extent into these reservoirs from which he draws throughout his career. Thus Chapters 1 and 2 provide a background of the Spanish heritage and childhood experience from which Buñuel emerged. It also considers in some detail surrealism and the Spanish vanguard, both of which are directly responsible for the achievements of Buñuel's early films. Chapters 1 and 2 also summarize the historical events leading to the hiatus and long stagnation of his career that made Buñuel's beginning seem even more spectacular.

The resurrection in Mexico of Buñuel's directing activities and his confrontation with the demands of commercial filmmaking are the central focus of Chapter 3. His Mexican period has, until recently, been the most misunderstood of his entire production because of the inaccessibility of these films. Now that some of them are more readily available, reports of their abysmal inferiority must be revised, for they include works of high quality such as *Essay of a Crime: Archibaldo de la Cruz,* a fresh and enduring work of film art. Yet the period as a whole remains an apprentice performance, an uneven but steady perfection of his craft.

The delayed development and prolonged apprenticeship which seemed to snuff out Buñuel's career may help explain the staggering fact that almost all of his mature films may be described as works of mastery, not only of technical problems, but of the expression of his thoughts and humor. Each of the eleven films analyzed in Chapters 4 and 5 has its weaknesses but represents in some measure Buñuel's unique and forceful contribution to filmmaking.

Buñuel's career spans the history of cinema. Just as film first turned to other art forms, primarily to novels and plays, for inspiration, Buñuel's work emerged from literary, cultural, and artistic traditions which he never abandons. Buñuel's films are never merely expressions of visual art. His disdain for, yet mastery of, film technique is, in fact, renowned. Yet Buñuel's manipulation of visual images in unexpected ways is always done in order to bring new understanding of what he considers to be our violent, destructive, fatally conformist society. Just as the art of portraiture was never the same after Goya's devastating rendering of the visages of the Royal Family, cinema has had to acknowledge the shocking and merciless satire of Buñuel who is, in many ways, Goya's twentieth-century heir.

Throughout this book, page references otherwise unidentified are to Jose Francisco Aranda, *Luis Buñuel: A Critical Biography* (1975). Passages of dialogue from the films, unless otherwise credited, are translated directly from the sound track.

The author acknowledges with gratitude the valuable assistance of MacMillan Audio Brandon and Azteca Films for making copies of Buñuel's films available, and the help of the staff of Pacific Film Archives, Berkeley, California, in obtaining research material.

Chronology

1900 Luis Buñuel born in Calanda, province of Aragón, Spain, February 22.

1906–1915 Attends Jesuit schools in Zaragoza.

1917 Attends Residencia de Estudiantes in Madrid.

1925 Goes to Paris.

1926 Assistant director, *Mauprat,* directed by Jean Epstein. Meets Jeanne Rucar.

1927 Assistant director, *La Sirène des Tropiques,* directed by Mario Nalpas and Henri Etiévant.

1928 Assistant director, *La Chute de la maison Usher,* directed by Jean Epstein.

1929 Begins shooting *Un Chien andalou* in March, premiere in June. Joins the Surrealist group in Paris.

1930 *L'Age d'or* premieres October 28 at Studio 28. Signs contract with MGM and goes to Hollywood.

1931 MGM cancels contract, and Buñuel returns to Paris.

1932 Ceases contact with Surrealists and returns to Spain to film *Las Hurdes.*

1933 Marries Jeanne Rucar. Works for Paramount in Paris.

1935 Executive producer of Filmófono in Madrid.

1936 Attaché to the Spanish Embassy in Paris. Works on documentaries of the Spanish Civil War. Collaborates with director Esther Schub on *España, 1937.*

1938 Supervises war documentaries in Hollywood.

1939 Joins the Museum of Modern Art Film Department in New York.

1942 Resigns from the Museum of Modern Art.

1944 Producer of Spanish versions of films for Warner Bros. in Hollywood.

1946 Begins shooting *Gran casino* in November in Mexico.
1947 Premiere of *Gran casino*.
1949 *El gran calavera*: shooting begins in June; premiere in November.
1950 *Los olvidados*: shooting begins in February; premiere in November. *Susana*: shooting begins in July.
1951 *Susana* premieres in April. *Los olvidados* wins prize for best direction and International Critics Prize at Cannes Film Festival. *La hija del engaño*: shooting begins in January; premiere in August. Begins shooting *Una mujer sin amor* in April and *Subida al cielo* in August. In March begins shooting *El bruto*.
1952 Premiere in June of *Subida al cielo*, which wins prize for Best Avant-garde film at Cannes Film Festival. *Una mujer sin amor* premieres in July, when shooting begins for *Robinson Crusoe*. Begins shooting *El* in November.
1953 *El bruto* premieres in February. Shooting begins on *Abismos de pasión* in March. *El* premieres in July. Begins shooting *La ilusión viaja en tranvía* in September.
1954 Begins shooting *El rio y la muerte* in January. Premiere of *La ilusión viaja en tranvía* in June; *Abismos de pasión* premieres in July. *Robinson Crusoe* premieres in the United States in July. Serves as juror at Cannes Film Festival, with Jean Cocteau presiding.
1955 Begins shooting *Ensayo de un crimen* in January. Premiere of *El río y la muerte* in February. *Ensayo de un crimen* premieres in April. Begins shooting *Cela s'appelle l'aurore* in August.
1956 Premiere of *Cela s'appelle l'aurore* in May, of *La Mort en ce jardin* in September.
1958 Begins shooting *Nazarín*.
1959 Begins shooting *La Fièvre monte à el Pao* in May. *Nazarín* premieres in June, wins Gold Medal at Cannes and the André Bazin prize at Acapulco Film Festival.
1960 Premiere of *La Fièvre monte à el Pao* in January. *La Joven* premieres in London Film Festival, in November, wins honorable mention at Cannes.
1961 *Viridiana* premieres in May at Cannes, where it shares Gold Medal.
1962 *The Exterminating Angel* premieres in May. Awarded prize

by International Film Critics; wins Grand Prix at Rassegna del Cinema Latinoamericano in Sestri-Levante.

1963 Begins shooting *Le Journal d'une femme de chambre* in October. *Exterminating Angel* wins André Bazin Prize at Acapulco Film Festival.

1964 Premiere of *Le Journal d'une femme de chambre* in March.

1965 *Simón del desierto* wins International Film Critics Award and Silver Lion of St. Mark at Venice Film Festival.

1966 Begins shooting *Belle de jour* in October.

1967 *Belle de jour* premieres in May. Wins Golden Lion of St. Mark at Venice Film Festival.

1968 Begins shooting *La Voie lactée* in August.

1969 *La Voie lactée* premieres in March. Begins shooting *Tristana*.

1970 *Tristana* premieres in March.

1972 *Le Charme discret de la bourgeoisie*. Shooting begins in May, premieres in September.

1974 *Le Fantôme de la liberté*.

1977 *Cet obscur objet du désir*.

1

Apprenticeship: The Formative Years

Biographical Notes

EVENTS AND CIRCUMSTANCES OF BUÑUEL'S YOUTH have, to a large extent, determined the nature of his art. Ordinarily uninteresting facts, such as his parents' ages when married, are, in his case, pertinent. That his father was forty-seven when he came home to Spain from America and married a beautiful teenager just turned seventeen may help explain why relationships between older men and young women *(Viridiana, Tristana, The Young One)* interest Buñuel.

Like the Spanish painter Goya, Luis Buñuel was born near Zaragosa, the capital of the province situated in the region of Aragón. His father, who fought in Cuba in the 1898 conflict between Spain and the United States, returned to marry and settle in Calanda, a village sixty-nine miles southeast of the provincial capital. Buñuel recalls that his childhood "slipped by in an almost medieval atmosphere."[1] Contributing to this atmosphere, which pervades Buñuel's art, is the legend of the Miracle of Calanda, which gave Buñuel's birthplace a certain notoriety. The legend of Calanda has it that in 1640 a young man's faith in the Virgin was so strong that his leg, lost in an accident, was restored to him after he rubbed oil from a prayer lamp on his right thigh where the leg was amputated. This legend may help explain why Buñuel's interest in Tristana's leg so far exceeds that in the novel on which *Tristana* is based.

Perhaps the strongest influence on the young Buñuel was his Jesuit education, which began when he was eight and extended into his adolescence. The educational program followed by the Jesuits at that time was essentially designed in 1773—an austere routine be-

The figure of Death from Fritz Lang's Destiny (Der Müde Tod, *1921), the film that led Buñuel to dedicate himself to cinema.*

ginning with obligatory Mass, recited, of course, in Latin. The catechism students were required to memorize was the Astete version, which dates from 1599. Mass was followed by a frugal breakfast, then classes. After classes, students lined up to march in absolute silence to the open patio of the school building, where they were allowed recreation. Although he was a good student, eight years of discipline and dogma produced in Buñuel a profound sense of revolt and rejection: "At sixteen I lost my religious belief," the filmmaker admits.[2] This sense of rebellion is later mirrored in his portrayals of such religious characters as Nazarín and Viridiana.

The importance of these years is difficult to over-estimate. The young American audiences of today to whom Buñuel's anticlericalism seems by now a dead issue are generally unaware of what it is like to mature in a country whose official religion has been vigorously established and imposed to the exclusion of all others for centuries. That Buñuel's religious training produced in him a taste for blasphemy and revolt is not particularly uncommon, for, as a Spanish saying goes, "Blasphemy is only a form of thinking for any intelligent Spaniard." While he rejected the church, Buñuel looked forward to church holidays, which meant returning to Calanda, where his family owned land and kept a house. He often participated in the activities of Holy Week, celebrated in Calanda by the procession of drums which accompanied ceremonies and parades for four days and three nights. Thus the drum rolls on the sound tracks of such films as *Simon of the Desert* and *Nazarín* were part of Buñuel's childhood experience. As in the processions in Calanda, the drums in these films announce the gravity of events about to occur.

Not all of Buñuel's boyhood was discipline and rigor. His special joys were music—he began playing the violin at thirteen—and theater. Among the anecdotes his sister recalls, one of the most revealing is of Buñuel's productions of plays with a theater set brought to him by his parents from one of their frequent visits to Paris. The characters included in the set were a King, a Queen, a Jester, and Courtiers. To this regal cast, Buñuel added a lion and a replica of the Eiffel Tower. His sister's account reveals her brother's discretion and diligence in the preparations, which he began a week before the shows. "He rehearsed with his chosen ones who, as in the Bible, were few, though many were called" (pp. 18–19). Only those who had reached the age of twelve were invited to the productions, held in the barn.

Another of Buñuel's early passions, along with music and theater, was animals. His sister affirms that "we all loved and respected everything that lived, even vegetable life. I believe that they also love and respect us. We could walk through a forest of wild animals, . . .without fear of molestation." Even spiders, which they considered "horrid and fearful monsters," became a favorite topic of family discussion due to "a strange Buñuelesque morbidity" (p. 20). The collection of animals to be found in the Buñuel household was truly wide-ranging and included monkeys, parrots, snakes, toads and frogs, a ram, a hatful of mice, and a rat that lived in a parrot cage and which, in spite of its treatment "as one of the family" (p. 19), was poisoned and died a martyr's death. Buñuel's love of animals has never faded and is apparent in most of his films, in which one creature or another makes an unexpected appearance. Just as the cook in the Buñuel home who was surprised to find an African lizard in the house, astonished critics wonder at the meaning, for example, of a bear and a flock of sheep in *The Exterminating Angel* or the insect in *Archibaldo de la Cruz*.

The most important legacies of his rural Spanish upbringing and his Jesuit education are what Buñuel calls the "two basic sentiments of my childhood, which stayed with me well into adolescence. . .a profound eroticism, at first sublimated in a great religious faith, and a permanent consciousness of death" (p. 13). The ambiguities of passion and the enormous sexual energy expressed in Christian piety and submission are among some of Buñuel's most characteristic motifs—from *El*, whose opening scene is a foot-washing ceremony in church accompanied by organ music, to later masterworks such as *Belle de jour* and *Tristana*. Death, although less an obsession than eroticism, is important in Buñuel's films as the frequent result of the violence his personages inflict on each other and themselves.

Any synthesis of biographical information such as this omits a complete panorama of the artist's boyhood years, to mention only those details which bear directly on his later works. What seems most important in retracing Buñuel's early upbringing is that it was not, for a Spaniard, especially remarkable. In his perception of love and death as the two strongest preoccupations of youth, Buñuel insists that he was "not an exception among my compatriots, since this is a very Spanish characteristic" (p. 13). As he points out, the art of his country is rich in eroticism and profoundly preoccupied with death.

Finishing his preparatory education at age sixteen, Buñuel was uncertain of what he wanted to study. His chief interests were music and natural history. Determined that his son would not study music, a career often leading to starvation, Buñuel's father urged him to seek a degree in agricultural engineering at the University of Madrid. Thus, in 1917, Buñuel, whose upbringing in provincial Spain meant that he had not yet "been a part of modern society," journeyed to Madrid "as a crusader who suddenly found himself on Fifth Avenue, New York City" (p. 21).

The Spanish Vanguard: 1917–1925

Madrid in the 1920s was a center of intellectual activity that Buñuel was eager to join. Any interest he may have had in agricultural engineering soon vanished. Having always been intrigued by insects, he turned to entomology and studied for a year with the director of the Museum of Natural History in Madrid. But soon he realized that he preferred "to chat with my friends in the café rather than to sit at the table with the microscope" (p. 22) at the museum. His group of friends included such young men as Rafael Alberti, García Lorca, and Salvador Dalí, who were to be numbered among some of Spain's best poets and painters of the century. They had a decisive influence in the formation of Buñuel's mind and art, for it was they who awakened in him new interests and made it possible for his life to take a new direction.

Buñuel changed his field of study from engineering to humanities, so that by the time he graduated and left for Paris in 1925 his cast of mind and attitudes toward art were fully formed. A panoramic review of Madrid in the 1920s is not appropriate here. But to understand how Buñuel left Spain with sufficient artistic maturity to make his most revolutionary film before he met Breton and other surrealists, who proclaimed it as a surrealist work of art, it is necessary to review the influences with which Buñuel came in contact in Madrid and their role in shaping his conception of art.

Artistic innovations began to invade Madrid soon after the First World War. One of the first and most receptive minds to receive new signals from abroad was that of Ramón Gómez de la Serna, whose literary cenacle held forth at the Café Pombo beginning in 1915. Into this gathering, which Ramón referred to as the "Holy Crypt of Pombo," were welcomed some of the most original minds of the day. Since 1919 Ramón had been writing what he called "*greguerías*," epigrammatic little statements composed, he said, of humor and metaphor. The *greguerías*, which reduced poetry to its essential element, the image, helped dispense with the distinctions between prose and poetry and thus prepared the way for the surrealist prose poems which began to circulate in the 1920s. It was with Ramón that Buñuel planned some of his first film projects, none of which was ever realized.

At home, Ramón occupied an extraordinary room whose walls were papered with photographs and from whose ceiling hung spheres covered with bits of mirrors. Littering the room were objects of all sorts which he had found at the flea market. Ramón's constant companion in this room was a mannequin of a woman whose garb he changed, or eliminated, according to his whim. This remarkable man published an avant-garde literary journal and gave lectures that were more like performances, one of which he delivered from a trapeze, another from the back of an elephant. Buñuel's irrepressible humor finds its most immediate antecedent in Gómez de la Serna, whose mannequin may have suggested the one that Archi dresses to look like his girl friend in *Archibaldo de la cruz*.

The innovative and bizarre displays of Ramón Gómez de la Serna were followed by other, more theoretical vanguardist movements, such as the *creacionismo* of Vicente Huidobro, the Chilean poet, and its successor, the *ultraísmo*, of Gerardo Diego. If *creacionismo* represented the incorporation of Cubism into Spanish poetry, *ultraísmo* was a synthesis of various vanguardist theories, including Cubism, Dadaism, and Futurism. Publishing, in 1918, one of the few manifestoes of the Spanish vanguard, the *ultraístas* continued to expand the vocabulary of poetry to include mathematical and scientific terms. The *creacionistas* had dismissed sentiment as unworthy of a builder of poems. In place of tears and lamentation, the *ultraístas* substituted the language of geometry and physics. They gave their books such titles as *Hélixes* and *Seafoam Handbook*. This detachment and preference for scientific attitude rather than sentimentality later found its way into surrealism and helps to account for what critics describe as Buñuel's curious objectivity in scenes such as the death struggle between scorpions and a rat in the opening frames of *L'Age d'or*.

Ultraísmo sustained the interest of Spanish writers for about four years. During this time dozens of small literary magazines appeared and disappeared in Madrid. When one of the most significant of the journals, *La Gaceta literaria*, was established in 1927 by the poet-critic Guillermo de Torre and Giménez Caballero, Buñuel was chosen as film editor and was given a page devoted to film criticism.

Since 1922, Buñuel had contributed prose pieces to literary journals. Some of his writings are important indicators of the extent to which he had absorbed the avant-garde ideas of his generation. He shared a poetic vocabulary strikingly similar to that of his friend the poet García Lorca. Lorca, in a brief sketch entitled "Santa Lucía y San Lázaro" (1927), was writing images suggested by the human eye: "Saint Lucy's eyes in the sea, in the watch-face. . .in the stump of the just-felled tree."[3] In the same year, Buñuel wrote a prose poem called "Ice Palace" in which he, too, is intrigued with eyes, especially his own: "Only in a puddle the eyes of Luis Buñuel were croaking" (p. 255). Thus, while literary variations on the theme of eyes had been published in Spanish avant-garde magazines, the opening shocker of an eyeball being severed in *Un Chien andalou* was entirely new in film.

Images of mutilation were already part of the surrealist lexicon. Lorca, for example, had, in 1925, written a film scenario, *Buster Keaton's Walk*, in which the famous clown stabs his four children. In 1927, Lorca wrote two more prose poems on the theme of decapitation. Buñuel experiments with similar images of gore and mutilation in several prose sketches, including "The Comfortable Watchword of St. Huesca," in which the central figure is a lump of meat. The lump of meat appears metamorphosed in many forms—walking, vomiting, and hanging from the cross where St. Huesca was crucified. Twenty years later a lump of meat appears with similar autonomy in *Los olvidados*, signifying both physical and emotional hunger.

After a period of gestation during which the Spanish vanguard was engaged in rich and varied activity, surrealism, by far the most fertile and productive of the vanguard movements, began to emerge slowly in Spain. Arising in Paris from the ashes of Dada and christened in 1924 by André Breton in his first *Surrealist Manifesto*, surrealism encountered much resistance in Spanish literary circles.

Objective assessment of surrealism in Spain has only recently begun, so that the importance of the movement in Spain is not yet entirely understood. Two points, however, are clear: surrealism in Spain was not an organized movement as it was in France and it was cultivated sporadically, even defensively, by poets at different moments. Some students of surrealism in Spain find its influence only marginal. Others maintain that Spanish writers not only produced surrealist works of artistic merit but inherited an artistic tradition from Goya, Galdós, and Valle-Inclán, which provided them with precedents in the same way that Lautréamont and Rimbaud inspired their French heirs, Breton, Eluard, Soupault, and Aragon.

Spanish artists were undoubtedly influenced by French surrealists. Translations of Lautréamont's *Chants de Maldoror* in 1909 and of Rimbaud's poems in 1919 were followed by Louis Aragon's speech at the Residencia de Estudiantes in 1925, in which he announced himself as a "germ carrier, a public poisoner"[4] come to spread the spirit of revolt. In 1928, Dalí and two other Catalán artists issued their *Catalán Anti-Art Manifesto*. This document addressed itself to the state of Spanish art, which it found to be putrefied. The signers of the *Manifesto* listed names of artists of diverse groups whom they admired, including the French surrealists Breton, Eluard, and Aragon.

An accurate measure of the true importance of surrealism in Spain has been complicated by, among other things, the reticence of Spanish poets to acknowledge it. García Lorca sent copies of his violent prose poems to a friend but warned that they were not surrealist works. Although Spanish poets generally rejected "automatism," they experimented with other surrealist techniques, so that their interest in violence, images of decay and mutilation, juxtaposition of disparate objects, and cultivation of illogic and chaos is apparent in their experimental writing. The greatest works of the Spanish vanguard—Lorca's *Poet in New York*, Alberti's *About Angels*, and Aleixandre's *Swords like Lips*—are closer to the surrealist aesthetic than to any other.

There were, of course, differences between Buñuel and members of his generation of poets. Buñuel, for example, detested the sixteenth-century baroque poet Góngora, to whom Lorca and other writers paid special homage. He also decried the kind of poetry his friends wrote based on traditional Spanish verse and folk ballads. Both Buñuel and Dalí severely criticized Lorca's *Gypsy Ballads* as an example of a token compromise between traditional poetic forms and modern aesthetics. Buñuel, in fact, expressed his disgust for what he considered the dandyism of those poets from the South of Spain in an unpublished book of poems, *Andalusian Dogs (Perros andaluces).* This title was changed to the singular form to correspond to the portrayal of the often-infantile main character in *Un Chien andalou*, a film which has been described as Buñuel's biography of his own Generation of 1927.

If Buñuel disdained the poetry of Lorca, Alberti, and Cernuda as lacking aggressive independence from the art of the past, there was one enthusiasm he shared in equal measure with his colleagues—the cinema. In 1925, Lorca prepared his scenario *Buster Keaton's Walk* for presentation at a film showing at the Residencia de Estudiantes. Buñuel arranged for films to be viewed at the Residencia and later, in 1928, helped establish one of Europe's first film clubs there. The American comedies of Chaplin, Keaton, and Harry Langdon especially intrigued the audience of young intellectuals at the Residencia. Rafael Alberti, who later wrote poems to the heroes of the silent comedies, admits that, while he stopped going to the theater, "it was the cinema that really intrigued me."[5] In 1927, Dalí published an article entitled "Art Film-Anti-Art Film" which he dedicated to Buñuel. This article expresses reservations about the avant-garde "art film" and its evasion of reality. "The best intentions of Man Ray and Fernand Léger derive from an inexplicable, fundamental error. . . the possibilities of photography and cinema lie in this unlimited fantasy which comes from concrete things ['things themselves']." Here, a year before *Un Chien andalou,* Dalí expressed the theory, basically surrealist, that film should exploit the fantasies of reality itself rather than that of contrived abstract shapes. "Only anti-artistic cinema, especially comic cinema, produces films . . . of intense and entertaining vitality," declared Dalí.[6] With this essay Buñuel's collaborator announces the aesthetic of one of the most revolutionary films yet made, *Un Chien andalou.*

Buñuel shared Dalí's conception of the possibilities of cinema. His thoughts about his own future, however, were less certain, for he left Spain in 1925 without the slightest notion of what he was going to do. His father's death lifted career obligations from him, and his mother gave him the freedom—both with money and consent—to follow his own inclinations.

If Buñuel had in mind no clear direction when he arrived in Paris, he had definite notions of what art should do and the forms it should take. He confesses that he momentarily vacilated with his Spanish colleagues about surrealism—"At one moment I laughed at it." Yet, like they, he had read Lautréamont, listened to Breton, and had published prose poems that closely reflected surrealist aesthetics. Thus it was that, even before he left Spain, Buñuel, according to his own admission, was "already half surrealist."[7]

Buñuel's formative years within the Spanish vanguard provided him with the theories, the poetic vocabulary, and the attitudes toward art that were the basis for his first phase of filmmaking. The themes and images, his early literary experiments, even the title of his book of poems, were those he was to elaborate in his visual art. When he arrived in Paris, Buñuel quickly set about acquiring what he did not learn in Spain—the technical knowledge of filmmaking.

Paris: 1925–1930

Buñuel recalls that he spent his first months in Paris reading newspapers. He also learned French and English and went to movies. His pretext for coming to Paris was to seek a position with the International Institute for Cultural Cooperation, for which a Spanish friend and diplomat had recommended him. Through another Spanish friend Buñuel met the pianist Ricardo Viñes, who helped him get his first job as set director for a stage production of *El retablo de Maese Pedro*, with music by Manuel de Falla. It was only after arriving in Paris and seeing Fritz Lang's *Destiny* that, realizing the enormous potential of film as an art form, he decided to make films (p. 32). His Spanish friend and colleague, Guillermo de Torre, coeditor of the avant-garde magazine *Ultra*, introduced him to Jean Epstein who, like Buñuel, had contributed to *Ultra* and was one of the most promising and imaginative young directors of silent film.

Jean Epstein, who shared Buñuel's background in literature and science, was one of the earliest theoreticians of the cinema. He had worked in the laboratory of Auguste Lumière who, with his brother Louis, projected the first film before a public audience in 1895. After collaborating on the official documentary of the life of Pasteur, Epstein had become celebrated because of his mobile camera work in *Coeur fidèle* (1923). When Buñuel met him, Epstein was forming what he called his "Académie du cinéma," a group of interns who learned their trade by helping him make films. Buñuel was invited to join this group, and thus he began his career as an assistant director. To understand how Buñuel became known as an innovator with his first film, it may be helpful to review what other directors of the day were attempting to do.

Buñuel assisted in directing Epstein's *Mauprat* (1926) and *The Fall of the House of Usher* (1928). The latter, based on Poe's horror tale, was filmed on location in England. Its dark passion, controlled violence, and the resurrection of Lady Usher were not without appeal to Buñuel. By this time, however, Epstein had become captive of an impressionistic style dependent upon melodramatic use of lighting and visual flamboyance. Soon he began neglecting content for form and relied on technical tricks to enliven uninspired scenes.

Epstein's interest in light and motion was shared by other avant-garde filmmakers, such as the Cubist painter Fernand Léger, and Man Ray, the American expatriate photographer. These two artists translated their ideas into film language and brought fresh visual imagery to the new medium. Léger's *Le Ballet mécanique* (1924) was the first example of *cinéma pur*, independent of any narrative, while Ray's *Emak Bakia* (Basque for *Leave Me Alone*), with its unrelated imagery and juxtaposition of the conventional and the bizarre, is among the first surrealist films. Repetition in this film of sequences of action—a woman's legs getting out of a car three successive times and a close-up of sheep interrupting a scene of a car driving down the street—announce the playful appearance in *Exterminating Angel* of a bear wandering up the stairway of the Nobile mansion and other scenes that are inexplicably repeated.

Events are also repeated in René Clair's *Entr'acte* (1924), a short piece made to be shown between the two acts of a Dadaist ballet. Based on a script by the Dada painter and poet Francis Picabia, *Entr'acte* became famous for its hilarious final scene in which a hearse drawn by a camel goes out of control and speeds downhill, spilling its coffin. The procession of mourners following the hearse hurries to keep up, but the mournful trek is transformed into a chase reminiscent of those of the American comedies. Having seen *Entr'acte*, Buñuel remarked, years later, upon the predictability of a coffin scene in Ingmar Bergman's *Wild Strawberries*.[8]

Among the most innovative directors of the day was Abel Gance, who, though not considered avant-garde, brought far-reaching technical experiments to the screen. In 1915 he shot a film about a hallucinatory drug through a distorting lens, the first of many attempts to produce special effects. Gance also pioneered the use of multiple screens, and his idea of strapping the camera to the cameraman's chest while filming *Napoléon* anticipates the recent *cinéma verité*. Gance also developed the use of very rapid cutting, with which he conveyed a character reliving an experience in *La Roue* (1923).

From Gance Jean Epstein had learned much of what he knew of film technique; so, when Epstein suggested one day that, as his apprentice, Buñuel make himself available to Gance, he was amazed by the adamant refusal of a neophyte to work with one of the giants of the film industry. Fired on the spot as an arrogant upstart, Buñuel was again on his own. He began following more closely the activities of surrealists and planning with Dalí the script for his first film.

Buñuel did not share the opinions on filmmaking of the avant-garde directors of his day. In fact, *Un Chien andalou* was made in protest of the reliance upon photographic tricks that produced skillful but empty cinema. Buñuel's film aesthetic was based on the conviction that bizarre angles, superimposition of images, and flamboyant tricks were distractions to be controlled, and his lifelong work continues to reflect this view. Rather than the visual innovations of the avant-garde, Buñuel's models were films such as *Greed, Destiny,* and *Fantomas*, all variations on themes of horror. In 1927, Buñuel wrote admiringly of Erich von Stroheim's *Greed* (1923) as "the most unsettling, daring, and jovial of all that cinema has been able to produce." Scenes of the lovers' first kiss while standing by a sewage outlet and the murder surrounded by the glitter of Christmas decor in the story of an alcoholic were, to Buñuel, "Magnífico, repugnantemente magnífico."[9]

The film that made Buñuel (and, it is said, Hitchcock) dedicate himself to cinema, Fritz Lang's *Destiny*, is a series of three episodes about the inevitability of death. The refined cruelty of the film's Venetian tale, the cool restraint of the most moving scenes, and the ambiguous ending of *Destiny* all became characteristic of Buñuel's style. Most of the action takes place within a dream in which a young girl attempts to win her lover's life by outwitting Death. The girl fights against overwhelming odds, but fight she must. Lang's philosophy seems to be that one must combat the enemy, but without illusions, an attitude Buñuel later expresses in his treatment of the three ascetics, Simon, Viridiana, and Nazarín.

Other early films which may have influenced Buñuel include

Witchcraft Through the Ages (1921), a documentary tract by the Danish director Benjamin Christensen which presented a mixture of humor and the macabre with cool detachment. This film was a favorite of the surrealists, as was Louis Feuillade's *Fantomas* (1913), the crime thriller whose master criminal went about his hideous deeds in black cowl and cape.

Buñuel's earliest models were not the avant-garde experiments but commercial neo-realism and horror films. Along with the American comedies which he knew and loved, the horror movies pictured passion, violence, repressed desires, and criminal instincts—topics of great interest to the surrealists but topics that were no longer being dealt with imaginatively. With all the new photographic techniques, the abstract elements of film itself—motion, lighting, and spatial arrangements—superseded human passion in the films made by avant-garde poets and painters. Jacques Brunius, Buñuel's collaborator on *L'Age d'or*, points out that the importance of *Un Chien andalou* was that it restored content to films increasingly preoccupied with form.[10] The presentation of the content of *Un Chien andalou*, of course, was illogical and chaotic, determined by surrealist aesthetics.

Buñuel's statement that *Un Chien andalou* would not have existed without the surrealist movement, [11] probably applies to his entire *oeuvre*; for, although he associated with surrealists in Paris for only about a year, Buñuel's lifelong preoccupations are the fundamental principles of surrealism. "In 1929," he recalls in his autobiography, "I entered the Surrealist group of Paris. Its moral and artistic intransigence, its new social political field, fit perfectly with my temperament" (p. 56). A brief review of some of the attitudes to which Buñuel refers may provide some keys to understanding the major themes of his art.

Surrealism was a philosophy, a means of perceiving reality founded by André Breton, ex-medical student and avid reader of Freud. He dedicated the movement to the investigation of dreams and their application to reality. His goal was the fusion of two apparently contradictory states of mind—waking and dreaming—into what he called "surreality."[12] Surreality is of primary importance in Buñuel's film art, for it accounts for his use of symbols. Objects in Buñuel's films have both literal and symbolic meaning. Just as surrealist poets sought as exact a language as possible, mirroring the sharpness of dream images, Buñuel, too, avoids generalizations and abstractions. His symbols relate directly to reality, yet they often reflect the surrealist axiom that reality is multiple, and signify more than one meaning. Much of the richness of Buñuel's art derives from his deliberate use of ambiguous symbols which illustrate his conviction that there is no chosen, definitive, or absolute reality but many emerging and often contradictory realities.

The surrealist notion of surreality, in which dreams and waking action fuse into one state of mind, particularly lends itself to cinematic treatment and becomes one of the basic tenets of Buñuel's style. The symbols, visions, and dream sequences of, for example, *Los olvidados, Viridiana,* and *Belle de jour* are as "real" as the waking states of the characters who experience them. Adopting Breton's view that these two states should be seen as parts of a whole, Buñuel films his characters' dreams and hallucinations with the same realism and detail as he does their waking action. Confusing the viewer by making dreams indistinguishable from waking states, Buñuel conveys his belief that the two states of mind have equal importance and reality.

The investigation of dreams opened the way for the expression of desires repressed by a society guided by reason and convention. Revelation of these desires accounts for the surrealists' preoccupation with eroticism and its many forms and variations. Foot-fetishism, displayed in *L'Age d'or* by a woman sucking a statue's toe, is one of Buñuel's most frequent erotic motifs, and images of feet and legs flash constantly through *Los olvidados, El, Diary of a Chambermaid,* and *Viridiana.*

Not only dreams but other irrational states of mind including hysteria, madness, sleepwalking, and hallucination interested surrealists as sources of knowledge as legitimate as reason. Following Freud's thought, surrealists found irrational and spontaneous emotions the driving force of conscious life. Thus, for Breton, beauty did not exist except as an electrifying force, "convulsive," in his words, and love must be mad passion *(l'amour fou).* The symbols of unfettered emotion were often, for surrealists, embodied in animals. In addition to Buñuel's personal fondness for animals, their prominence in his films may in part derive from their special significance in surrealist symbolic language as creatures unconcerned by such notions as propriety and restraint. The young bear who noisily ascends the stairs in *Exterminating Angel* and the grasshoppers, both in *Archibaldo de la Cruz* and in the hand of Simon of the Desert, are innocents, free spirits in a world of protocol and repression.

Inevitably, preference for fantasy over reason in a rationalistic society led to conflict. Surrealists opposed every conventional value and institution, including, before long, some "narrow-minded revolutionaries" who hampered their attempt, as Breton stated it, "to give mankind some faint idea of its abilities and to challenge it to escape its shackles,"[13] by which he meant to break up conventional social, moral, and artistic habits of thought and perception.

Surrealists, then, were devoted to revolution, and from this basic attitude derives the spirit of revolt that runs throughout Buñuel's art. *Un Chien andalou* was, as Ado Kyrou described it, the first "film non-attractif"[14] because of its directors' contempt for conventional standards of art. Buñuel's declaration that his first film was nothing but "a desperate cry for murder" (p. 63) voices the surrealists' hostility, not only toward society, but toward the preoccupation with technical as opposed to spiritual values displayed in the avant-garde cinema of the 1920s. Throughout his life Buñuel, to the consternation of his cinematographers, has disdained use of exaggerated camera angles, melodramatic lighting, picturesque landscapes, and any other visual distraction from the ideas he is trying to convey. Maintaining his indifference to any ideology that compromises his art, Buñuel revealed his priorities unmistakably in a declaration in 1958: "To my way of thinking there is not one indication in . . . recent years, either 'capitalist' or 'communist,' that encourages any hope of the spiritual improvement of cinema unless it be in its technical aspect, where the progress of both is unquestionable."[15] This reply, written in answer to a questionnaire, clearly reveals Buñuel's consideration of technical concerns as secondary in importance compared with content. He refuses, as did Breton, to forsake artistic integrity in the interest of either of the prevailing political ideologies. The anticlerical, antiartistic, iconoclastic form and content of Buñuel's early films follow naturally from the surrealists' opinion that prevailing political, social, and moral institutions were hopelessly decadent.

The "crise de conscience" which Breton hoped surrealism would provoke is also the objective of Buñuel, who uses the cinema to coincide with Breton's goal, stated in the second *Surrealist Manifesto*, "to expose . . . the factitious character of the old contradictions hypocritically calculated to hinder every unusual agitation on the part of man . . . "[16] Buñuel's methods range from shock and revulsion to humor, of which he has always been a master. Surrealists were especially fond of using humor as a weapon to combat hypocrisy and convention, finding easy targets within a pompous society. In his famous *Anthology of Black Humour*, Breton pays tribute to the wit of authors such as Swift, Lewis Carroll, and Kafka and identifies black humor as an expression of revolt. *Un Chien andalou* was, according to Buñuel, only a series of gags. It was the first of many films whose searing social criticism is delivered by means of parody, caricature, irony, and the comic grotesque.

Surrealism is the philosophy on which Buñuel's vision of life rests. As a radical critique of society and intellectual traditions, surrealism provides a point of departure for the director's corrosive views of human endeavor. Yet surrealism is not an entirely negative force: Buñuel also gained from it a moral sense. In 1954 he wrote, "It is surrealism which has revealed to me that in life there is a moral code from which man cannot extricate himself. It has enabled me to learn for the first time that man is not free. I believed in the absolute liberty of man, but I have seen in surrealism a discipline to be exercised. This has been a great lesson in my life as well as a marvelous and poetic step forward."[17] If Buñuel's images of decay and dismemberment express the surrealists' disgust with bourgeois society, his moral outrage derives from that of the surrealist movement, which explored new ways to reveal the human character.

The ideal medium for conveying the surrealist view of life was, according to some, the cinema. In an article entitled "Cinema and Surrealism" (1925), René Clair voices tentative hope that "even if the cinema cannot be a perfect medium of expression for surrealism, it still remains, in the spectator's mind, an incomparable field of surrealist activity."[18] An anonymous remark in the April 1925 issue of *Surrealist Revolution* expressed similar faith in cinema as "la mise en oeuvre du hasard." Breton's practice of dropping in at movies, leaving when he began to tire of the action to go to another, and so on, indicates the kind of film surrealists were seeking—a constant succession of images without theme or narrative structure. This is what they were offered by René Clair in *Entr'acte*, in which the antics of American comedies were combined with defiance of the laws of logic. Things in the film are never what they appear to be—a chessboard becomes the Place de la Concorde, and cigarettes line up to become the Parthenon—a principle which coincides with the surrealist belief that reality is multiple.

Surrealists did not always agree on what constituted a good film, but they all liked Charlie Chaplin and generally disliked *La Coquille et le clergyman (The Seashell and the Clergyman)*. This film, based on a script by Antonin Artaud, was intended to be a surrealist work, but it proved to be a self-conscious effort. The story of the temptations suffered by a celibate priest was not photographed realistically but with exaggerated angles and photographic tricks which made it appear pretentious. There were other surrealist films, such as Man Ray's *L'Etoile de mer (The Starfish)* based on Robert Desnos's poems featuring a starfish as the central motif. None of these films, however, struck the surrealist cenacle, or the public at large, with the unexpected force of *Un Chien andalou*.

When the showing of *Un Chien andalou* was announced by Studio 28, André Breton, who had never heard of the two directors, assumed that they were impostors and gathered his troops to plan a demonstration against the film. Georges Sadoul, in an interview years later with Buñuel, recalled that Breton instructed his followers to appear at the Studio and make as much noise as possible, as they had done the previous year at the showing of Germaine Dulac's *La Coquille et le clergyman*. "But at the last moment," explains Sadoul, "André Breton felt some scruples. Before the demonstration he went to see your film completely alone in a dark overcoat. He returned enthusiastic."[19] Thus *Un Chien andalou* represents the credentials with which Buñuel entered the cenacle of French surrealists rather than the product of his association with it.

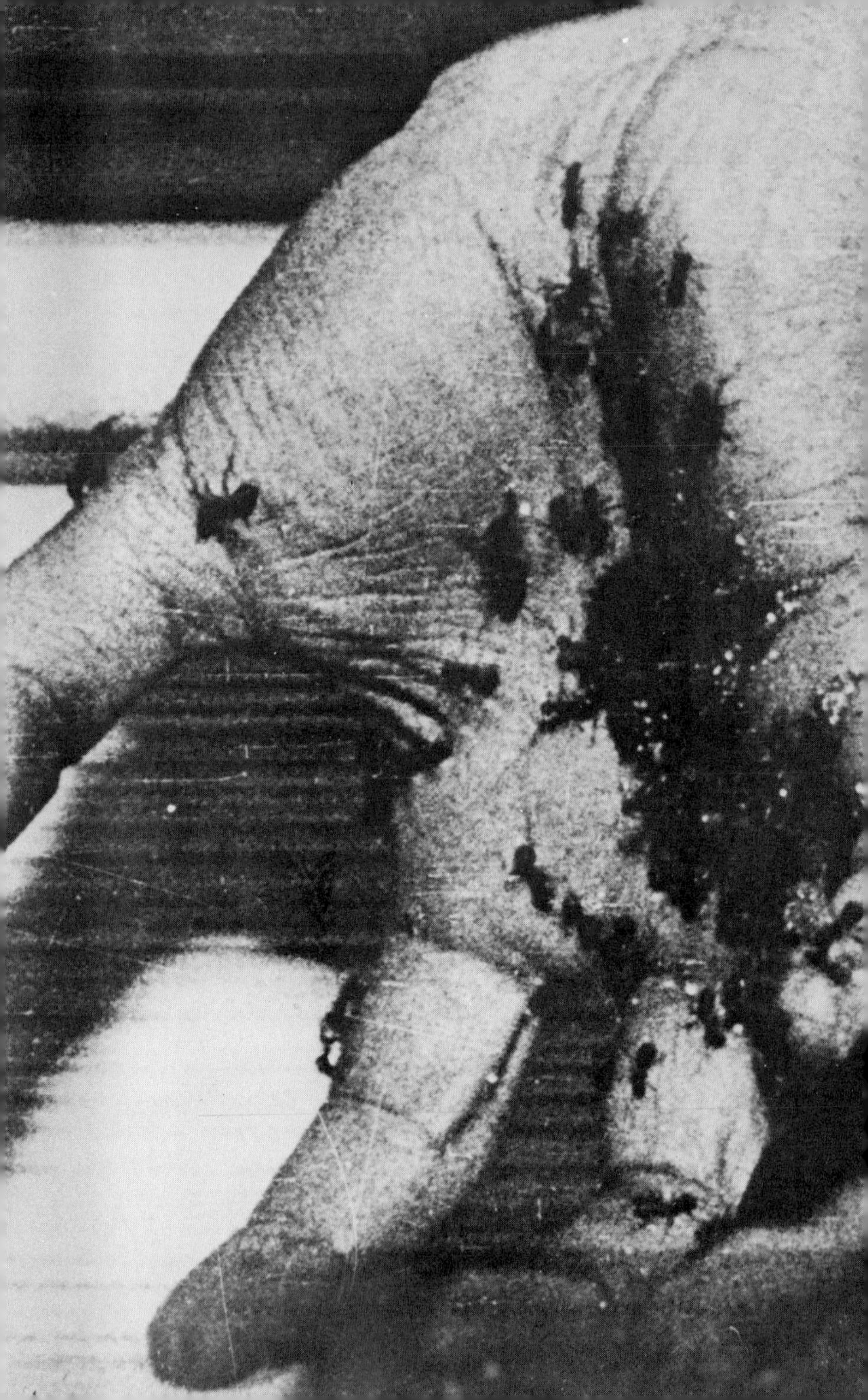

2

The Heroic Exploration and The Silent Years

An Andalusian Dog (Un Chien andalou) (1929)

IF, as Jacques Brunius states, avant-garde film paralleled in the film industry the role of the opposition in politics,[1] then *Un Chien andalou* was a revolutionary act aimed at convention, both social and cinematic. Expecting audience outrage at such a blatant attack, Buñuel attended its debut armed for defense with pockets full of pebbles. To his amazement, the work was greeted not with anger but applause. One member of the audience, Cyril Connolly, remembers that viewers were stunned: "With the impression of having witnessed some infinitely ancient horror, Saturn swallowing his sons, we made our way out into the cold of February, 1929."[2] Connolly's perception of horror has often been echoed by viewers and critics, yet, like the Mona Lisa's smile, *Un Chien andalou* has given rise to a staggering range of interpretation. "A poem" for Freddy Buache,[3] it is "an incoherent film" for Fréderic Grange.[4] Jacques Brunius's feeling that the work comes near to being a dream[5] is echoed by Raymond Durgnat, for whom it is "seventeen minutes of pure, scandalous dream-imagery."[6] Buñuel's special target may have been film critics, in the view of J. H. Matthews, who finds *Un Chien andalou* "an attack upon systematization in film commentary."[7] Buñuel himself was less than helpful when he wrote in 1947 that "nothing in the film symbolizes anything."[8]

What did it all mean? In his autobiography, Buñuel is more enlightening: "In the film are amalgamated the aesthetics of surrealism with Freudian discoveries. . . . Although I availed myself of oneiric elements, the film is not the description of a dream. On the contrary, the environment and characters are of a realistic type. Its fundamental difference from other films consists of the fact that the

A famous emblem of surrealism from Buñuel and Salvador Dali's Un Chien Andalou *(1928).*

characters function, animated by impulses. . . . At times these characters react enigmatically, as far as a pathological psychic complex can be enigmatic" (pp. 56–58).

As *Un Chien andalou* contains no dogs and no Andalusians, the title remained a mystery until recently when Buñuel's biographer, comparing the director's unpublished poems entitled "El perro andaluz" with the film, has offered a plausible explanation. Buñuel, protesting his Spanish colleagues' admiration for Góngora and their lack of social awareness, wrote the violent poems of "El perro andaluz" denouncing the cult of beauty his friends still served. By changing the definite article of the title, Buñuel stressed that he was not writing the "psychopathological biography of a specific poet, but of the southern group, as a social entity."[9]

The famous opening sequence of *Un Chien andalou*, a close-up of a razor slicing a woman's eye, has, no less than the title, aroused infinite speculation on its meaning. Buñuel stressed its formal function: "To produce in the spectator a state which could permit the free association of ideas, it was necessary to produce a near traumatic shock at the very beginning of the film; hence we began it with a shot of an eye being very efficiently cut open. The spectator entered into the cathartic state necessary to accept the subsequent events of the film" (p. 67).

No doubt the scene is, so to speak, an eye-opener. Strategically placed as the first image of the film, it establishes violence as the tenor of the work. As a surrealist scene, its symbolism is multiple, but one of the most evident meanings of a blade slicing an eyeball is that of rape. Raymond Durgnat goes only so far as to find cutting "a destructive activity,"[10] without taking into account the sexual significance of a male (Buñuel himself, in fact) wielding the razor on a woman. Two French critics, however, explore different meanings of the image. Xavier Gauthier recalls that Freud interpreted fear for the eyes as castration fear;[11] Pierre Renaud finds that the repugnance of the image, together with its sexual connotation, may be a justification of homosexual behavior.[12] While this renowned opening image suggests several possibilities of sexual violence, the only certainty is that the image is not, as J. H. Matthews asserts, "gratuitous."[13] It serves as the opening salvo for a series of scenes, or gags, as Buñuel called them, dealing with erotic fulfillment and death.[14] In spite of the apparent incoherence of *Un Chien andalou*, the film is almost anecdotal in the presentation of its narrative.

The scene of mutilation which serves as a prologue is introduced by the famous first line of fairy tales, "Once Upon a Time." The echo of tradition Cyril Connolly noted when he spoke of having witnessed something ancient may have been stirred by this line, but in *Un Chien andalou*, this echo is ironic, announcing not a familiar legend but an excruciating view of laceration. The exposition which follows continues the tone of violence. The central character, an unnamed cyclist, is an anonymous young man on his way through life. He wears over his suit articles of clothing denoting effeminacy—a large white collar, a short white skirt, and a white cap pinned in his hair. When he falls from his bike, a young woman runs to comfort him. The next scene, in which the woman contemplates the cyclist's clothes laid out upon the bed, suggests that the wearer, being absent, is not adequately fulfilling his role. The young woman turns from the bed to find the cyclist terrified by what he finds in his hand: ants, recalling the cliché "itching with desire." The young man desires the woman, but she is fearful and uncertain. Playful visual metamorphosis of a woman's underarm hair into a sea-urchin serves as a transition into the next sequence—another disturbing scene focusing again on a hand.

An androgynous young woman, surrounded by a crowd of onlookers, pokes a severed hand with a stick. The onlookers, perhaps reflecting society confronted with sexual ambiguity, are angry and must be restrained by a policeman. The androgyne clasps the striped box, which the cyclist has worn about his neck. The cyclist and his girl friend watch from a window while the androgyne picks up the hand and puts it into the box as if depositing a treasure. She is obviously protecting the mutilated member, an act which may establish her as the personification of sexual anxiety and fear. The cyclist, still watching, becomes increasingly excited. When the androgyne is flattened by a passing car, he becomes pensive, then sexually aggressive. Fondling his girl, our hero appears to be in ecstasy, blood running from the corner of his mouth. But as he advances, he is foiled again, this time not by his own fear, but by the detritus with which cultural conditioning has burdened him. He pulls the now-infamous load of two priests, lying prone and praying aloud, two pianos, and two putrid donkeys. While he struggles to cope with this hilarious concoction, the girl escapes. Seeing her go, he drops everything and runs after her, but it is too late. His hand is caught in the door and he is back where he started—anxious, with ants crawling from the palm of his hand, servile, and dressed in frills.

A title, deliberately dislocating time, introduces the next sequence: "Towards Three in the Morning." A new character appears, apparently bringing memories of childhood and punishment to the fearful cyclist. The man insists that the cyclist remove his frills and striped box (the protective case for his fragile sexuality, the severed hand). Perhaps recalling school discipline, the cyclist is now made to stand against the wall. Another title appears, "Sixteen Years Before," as if to push farther back into the cyclist's memory. The stranger walks toward a school desk, picks up two books, and hands them to the cyclist. The books, possibly suggesting more cultural dead-weight, suddenly turn into revolvers and the young man, now armed, faces his intimidator as an angry young man who turns his acquired knowledge into weapons against his oppressors. He shoots, and as the stranger falls we see that he is the cyclist's double. His efforts to defend himself against intimidation have destroyed him. As he dies, he envisions the back of a nude female. He tries to grab her, but he falls. Some men come and carry away his corpse unceremoniously. He remembers his girl friend and sees her room, but then the camera zooms in on a spot on the wall which turns out to be a death's-head moth, an ominous sign. The girl friend appears glad to be rid of him, anyway, and sticks out her tongue as she leaves. She meets a new man, virile, self-assured, confident, and handsome. They kiss and walk along the beach, kicking aside the cyclist's frills that litter the rocks below their feet.

Love, however, does not triumph. *Un Chien andalou* ends as it began, with an ironic subtitle. Far from announcing renewal of love, the title "In the Spring" reveals a scene of slow death. The two lovers are up to their chests in sand, at the mercy of the elements and of insects that begin to crawl over them. Thus love, impossible to express because of inhibitions, finally blossoms only to be buried in the sand.

Un Chien andalou, which lends itself to multiple interpretations, was hailed by surrealists as the first example of *cinéma automatique*, a free-flowing sequence of images uncontrolled by logic. Previous directors had suggested psychological states by means of distorting lenses, superimposed images, blurred focus, and other photographic devices. Buñuel was the first to film visions and fantasies in what Claude Beylie describes as "a rather prosaic realism."[15]

Buñuel's innovation was not so much his imagery—images of eyes, including mutilated ones, can be found in the poems of the Spanish surrealist Juan Larrea and in the early prose poems of García Lorca. But Buñuel's rendering of mental states such as hysteria, fear, ecstasy, and dreams with the same realistic treatment of, say, buying a loaf of bread, was a creative invention supremely achieved in *Un Chien andalou*.

Buñuel's first film, however, is not merely a technical innovation but also a highly personal vision of its director's experience of reaching maturity in Spain. Dalí and Buñuel, holding the same artistic views, sadly watched their generation, the best of Spain's poets of this century, struggle with the past and become defensive about adopting new art forms. Nor is it coincidence that the cyclist's load contains priests, for the presence of religion in Spain is inescapable, even to those who reject it. While themes of eroticism and death predominate in *Un Chien andalou*, its undercurrent of social and religious satire did not escape the notice of Jean Vigo, who did not hesitate to call it "a film of social consciousness."[16] Even the donkey carcasses are reminders of days spent in Madrid. On walks to the outskirts of the city Buñuel and his friends often viewed dead and dying animals dumped, as old cars are now, by their owners and left to rot. Thus *Un Chien andalou*, a milestone in the history of cinema, emerges from its director's adolescence in Spain and announces the themes and techniques that were to preoccupy Buñuel for half a century, through the rest of his career.

The Golden Age (L'Age d'or) (1930)

If any film produced more outrage than *Un Chien andalou*, it was its successor, *L'Age d'or*. This time Buñuel seemed to have gone too far. While *Un Chien andalou* had been a personal vision of erotic obsessions and anxiety, *L'Age d'or* went beyond the personal to indict social institutions and beliefs that repress individual spontaneity. Reaction to *L'Age d'or* was violent: its first showing provoked loud protest and ink was thrown on the screen. Public outcry and official prohibition of it caused surrealists to rally to its defense and publish their most complete statement on film art, the "Surrealist Manifesto on *L'Age d'or*." This aggressive document hails *L'Age d'or* as the moral equivalent of the stock-market crash, a herald of epidemic social decay. The surrealists saluted Buñuel's portrayal of love as a passion that would transcend depression and pessimism: "The step from pessimism to action is determined by love." By love the surrealists meant passion unrestrained by social convention and capable "of total sacrifice: position, family, honor."[17] In short, they hoped love would generate passion strong enough to act as a weapon against conventional morality.

While attacking the establishment at large, *L'Age d'or* also reflects the upheaval taking place within the surrealist movement. Until 1930, the official surrealist publication had been called *The Surrealist Revolution*. As militance increased, the group changed the title to *Surrealism at the Service of the Revolution*. This spirit of open revolt accounts for the shift from inner monologue in *Un Chien andalou* to the wider social scope of *L'Age d'or*. Deep commitment to social revolution not only caused a schism in surrealist ranks but also set the course for Buñuel's art. If erotic desire in *Un Chien andalou* appears as a cause of personal frustration, in *L'Age d'or* it becomes a means of social attack.

That the theme of *L'Age d'or* is wider than "an admirable and unique appeal to love," as described by Ado Kyrou,[18] is apparent in the film's prologue and final sequence, both of which express convictions about society and human nature in general. The documentary-style prologue treats the viewer to the scene of a death battle between two scorpions and a rat. The only clue to the meaning of these frames is in the accompanying titles which read like lines from a textbook on arachnids. One such title states that a scorpion which has just attacked another is "not at all sociable."[19] The viewer of this zoological prologue is repulsed. By subtle analogy between insect and human behavior, Buñuel, who knows how to use documentary for moral purposes, announces the violence that continues through much of *L'Age d'or*.

The scorpions and their victim, the rat, do not seem unlikely creatures to introduce this film. The following scenes are of a group of bandits reduced to animaloid existence who barely manage survival on a desert island. Like the inhabitants of *Las Hurdes*, his next film, they suffer from untreated wounds, malnutrition, pain, and hunger. Their leader stares, like the feebleminded of *Las Hurdes*, at one of his comrades who is dying and wonders how he and his men will confront a group of Majorcans who approach the island. The bandits' vain effort to mobilize themselves ends with their total collapse in exhaustion.

The group of people identified as Majorcans arrive on the island.

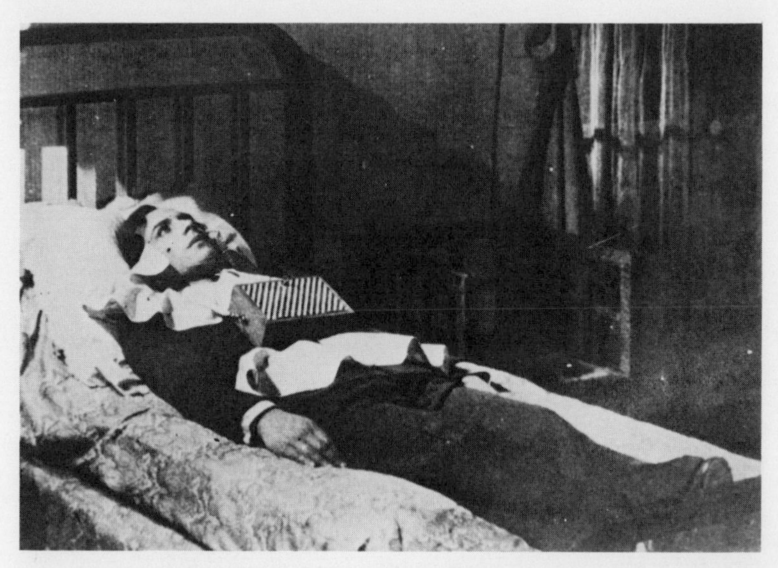

Key scenes in two surrealist classics: (above) The man with the striped box in *Un Chien Andalou;* (below) The bishops become skeletons in *L'Age d'or*.

Their visit is introduced by one of Buñuel's most famous images—the four archbishops who after blessing the beach, decked in their ceremonial robes, soon turn into skeletons in the sand, their mitres still tight on their skulls. The scene strongly suggests the conquest by Spaniards of some distant New World reef, claiming it for God and King. The Majorcans are all members of the establishment and include priests, army officers, and a government official. The assemblage gathers to pay respect to the mitred skulls on the rock and to listen to a speech by the governor. Suddenly, however, the ceremony is interrupted by screams of people witnessing a scandalous act: two lovers roll about in a mud puddle, embracing passionately. It is unmistakably a case of *l'amour fou*, or mad passion, the kind of joyous paroxysm in which surrealists place their hope for the renewal of energy misspent on conventional behavior.

The forces of social order quickly stop this erotic frenzy. The man is handcuffed and led away as the ceremony proceeds and the Majorcans dedicate a stone to the four bishops. The governor places a little pat of cement on the stone and, as the camera zooms in for a close-up, we see the cement is in the form of excrement, recalling the throne of excrement on which the Creator sits in the second Canto in Lautréamont's *Maldoror*. The Majorcans' stone is not only commemorative, but is the foundation of a city. As an aerial view of Rome is flashed on the screen, the implied analogy between the Christian founding of the Holy City upon a rock and the Majorcan excrement piled on the stone is inescapable.

More titles, in the textbook tone of documentary, introduce an ironic travelogue. "A Few Aspects of the Vatican, Firmest Pillar of the Church" announces a view of the Vatican facade as the camera closes in upon the building's architectural detail. A note stuck in a broken window pane indicates that the place is for rent: "I've spoken to the landlord," the note reads. "He's letting us acquire a long lease on very favorable terms." The note ends with the trivia of arranging a rendezvous. Another title announcing the fact that "the Very Ancient Imperial City has joined in the Hubbub of Modern Life" (script, pp. 31–32) is followed by scenes of destruction and traffic congestion. Several visual gags—a man kicking a violin down the street, a bearded man with a stone on his head mimicking a statue in the same pose—add to the comic presentation of the Holy City.

Soon the hero, the man in love, comes into view, still handcuffed between two policemen. Everything he sees—signs advertising ladies' stockings and handcream which display pictures of feminine hands and legs—fires his erotic imagination. A photograph resembling his lover serves as a transition as the scene cuts to the girl's room where she, too, is fantasizing. The girl's parents are having a party and her mother, the Marquise, tells her, "Hurry up, the Majorcans will be arriving at nine o'clock" (script, p. 36). At this point a large Jersey cow is discovered lying on the girl's bed. The girl dismisses the beast as if it were a pet poodle. It lumbers off, the bell around its neck continuing to clink long after it is gone. Like erotic desire, the presence of the cow is impossible to ignore, no matter how hard we try.

The expository segment of *L'Age d'or* ends with a cut back to the street where the hero, insulting passers-by and behaving in a generally surly fashion, finally reveals his identity. Like the director himself, who came to Paris as a delegate to something called the International Commission for Cultural Cooperation, the prisoner pulls from his pocket an official document which names him first delegate of the "International Assembly of Goodwill" (script, p. 43). Thus we find that the lovers, like Buñuel, are members of the same establishment which they have scandalized by their behavior. The policemen are nonplussed and release the hero, who calls a taxi. Taking a last jab at respectability, he runs up to kick a blind man before driving off in the taxi.

The major developments in *L'Age d'or* take place in the third segment, a portrayal of an aristocratic gathering at the mansion of the girl's parents. This scene, perhaps an early prototype for *The Exterminating Angel*, is one in which Buñuel excels. His intimate knowledge of upper-class protocol and conversational trivia is revealed in the understated humor with which he renders this social group. The elite, trained to maintain poise and composure under any circumstances, respond like robots to life. They are oblivious to a series of disasters that interrupt the gathering. No one heeds a farm cart pulling two drunken workers through the ballroom. A valet continues serving punch as a fire breaks out and a servant faints. The gamekeeper murders his son, which momentarily causes varied reactions, none of which last long enough to disturb the proceedings of the party.

Up to this moment in the film, erotic passion has been one of several gags used for shock value. The lovers' frenzied rolling in the mud was followed by the man's onanistic visions of advertising signs, and his kicking a dog and a blind man. These actions, together with one character kicking the violin and another with the stone on his head serve, primarily, as jokes calculated to scandalize. So far, the reaction of the establishment has been predictable. The lovers are separated; the man is arrested and handcuffed.

In the central segment of *L'Age d'or*, eroticism becomes the major preoccupation of the film. Even as predominant action, however, erotic passion concerns the director not as an emotion in itself, but in its social impact. The lovers are reunited at the gathering of the *haut monde* not to continue their love story, which, in fact, ends when the girl transfers her affection to another man, but in order to develop the theme of sexuality as a challenge to conformist and repressive culture. As Morse Peckham has pointed out, the Judeo-Christian proscription of eroticism makes erotic behavior, especially pornography, a well-suited means of cultural attack.[20] Buñuel has, with some pride, agreed that some of his films are pornographic, and *L'Age d'or* makes clear that, for Buñuel, pornography exists as a weapon against conformity rather than as a means of sexual arousal. Yet to suggest genital activity, Buñuel does not resort to nudity. When the lovers at last escape to a corner of the garden, Buñuel resorts to comic resolution of their frustration. The lovers grope each other with such awkwardness that the scene becomes a parody of pornography. When the man leaves to answer an important telephone call, the girl satisfies her desire by sucking the toe of a nearby statue, an entirely harmless but unmistakable substitution for oral gratification. By commercial film standards of today, in which nudity is a stock commodity, Buñuel's subtle porno seems rather circumspect.

The erotic culmination of the action of *L'Age d'or* takes place not in privacy but, as in scenes of previous lovemaking, in the presence of an audience. The Majorcans are seated now before an orchestra. The lovers bite and stroke each other as the conductor directs the musicians performing the death scene from *Tristan und Isolde*. This passionate operatic music heightens the lovers' ecstasy while the polite audience sits unmoved by the tragic sounds. Respectable society, trained by the church to conceive of erotic desire only in terms of reproduction, is determined to ignore what Freud identified as the single most important source of human motivation.

Ignoring erotic passion, however, is not easy, as Buñuel has suggested by the image of the Jersey cow on the girl's bed. The sound of the cowbell is repeated when a pair of guests arrives at the party carrying a religious reliquary with them in their car. Another of Buñuel's most consistent themes, the sublimation of sexuality into religious activity, is evident here. The orchestra conductor, who is described as conducting "with tremendous passion" (script, p. 66), finally succumbs to the emotion of the music. Flinging away his baton he approaches the lovers, sobbing and holding his head. The young woman, apparently moved with pity for the desperate conductor, leaves her lover to embrace and kiss the aging musician.

This scene, with the girl's betrayal of her lover, presents a potentially serious conflict whose outcome could be fatal. But Buñuel avoids melodrama by resourceful use of humor. Using an old gag from comic films, the lover jumps up in protest only to hit his head on a low tree branch. He staggers off, almost unconscious, past the girl and the conductor, now entwined. He soon reappears in the young woman's room in a fit of rage. But instead of trying to kill his rival, a traditional resolution of betrayal, he turns his anger upon whatever he finds in the room. In fury he tosses out the window a series of unrelated objects including a large plow, a flaming tree, an archbishop, and a giraffe. The feathers from a pillow serve as the transition to the final scene of the film. As feathers turn into snow, a medieval castle looms into view.

The high comedy of the lover's desperation now changes abruptly and the horror and savagery of the scorpions and rat are restored. The main characters of this final scene are identified as "four well-known and utter scoundrels" (script, p. 69). The titles used to introduce each new segment of the film describe the four men as libertines and criminals. One, dressed in robes and looking very much like Jesus, is identified as the Duke de Blangis, the murderer in the Marquis de Sade's *One Hundred and Twenty Days in Sodom*. As he steps out of what is described as the Chateau of Seligny, he makes "a gesture of blessing, then clasps his hands together in prayer (script, p. 70). His fellow orgiasts, who have spent the last 120 days in unspeakable depravity in the castle, hobble along behind him. In the original screenplay, these men were identified as President Curval, the Financier Durcet, and "the Bishop of K., dressed like a sixteenth-century priest" (script, p. 71). Thus Buñuel's assemblage includes, as did the group of Majorcans, representatives of political and religious institutions. Their crimes become evident as an adolescent girl stumbles out of the castle, wounded. The Duke, with the tenderness generally associated with Christ, picks her up and assists her back into the castle. A terrible shriek is heard from within and the mock Christ reappears, "tragic piety in his face"; the scene ends with a view of the cross as a kind of trophy stand decorated with "the scalps of many women" (script, p. 71).

In this epilogue, Christianity is deeply implicated in the murder of women and appears as a force which sustains evil. The titles inform us that, to the Duke and his cohorts, "the life of a woman—what am I saying—of one woman, of all the women in the world—counts for as little as a fly's." By traditionally repressing sexual expression and equating it with sin, Christianity not only denies basic human needs but becomes itself a criminal institution cruelly exploiting sexuality for its own purpose. In spite of its cult of the Virgin, Christianity is portrayed in *L'Age d'or* as being composed of a group of orgiasts for whom women are merely victims. The exploitation of women by a depraved Christian morality is a theme that echoes throughout some of Buñuel's best films.

L'Age d'or, which began as a documentary on scorpions and continues primarily as a slapstick comedy, ends with a scene of cruelty comparable to those imagined by de Sade. De Sade is not Buñuel's only model for the orgy scene. God the Creator appears in a similar state in the third Canto of *Maldoror*, where the "Supreme Drunkard," in Lautréamont's phrase, is described as "befouled in the goblets of an orgy."[21] The final, memorable scenes of *L'Age d'or* make clear that this film, as Ado Kyrou explains, is not primarily a cinematic poem of *l'amour fou*[22] but a moral indictment of a culture which represses spontaneous behavior. Sexuality is the dominant example of repression, yet other spontaneous acts are also policed and restrained. A society which represses freedom and innovation is no longer a living entity, but a fossil, as Buñuel suggests by the skeletons of four of its potentates upon a rock. Eroticism unexpressed becomes sadism, as suggested by the figure of Jesus as a criminal tenderly victimizing women. In spite of the laughs provided by the film, the savagery of its opening and closing frames makes this work much more than a surrealist hymn of love. Buñuel's interest lies in passion not only as romantic experience but also as a means of achieving freedom, and *L'Age d'or* is a moral document of the violence with which free sexual expression is met by Western culture.

Aftermath of *L'Age d'or*: More Biographical Notes

Word of *L'Age d'or* traveled fast. The film helped Buñuel secure a contract in 1930, but twelve years later he was denounced and lost his job for having made it. The principal actress in *L'Age d'or* was given a contract by Metro-Goldwyn-Mayer. Buñuel was offered a contract but he refused it, suspicious of the film industry. "I didn't want to be a professional director," he explained. "I used it as a means of expression, but the industry disgusted me."[23] Buñuel agreed to go to Hollywood only as an observer (for which Metro engaged him on a six-months' basis). There he hoped to learn about film production, for Hollywood at this moment was the center of enormous activity; and, as Jacques Brunius notes, even experimental cinema depended for its effectiveness on a basic technique, "equal at least to that of Hollywood." Many European studio technicians, cameramen, sound engineers, and, of course, actors and actresses made their way to Hollywood or, "Neubabelsburg."[24]

Buñuel, however, did not thrive in the Hollywood atmosphere of big studios and star systems. He recalls observing a set where Greta Garbo was working. The star took a look at the stranger on her set and had him tossed out. After this, Buñuel only went to the studio to collect his paycheck. One day an employee of Irving Thalberg, head of Metro, asked Buñuel, since he was Spanish, to look at a film of Lili Damita's. Buñuel insisted he was hired in Paris and made films in Paris, but the supervisor insisted. Buñuel, infuriated, walked out. His contract was canceled, and by April of 1931 he was back in Paris. To the director of *Un Chien andalou* and *L'Age d'or*, the brief sojourn in Hollywood was largely irrelevant. After *L'Age d'or*, reports Pierre Kast, Buñuel wanted to make *Wuthering Heights* and had prepared a script, but it was refused by the producer to whom Buñuel proposed the project.[25]

During this time, Buñuel shuttled back and forth frequently from Paris to Madrid. He sat in a café with a good friend, an anarchist named Acín who wanted to buy a lottery ticket but lacked the cash. Buñuel advanced him the money, but added that if Acín won, he could provide the money for a short film on a backward region of Spain called Las Hurdes. Three months later, Acín won the lottery, paid his friend, and Buñuel's next film, *Las Hurdes (Land without Bread)*, was under way.

Las Hurdes (Land Without Bread) (Tierra sin pan) (1932)

Las Hurdes is Buñuel's consummate horror film, not because it evokes any ingenious thrills, but because its horror is a document of living fact. With his background in entomology and his conviction that the surreal is based on reality itself, documentary seems a fitting mode of expression for the mind of Buñuel. The documentary has interested other experimental directors. Jean Epstein filmed the life of Pasteur in 1925. Jean Painlevé, a biologist who was also attracted to surrealism, aimed the camera through a microscope to reveal micro-organisms in their underwater habitat. The recording of reality was, after all, the first and most obvious use to which moving pictures were put. So when Buñuel was offered financial backing by a friend, the idea of shooting a documentary seemed a natural synthesis of his capabilities as a filmmaker, his antiartistic attitudes toward the cinema, and his astute observations of the reality of Spain.

Buñuel became interested in a doctoral study written by Maurice Legendre on a remote and backward region of Spain called Las Hurdes. Legendre, the director of the Institut Français in Madrid, had visited the region for twenty years, collecting exhaustive notes (1,200 pages, Buñuel recalls) on what he found there. With his crew of four—Eli Lotar, cameraman, Pierre Unik, Pierre Vogel, and Sánchez Ventura—Buñuel went to Las Hurdes. On April 20 he began filming and on May 24 he had completed shooting the footage for what has been judged one of the twelve best documentaries ever made.[26]

Both the narration and the cinematography of *Las Hurdes* are entirely in documentary style, that is, objective, straightforward presentation of fact. Buñuel's observations are primarily of two kinds—socioeconomic and cultural. The socioeconomic facts of life in Las Hurdes comprise the body of the film. We learn that the staple food of the *hurdanos* is potatoes, sometimes supplemented with beans. Only the few who own pigs can afford to eat meat. When a hog is killed, once a year, the meat is gone in three days. The *hurdanos* keep a few goats, but goat meat and milk are reserved for the sick. Bread is not produced in Las Hurdes. Teachers sometimes bring it to the pupils at school, but since their parents do not know what it is, they take it from their children and do not allow them to eat it. In the spring months, when potatoes run low, unripe

The natives of *Las Hurdes:* (above) schoolchildren washing unfamiliar bread; (below) a family of dwarves.

cherries are eaten, causing dysentery to be widespread among the population.

Most of the miseries of *Las Hurdes* are those that basic measures of hygiene and health care would eliminate. Common diseases include, besides dysentery, goiter and malaria. Mental disease is also rampant. Incest resulting from overcrowded living areas and lack of education is so frequent that many of the *hurdanos* are cretins and mental retardates.

This picture of collective degradation is completed by a presentation of the economic plight of Las Hurdes. Too rocky and arid for agriculture, the land is cultivated in small plots with primitive implements. The main productive activity of the area is bee-keeping. The hives, however, are owned absentee and are periodically transported outside the region, thus providing no more than marginal subsistence for the *hurdanos*. Groups of ten to forty men are often seen leaving Las Hurdes to seek work in outlying towns, but as migrant laborers they can only help with harvesting or become beggars. They return, the commentary informs, as they left, without money or bread.

Details of material deprivation, however, provide information only on one level of reality. It is in the cultural facts of Las Hurdes that Buñuel reveals his most profound and moving insights. The documentary begins with a scene entirely as repulsive as those of his first two surrealist films. From a cord suspended across the main street of a village, chickens hang by the feet. Echoing some primitive urge for display of prowess, newlywed males of the village gallop headlong down the street, yanking the heads off the chickens as they pass. This scene of the *hurdanos* at play reveals perhaps better than the views of their misery the savagery to which civilization has reverted in Las Hurdes. For, if the diseases, poverty, and filth in which the people of the area live can be remedied, cultural attitudes such as a taste for cruelty are not as readily controlled and must be molded over a long period of time by the educative process. And the education given the children of Las Hurdes is itself found to be a hideous distortion of values that do not apply to the reality of the place.

In one of the key sequences of the film, children are seen sitting, barefooted and in rags, in front of a blackboard. Buñuel states that, wanting to shoot a scene of a pupil learning to read, "We opened a book at random that we found on a desk."[27] The surrealists' belief that chance reveals destiny is born out when the child goes to the board and writes the passage he takes directly from the random selection from the book: "Respect the property of others." The irrelevance, even the cruelty of an education based on capitalist morality in a world where ownership, even of a crust of bread, is unknown, is the unavoidable conclusion to be drawn from this scene. Thus the film, through irony and understatement, not to mention coincidence, goes beyond documentary to social criticism and indicts a European society so obsessed with private property that starving peasants are fed on capitalist refrains instead of bread.

The role of religion in *Las Hurdes* seems to parallel that of education. The opening shot of the film is of a house over whose door is inscribed "Ave María Inmaculada, conceived without sin" (script, p. 9). Religion, however, has barely left its traces on this forsaken region. A monk, living in a valley with his followers, and the ruins of an ancient monastery are the only vestiges of Christianity in Las Hurdes. In the villages, however, the only reminders of luxury are the churches. Compared with the windowless, one-room, dirt-floored enclosures where whole families live and sleep together on beds of sticks, the interiors of the churches, with their carved wooden altars and paintings, are rich indeed.

Lest the viewer begin to feel that this subhuman existence is being led by a race apart, Buñuel reminds us that the *hurdanos* are like the rest of us, especially in their grief. Unable to feed domestic animals, the *hurdanos* do not own livestock and thus have no means of transport. A father, whose child has died, places the wrapped body in a wooden trough and floats it down a stream to a burial ground. Bodies of adults are strapped on a ladder to be carried to a distant cemetery covered in tall grass where small chunks of wood tied together to make crosses are stuck into the weeds. The film ends as a woman selling prayers for the dead goes down the street ringing her small bell. Advertising her services she calls out, "Nothing keeps you awake better than thinking about death. Say a prayer for the soul of . . . "—as if the *hurdanos* had little else to live for but death (script, p. 15).

What Buñuel has done with documentary has been not only to inventory the medical, social, and economic facts of the lives of an isolated cluster of people. Through meticulous editing and the astounding manipulation of music, he states a case for criminal neglect that he lays at the feet of Western civilization, which prospers not far—sixty miles—away. The books the children use for readers in school show to the ragged waifs a picture of a typical bourgeois woman, wellfed, welldressed, and content. The cause of the malaria which kills many *hurdanos* is so well known that Buñuel includes a sketch of its carrier, the anopheles mosquito, along with the comment that it is found in nearly all the houses of Las Hurdes. By following the shot of the church altar with a shot of the interior of one of the better homes of the region, Buñuel forces the viewer to consider the enormous contrast between the comfortable church and the miserable hovel.

Barely containing his rage, the director relies on the visual facts to carry his message. The commentary departs only twice from its detached narration to underline the obvious. To a scene of dwarfed and deformed retardates the narrator adds that "the degeneration of this race is due principally to hunger, lack of hygiene, misery, and incest" (script, p. 14). The schoolroom scene evokes the narrator's amazement that "these hungry children are being taught, like those everywhere else, that the sum of the angles of a right triangle is equal to two right angles" (script, p. 11). These direct statements, however, do not capture the mind of the viewer with the force of the last scene, in which a view of a family sleeping side by side like a litter of animals is accompanied by music from Brahms' *Fourth Symphony*. The juxtaposition of the exalted music with the degradation of the visual images is a staggering implication that the grandeur of cultural achievement is hollow in the face of such wretchedness. The spiritual uplift of the *Fourth Symphony* is absurd while a segment of humanity is allowed to become the cesspool that is Las Hurdes.

Underlying the moral outrage of *Las Hurdes*, there emerges another theme that preoccupies Buñuel repeatedly throughout his art; that is, the theme of the lost souls, abandoned to their fate in a hostile environment. In *L'Age d'or*, Pemán and his brigands are outcasts, clinging to survival on a desert island. The *hurdanos* have also been abandoned on a cultural island, a kind of no-man's-land, by an indifferent society. They share the fate of the bandits, for there is no rescue in sight for them. While marooned and weak, they grasp at the only help offered from outside—useless abstractions about geometry and private property, and an equally irrelevant religion.

Survival in a hostile world is seen to be the primary effort of the nameless but real characters of *Las Hurdes*. In later works, Buñuel examines the theme in the context of individuals. A small band of hunted refugees escapes into the jungle in *Death in This Garden*. They lose their persecutors only to become victims again, now of insects, hunger, and fear. Ultimately they find only madness and death. Stressing the theme of isolation, two of Buñuel's films are set on islands—Robinson Crusoe masters his environment but struggles with solitude. The political corruption endemic to the island of El Pao, in *Fever Mounts on El Pao*, finally overtakes the ambitious young hero, who has struggled to free himself of it. One of Buñuel's most memorable characters, Simon Stylites, stands in self-imposed exile on the top of a column in the middle of a desert. His preference for refuge from the raucous life of modern society is seen as both futile and absurd. Another self-imposed exile, Nazarín, finds that he cannot both serve humanity and remain aloof from it. Viridiana, too, starts out in the protective isolation of a convent. The faint hope offered by the film is that she appears to gain the courage to leave her mental desert island to join her fellow human beings. By the theme of lost souls Buñuel seems to suggest that neither individuals nor whole societies can remain isolated and retain their full humanity. Survival, he appears to conclude, depends on the ability to remain in contact with human culture.

Las Hurdes not only develops one of Buñuel's major themes, but it is a pivotal work and forms a link between his first two surrealist experiments and his later commercial films. In spite of its pure realism, *Las Hurdes* is a surrealist documentary, for the director forces the viewer to draw conclusions based upon a new awareness of the attitudes he creates. While some critics find that *Las Hurdes* falls outside surrealist aesthetics, most consider it a direct continuation of *Un Chien andalou* and *L'Age d'or*. When asked to explain the relationship between surrealism and his documentary, Buñuel affirmed, "I made *Las Hurdes* because I had a surrealist vision and because I was interested in the problem of man. I saw reality in a different way than I would have seen it before surrealism."[28] If the realism of *Las Hurdes* is far from the dreamlike, chaotic montage of the first two films, this documentary shares with them certain techniques as well as their spirit of revolt.

The visual violence for which *Un Chien andalou* is renowned also introduces *Las Hurdes* and is repeated in the body of the work. The repugnance of the two putrid donkeys of *Un Chien andalou* is transcended by the scenes of the slow death of a donkey carrying beehives in *Las Hurdes*. The loaded beast stumbles and falls, the hives break open, and the donkey, covered with honey, lies helpless while the bees cover his hide. Within a few short minutes, he lies dead from the stings.

The almost didactic use of close-up insect study which introduces *L'Age d'or* is again seen in *Las Hurdes*. While the scorpion prologue suggests an analogy with the human behavior which follows, the lesson on the anopheles mosquito is intended to imply knowledge already so widespread that it is elementary and should thus be applied in *Las Hurdes*, where the insect breeds everywhere.

As Charles Pornon has remarked about *L'Age d'or*, *Las Hurdes* shocks not because of formal virtuosity or visual fantasy but because of its content and meaning.[29] Clearly the intent of *Las Hurdes* is identical with that of *Un Chien andalou* and *L'Age d'or*. As a challenge to a morality that does not respond to basic human needs, Buñuel's documentary is an even more searing indictment of social institutions than either of the first two films. As in the earlier works, Buñuel relies on indirect means to express himself. But through irony, contrasting images, and the narrator's detached tone of voice, the director's intentions are clear. Just as we are not to take *L'Age d'or* for the love story it often appears to be, it is not the horrors of Las Hurdes we are to dwell upon, but the toleration of such horrors by a comfortable Spanish bourgeoisie.

However staggering the reality of *Las Hurdes*, the full meaning of the film does not lie in the physical reality of its images alone. Writing some years later in his autobiography, Buñuel clarified his conception of the documentary: "To my mind there exist two different kinds of documental films: one which can be called *descriptive* in which the material is limited to the transcription of a natural or social phenomenon. For example: industrial manufacture, the construction of a road . . . etc. Another type, much less frequent, is one which, while both descriptive and objective, tries to interpret reality . . . . Such a documental film is much more complete, because, besides illustrating, it is moving . . . . The great majority of documental films lack psychological value. Thus besides the *descriptive* documental film, there is the *psychological* one. I should like the making of documental films of a psychological nature" (p. 127). It is through the surrealist techniques of shock, violence, images of decay, and expression of rebellion against established institutions that *Las Hurdes* conveys the psychological values to which Buñuel refers.

If *Un Chien andalou* and, to a lesser degree, *L'Age d'or*, had perplexed their audiences, everyone understood *Las Hurdes*. It was banned immediately in Spain by the Spanish government and not released in France until 1937. At a semi-private screening at the Palace of the Press in Madrid in 1933, at which Buñuel himself read the narration and played the accompanying music on records, the public was angry. One of the outstanding physicians and intellectuals of the day, Gregorio Marañón, was indignant because Buñuel had not included some of the beautiful architecture that exists in Las Hurdes. His comment only illustrates the point made by the film regarding the insensitivity to suffering that Western culture has developed. Thus with *Las Hurdes*, Buñuel both continues a precedent he had already set and also establishes a new one. Like his second film, *L'Age d'or*, his third, subtitled "a cinematographic essay in geography," was so forceful that officials tried to keep it from the public. In its realism, *Las Hurdes* is understandable not only to sophisticated minds. It speaks directly, as his prior experiments did not, to the general audience. And herein lies the style that Buñuel adapts in his future films, for in *Las Hurdes* Buñuel has put realism at the service of the surreal, the technique with which he later creates the great achievements of his career.

The Silent Years 1933–1946

After his first three films, which have become landmarks in cinema history, Buñuel did not direct a film that bears his name for fourteen years. Such a lapse would doom most artists to lasting oblivion. Pierre Kast, describing this as a noncareer, remarks that there is nothing like it elsewhere in cinema.[30] Yet Buñuel lived one of the greatest survival stories, artistically speaking, of any major creative artist, enduring these long, silent years, perfecting his craft, and emerging from them to produce his best work.

After completing *Las Hurdes*, Buñuel came to see himself as a professional *cinéaste*, yet the direction his career was to take was still uncertain. He admitted his dilemma to Elena Poniatowska: "Finishing *Tierra sin pan*, I decided to dedicate myself entirely to the cinema. . . . I did not want to make professional movies. I used it as a medium of expression, but the industry disgusted me. . . . In Spain then there was no chance of doing things that interested me. I acted as a supervisor and directed without using my name."[31] This statement reveals Buñuel at an impasse. He wanted to make films, but had no interest in meeting the demands of commercial producers. He had, after all, made cinema history with three films seen by only a select, relatively tiny public. His next project, based on one of the surrealists' favorite Gothic novels, *Wuthering Heights*, had been rejected by producers. So Buñuel, without illusions about the film industry and restless after two years spent dubbing dialogues for Paramount in Paris, decided to take on a task he had not yet tried and become a producer himself.

As a Spanish film producer, Buñuel was again something of a pioneer. A friend, Ricardo Urgoiti, who owned a film company, Filmófono, invited Buñuel to produce films for a mass audience. In his autobiography, Buñuel terms the venture an "experiment" (p. 101). The film industry in Spain was still far behind the technical level of Hollywood or Paris, and Spanish filmgoers preferred inconsequential musicals based on traditional Spanish *zarzuelas* rather than imported movies. Buñuel accepted the job with the provision that his name not be used, and began the search for writers, directors, sound technicians, and lighting and cameramen.

The details of Buñuel's two years as a producer have been so thoroughly narrated by his biographer that they need not be repeated here (pp. 100–15). What is important, however, is to understand the impact of this experience on Buñuel's career. The mere fact that the blasphemous young surrealist militant, with three successful and uncompromising films to his credit, was now making musical comedies in Madrid was, on the face of it, stupefying. Yet, his stint as producer of commercial movies was to serve as Buñuel's apprenticeship in addressing himself to a larger audience than he had heretofore reached.

Buñuel found Filmófono a laboratory in which he could gain firsthand experience of every technical procedure. At the same time, he learned the discipline of working within the limits of popular taste. But the experience clearly lacked the flamboyance of his surrealist adventure. Buñuel admired the Spanish farceur, Carlos Arniches, yet the musicals based on his plays—*Don Quintín el amargado* (1935) and *Centinela, alerta* (1936)—broke no new ground. The other two of Buñuel's Filmófono productions, *La hija de Juan Simón* and *¿Quién me quiere a mí? (Who Loves Me?)*, were lackluster melodramas.

Buñuel refers to these four films as "without interest" and insists he has forgotten their titles.[32] Notwithstanding their minimal artistic level, Buñuel's submission to producing musicals and melodramas was an exercise in which he acquired qualities for which his best works are known—control, meticulous preparation, and restraint of the desire to shock the public, which he admits he set out to do in his early works. Although Buñuel attaches no importance to his collaboration in these films, had he not made them, it is doubtful that he would have been selected by Oscar Dancigers to direct films in Mexico; for the first two Mexican films were, like the Spanish productions, musicals, catering to the tastes of the masses. Surely these Spanish films sharpened his talent for humorous exploitation of bad taste, honing it into the sharp instrument of satire it became in later films such as *The Exterminating Angel.*

Buñuel's apprenticeship in commercial film was interrupted by the outbreak of the Spanish Civil War in 1936. In his autobiography, Buñuel states that he dropped his work to offer his services to the Spanish government, which sent him to Paris as an attaché to the Spanish embassy. Here he supervised the compilation of newsreel material of the war into the forty-minute documentary, *España, 37.*[33] A year later, in 1938, the Republican government sent him to Hollywood as a technical supervisor for two documentary films dealing with the war. One of these was to be called *Cargo of Innocence,* an account of the evacuation of homeless children from the ruins of Bilbao to the Soviet Union. With the Republican government suffering increasing defeat, however, these films were never produced.

At the end of the Spanish conflict, Buñuel found himself still in Hollywood and unemployed. Through Iris Barry, director of the Film Department at the Museum of Modern Art in New York, he found a position there making Spanish versions of documentaries for distribution in Latin America. Buñuel was grateful for work and, as he told André Bazin, had hopes of doing great things at the museum. But after four years there, he found that he was merely one of a team and began to chafe at what was essentially a laboratory job of reediting films for a Latin American public. The only work of this period Buñuel acknowledges as his own is *Triumph of the Will,* a short documentary, which was to be included in the *March of Time* cinemagazine series. In this film Buñuel put together footage from two documentaries about Nazi Germany. Scenes from Leni

Riefenstahl's tribute to Hitler, also entitled *Triumph of the Will* (1934), showing the emotional reception of the Führer riding with outstretched arms in an open car, are followed with scenes from Hans Bertram's *Baptism of Fire* (1939) of the systematic and savage liquidation of Poland.

The purpose was to show the enormous disparity between the hope Nazism offered and horrors it actually wrought. The effort, however, was unsuccessful. Buñuel tells of showing his documentary to Chaplin, who "rolled with laughter, pointed at Hitler and said the Führer was a bad imitation of Charlot" (Chaplin's French nickname). René Clair also saw the film and had misgivings about it. It was sent to the White House for official approval, but President Roosevelt agreed with Clair and "it was quietly sent to the archives."[34]

In November 1942, Buñuel resigned from the Museum of Modern Art because, he recalls, Dalí had, in his recently published autobiography, revealed Buñuel's identity as the author of the scandalous *L'Age d'or*. This may be true, for, while *L'Age d'or* brought its director and lead actress offers from Hollywood, it was banned almost everywhere. All known copies were confiscated in Paris in 1930. Yet, in view of its relative obscurity twelve years later—only a handful of people in the United States had seen it—there may be another, perhaps more compelling reason that forced Buñuel to sever relations with the museum. Buñuel must have understood that the position in America of any former member of the Communist party, as he and other surrealists had been for several years in Paris, was, at best, tenuous. Officials at the museum, which was supported by the Rockefeller Foundation, were especially wary of Communists in their midst, and this is probably the reason that Iris Barry unwillingly requested and received Buñuel's resignation. Departing on the day of the tragic invasion of Oran and its port, Mers-el-Kébir, Buñuel recalls that he was too depressed to explain to inquiring interviewers why he had quit.

Buñuel's career had indeed hit bottom. Given the tenor of those years, it seemed unlikely that any former Communist could work unmolested in the United States. To sustain himself, Buñuel narrated documentaries made by the Army Corps of Engineers on such topics as welding, explosives, and airplane parts. An offer to produce Spanish versions of films from Warner Brothers must have seemed attractive by comparison and, in 1944, Buñuel returned to Hollywood.

As an associate producer with Kenneth McGowan, Buñuel was well-paid at Warner's and saved enough money to spend a year at what he really wanted, "to do nothing."[35] Buñuel was not without friends in Hollywood. Two of his surrealist colleagues were there at the time. With one of them, Man Ray, Buñuel planned a script whose title, *The Sewer of Los Angeles,* may have reflected the state of his spirits at the moment. At the home of the other, René Clair, he met Denise Tual, who had helped produce Bresson's *Les anges du peché* in 1943. Her invitation to Buñuel to direct García Lorca's *La casa de Bernarda Alba* seemed to offer Buñuel hope: "I thought the sky was finally clearing."[36] Buñuel was eager to film what he considers the slain poet's best play. But even though he had been one of Lorca's closest friends and had known the poet's brother Paco, the family refused to grant the rights to the film and the project failed. Denise returned to France and Buñuel stayed in Mexico, where he had gone to make final plans for the project which he had to abandon.

For a director in the 1940s to desert Hollywood, mecca of the world film industry, to make movies in Mexico might appear rash and ill-informed. True, Sergei Eisenstein had visited there in 1932 in hopes of filming his abortive *¡Que Viva Mexico!* Yet the country's cinema industry was still marginal. Buñuel's decision to remain in Mexico, however, was not an entirely desperate one. Some of Spain's most distinguished writers and intellectuals, including Max Aub and poet Luis Cernuda, had sought exile there from the Spanish conflagration. Nor was surrealism unknown in Mexico. André Breton had visited there in 1938, bringing with him copies of *Un Chien andalou* and other works of surrealist art, to which Frida Kahlo, wife of Diego Rivera, and other talented Mexican artists had since become attracted. In 1942, another of Buñuel's surrealist associates, Benjamin Péret, and his wife, the immensely talented surrealist painter Remedios Varo, sought refuge in Mexico. Paris was still suffering from postwar shock in 1946, when Buñuel decided to leave the United States. Remaining in Hollywood promised a dismal future. Not only had he never been offered any films to direct there, but Buñuel detested the Hollywood star system and its cult of personality, in which the egos of a few actors and producers dominated all phases of production. Later Buñuel confessed his horror of what he called "l'engranage," the machinations of Hollywood.[37]

The years of silence were, however, not years of total loss for

Buñuel, for it was during this period that he developed two skills which were to mark his art in an important way. As a producer of musical comedies in Madrid, Buñuel not only completed his acquaintance with all aspects of filmmaking, but came to grips with the demands of commercial cinema. The making of *Las Hurdes*, an effort to broadcast information, is an indication that Buñuel, while not enchanted with the film industry, did not wish to spend the rest of his life making thrillers for sophisticated devotees of the avant-garde. His success in reaching a wider public would depend on the by no means simple task of achieving some kind of balance between the demands of commercial producers and his own artistic and moral dignity. Buñuel began to resolve this conflict between popular tastes and his own standards in the context of the *zarzuelas* he produced in Madrid, in which the observant spectator can detect a perverse surrealist humor in scenes which parody popular sentimentality. The necessity to cloak his surrealist vision with the appearance of the ordinary reality to which mass tastes were accustomed had enormous influence on Buñuel's art. This need helped establish his conception of realism, converting his films from chaotic nightmares in surrealist code into realistic narratives in which surrealist imagery is reserved for the delivery of carefully timed but highly charged jolts to the mind of a conventional public.

In addition to learning to express himself within the confines of commercial cinema, Buñuel absorbed much from his work with documentary film, from which he discovered further lessons in the editing of realistic material for the purpose of conveying an implicit point of view.

Buñuel's shift from the role of revolutionary to director of musical comedy was thus not the desertion of values it may have once seemed to his surrealist colleagues. These silent years might be compared to those in the life of a revolutionary who, forced underground, emerges fourteen years later purged of the indulgence of hermeticism and now fully capable of expressing his vision in whatever film language he wishes.

3

The Mexican Films: 1947–1960

BUÑUEL'S LONG ABSENCE FROM EUROPE aroused speculation among his friends that "he had been swallowed up by the commercial cinema of the New World where, in order to earn his living, he was doing obscure and third-rate work in Mexico."[1] Buñuel, in fact, was learning to express himself within the limits of commercial cinema. But, while he made some bad films there, he was by no means being "swallowed up"; nor was he doing strictly third-rate work. Many of his films made in Mexico are inconsequential. Only five of the nineteen films of this period can be considered memorable. Yet, as Carlos Fuentes observed, "No director ever has been able to say so much with so little as Buñuel during his Mexican years."[2] Within the restrictions of popular commercialism and financial restraints that required most films to be shot in two weeks, Buñuel not only directed one of his strongest works, *Los olvidados*, in Mexico, but made four other films there—*Robinson Crusoe, El, Archibaldo de la Cruz*, and *Nazarín*, which have been acclaimed by critics as among the finest of his career.

A glance at the Chronology in the front of this book reveals the uneven ebb and flow of Buñuel's career during his Mexican years. The famed *Los olvidados* was followed by two mediocre melodramas and an amusing farce. The entire fourteen-year period can be said to have ended about as it had begun for Buñuel, with the making of undistinguished movies. Yet, these years were extraordinarily important, for it was during this period that he evolved from being a director of films for highly sophisticated viewers to a commercial director able to convey his iconoclastic thought to a wide audience.

The Mexican films can be grouped in roughly chronological order into five categories. The first consists of musicals and melodramas, interesting to Buñuel only as commercial enterprises leading to

A high point of Buñuel's career—Arturo de Córdova and Delia Garcés' violent struggle in Él (This Strange Passion, *1953*).

better opportunities. The last, a trilogy of love and revolution, are some of his worst. Amid these failures, however, Buñuel consistently developed the themes of isolation, social reform, and pathological behavior that recur in his masterworks. The Mexican years were for Buñuel not only a time of apprenticeship in commercial cinema but of solid achievement as well.

Musicals and Melodramas

Gran casino (1946)

A melodramatic musical, *Gran casino* is conventional Mexican film fare of the 1950s. Views of oil wells in the tropics recreate the steamy atmosphere of Tampico. A tale of love and intrigue develops from a dispute over ownership of the wells. The two male stars are Jorge Negrete, a well-known singer of Mexican *ranchero* songs, and Libertad Lamarque, equally famed Argentinian vocalist. This cast left Buñuel with few possibilities so, he admits, "I had them sing throughout. It was like a match, a championship."[3]

Buñuel's surrealist humor surfaces from beneath the sentimentality from time to time. One of the fighters in a brawl smashes into a cupboard whose doors open and envelop him within. The hero and heroine approach each other and embrace; but Buñuel, avoiding the treacly cinematic kiss, focuses not on the lovers' lips but on a puddle at their feet instead. A stick pokes out of the oily ooze, recalling the stick that poked the severed hand in *Un Chien andalou*, while the couple kissing in the mud suggests the passionate lovers rolling in the mire in *L'Age d'or*. These irreverent moments are the distant echoes of dark humor still dedicated to the ridicule of bourgeois romanticism. This film was a commercial flop, however, and Buñuel did not direct again for two years.

The Great Madcap (El gran calavera) (1949)

The rapid pace of this zany comedy may stem from the fact that it was filmed in sixteen days. The opening scene is of a mass of legs and bodies lying entwined on the floor, the shoe-soles a quick clue to their owners' station in life. As the camera backs away we see that we are in a jail where a pile of sleeping drunks lie in a heap. One of them is Don Ramiro, a millionaire who mourns his wife by staying inebriated. His family hopes to shock him into his senses by pretending they are going broke. They move to a poor section of town where they take up menial jobs. Here Don Ramiro's daughter,

Virginia, meets and falls for Pablo, who announces street advertising over mobile loudspeakers. The advertisements, used for comic effect, are ridiculous, as when Virginia meets Pablo and their intimate lover's chatter is broadcast along with the advertisements. This device is used again in the culminating scene of Virginia's wedding.

Forced to marry a rich man, Virginia goes unwillingly to the ostentatiously decorated church. As the priest addresses his well-to-do audience, Pablo's loudspeaker blasts forth, maintaining a counterpoint of advertisements which provide a comic commentary on the sermon. This scene is echoed twelve years later in *Viridiana* when the beggar's prayers are drowned out by the sounds of construction. The angry wedding guests in *El gran calavera* head for the door, looking for the mobile loudspeakers. As the bride races to her lover's side, the guests take up the chase, as in the old American comedies.

It was this film farce which gave Buñuel the chance to make *Los olvidados.* The producer, Oscar Dancigers, agreed that if the director first shot *El gran calavera,* he would be free to work on his own project. With that kind of bargain, Buñuel rapidly completed *El gran calavera,* eager to resume, at long last, his career as a director of serious films.

Daughter of Deceit (La hija del engaño) (1951)

Daughter of Deceit and *A Woman without Love* are two studies of domestic trials and tribulations which are undistinguished except as early treatments of a theme that was to result in a later masterpiece. The relationship between an old man and a younger woman, which Buñuel dramatizes brilliantly in *Tristana,* began to interest him as early as 1951 when he made these two obscure, relatively unknown films.

Daughter of Deceit is a remake of *Don Quintín el amargado,* produced by Buñuel for Filmófono in 1935. The Mexican version of Carlos Arniches's play is much like its Spanish predecessor. Don Quintín's young wife is unfaithful and he sends her away. Before she leaves, however, the wife tells him that he is not the father of their daughter, Marta. Don Quintín sends Marta to live with Lencho and his wife. By the time Don Quintín learns from his dying wife that Marta is indeed his daughter, the girl has grown up. The passing of time and Marta's maturity is suggested in a clever scene full of erotic undertones. Her adopted father, Lencho, spanks little Marta as the scene fades out. Fading in again, the image is of Marta now grown up, but still being spanked by Lencho. The passage of time is thus indicated as the act of spanking loses its disciplinary function and takes on the suggestion of sexual play. The aging father, Don Quintín, eager to see his daughter and forgetting his bitter past, is jubilant when he finds her now happily married.

A Woman without Love (Una mujer sin amor) (1952)

In this film, infidelity by the young wife ends not with resignation and acceptance but with insult and recrimination. The wife, after her affair with a younger man, does not abandon her husband, but remains to care for him as he becomes ill. The passage of time all but heals old wounds. A bitter reminder disturbs the family, however, when the wife's son inherits money from an Argentinian man he has never known. The early transgression is never accepted and the film ends, as in *Tristana,* with expression of long-repressed resentment.

Social Panoramas

Mexican Busride (Subida al cielo) (1951)

While open expression of desire is punished by the puritan oligarchy in films such as Buñuel's *Susana,* sexual desire is recognized as a natural human function in the merry *Mexican Busride,* notable for its absence of Christian morality. In this surreal farce, a bus becomes a Mexican "ship of fools" carrying a load of passengers through unexpected detours of life.

The introductory scenes are of the central character, Oliverio, and his bride, who have just married in a village distinguished by its lack of a church. The wedding, held without a priest, is barely over when Oliverio's mother beckons him from her deathbed. He must go to the village where she lies near death and ratify her will. So Oliverio dutifully climbs aboard a bus, along with a varied array of passengers including a political candidate, a woman about to give birth, and a cruising seductress named Raquel—who is a direct descendant of the earlier Susana.

With the passengers and baggage an oval mirror is loaded onto the bus. Mirrors were, for the surrealists, reflectors of the unconscious, the "mirors de merveilleux." Like the dressing-table mirror in *L'Age d'or* that reflected the heroine's erotic daydreams, the mirror loaded on the bus suggests suppressed desires revealed through a dream that Oliverio has during the busride.

Transportation problems in two social panoramas: (above) Flood stops the bus in *Subida al Cielo* (1951); (below) A street fight stops the trolley in *La ilusión viaja en tranvia* (1953).

The ride is a series of encounters with chance, the surrealists' *le hasard* which they felt guides human destiny. When the bus gets stuck in the mud, all efforts to free it fail until a child leading a pair of oxen by a string pulls the vehicle out. A baby is born to the pregnant passenger, and the bus driver decides to stop by his mother's home to celebrate her birthday. Raquel, in a gesture repeated later by Tristana, hands Oliverio an apple. Like Saturno, Oliverio munches it in a scene foreshadowing their love-making on the bus which occurs as they climb the "subida al cielo" or ascent to the heavens.

By the time Oliverio reaches his mother she had died. He fulfills her wishes by inking her dead fingers and pressing them to the paper, thus imprinting her verification of the will after her demise. The key to this preposterous farce is, as the presence of the mirror suggests, a dream in which Oliverio appears to seek permission from his mother to satisfy his sexual desire.[4] In the dream his mother, perched on a pedestal, knits. In a surreal metamorphosis of images, the knitting figure of the mother suddenly changes into Raquel with her apple peel, who in turn becomes Oliverio's bride. Oliverio appears attached to the women first by the knitting yarn and then by the apple peel, both suggesting an umbilical cord.

Mexican Busride, a short film lasting only an hour and fifteen minutes, is one of only two farces Buñuel directed during the 1950s. To this fast-paced, gag-filled genre Buñuel adds touching death scenes and dream symbolism. The result is a lively but thoughtful mixture of Buñuel's favorite themes including eroticism, death, and life as the dominion of chance.

Illusion Travels by Streetcar (La ilusion viaja en tranvía) (1953)

This delightful farce about the adventures of a stolen streetcar is Buñuel's tribute to American comedies. All the standard gags are present—the comic pair of clowns who outwit the authorities, narrow escapes from disaster, the love of speed, and constant action, as in Buster Keaton's *The General.* Yet *Streetcar* begins with a straight face and a documentary tone, as the opening narration informs us that this film offers a veiw of "the enormous hive that is the city. This is a story of the working classes—those who travel on streetcars." Thus *Streetcar* is a proletarian comedy whose heroes are the common people of urban Mexico.

The two central characters—the pudgy Tarrajos and his pal

Juanito—are laid off work in the opening scene because their aged streetcar, 133, has been pronounced unserviceable and is being retired from use. They find the nearest bar to lament the departed vehicle and thus arrive late at a party where they take part in a play, a morality farce. Tarrajos, still drinking beer, is cast as a fat angel who shoots a paper dove and is banished from "the Catholic World." Angry at being ejected, Tarrajos now dons the devil's costume—steer horns tipped with bells. The scene changes to Eden, inhabited by Adam and Eve, who are dressed, like Tarzan and Jane, in animal skins. The devil, draped with a banner identifying him as "Serpent" lest the viewer mistake the locale, offers Eve an apple. God, who is wearing a long white beard and holding a globe, offers to send them a Redeemer. A character named Miguel comes to slay the Serpent and the play ends. This farce within a farce serves to set the irreverent but innocuous tone of *Streetcar*.

Tarrajos and Juanito leave the party and decide to resurrect their decrepit streetcar in order to give the girls a ride home in it. They find old 133, but by the time they return the fiesta is over. They give rides to those leaving late, changing the overhead sign of the car from "Hospital" to "Rastro," Flea Market. But when the first passenger gets off, a line of people is waiting for the car. They bang the door, enter, try to pay, and sit down with their packages. Slaughterhouse workers carry sides of beef carcasses and hogs' heads, which they hang from the riders' handles. The butcher stands in bloodied apron with long knives in his belt. A bizarre series of riders boards and departs—two old ladies with a bleeding-Christ statue, an American lady who suspects communism when the drivers won't let her pay. Other bourgeois passengers complain about labor when they learn the fare is free.

Soon a retired streetcar driver, Papa Pinillos, catches on to what has happened and tries to report the drivers to the transit company. The pair has been trying all day to return the car, but the stream of passengers never lets up. So, after many misadventures, Tarrajos announces that all riders must leave the car. The passengers at first refuse, but when they see the car is not moving, they get off. Meanwhile, old Pinillos has fainted, revived, called a cab, and is headed for the depot to report the wayward car.

At the depot office, Pinillos, a familiar face recognized by transit officials as a chronic complainer, is made to wait. The manager, disbelieving the old man's story, finally agrees to check the station in order to be rid of him. By now, of course, Tarrajos and Juanito have had time to return the car, which, the manager calmly points out, is in its accustomed place in the depot. Pinillos is beside himself. The last scene is a long shot of the old man waving his arms while Tarrajos, Juanito, and his girl friend Lupe walk away, their dialogue fading in the distance. Another chaotic journey, similar to the previous one in *Mexican Busride,* is over. The format of the wild adventure, with its numerous comic possibilities, is one well suited to Buñuel's rapid, episodic style. In later films, such as *The Milky Way* and *The Discreet Charm of the Bourgeoisie,* Buñuel puts this style to serious use.

The River and Death (El río y la muerte) (1954)

A masterly study of machismo, *The River and Death* may be Buñuel's least understood film. Because its language, situations, and tone are of the rural Mexican working class and because Buñuel restrains the caustic humor generally associated with his art, the film failed at the 1954 Venice Film Festival. Sophisticated audiences, unfamiliar with rural Mexico, considered the story a farce. J. A. Fieschi's refusal to take the work at face value leads him to conclude that since *River* is "the least ambiguous, least wicked," it is, therefore, "the least fascinating and least characteristic of Buñuel's films."[5] While the theme of exaggerated virility is treated seriously, the film is not without delicious moments of parody and black humor. The delicacy with which the subject is treated belies the director's hopes of moving the audience at which it is skillfully aimed. Jean Delmas feared the French public, not believing the reality before their eyes, would take the film for a joke, and warned. "I believe [Buñuel] wanted to convince."[6]

That the problem is a social one is clear from the opening panoramic view of the village populace on market day. The village, San Bibiana, is located on a river where for about a century, two families—the Anguianos and the Menchacas—have been feuding and killing each other. Why? Because one day a cow, just whose is now forgotten, was allowed to wander into the other family's pasture. The implied humor of this explanation is no less serious for its understatement.

In the best realist tradition, Buñuel cuts from the wide panorama of the open plaza of San Bibiana to the more intimate scene of two men having a drink in a tavern. One becomes angry at an idle remark, stands, draws his pistol, and shoots his friend. A jump-cut to a hospital room reveals the victim, Gerardo Anguiano, in an iron lung. Gerardo, the last male of the Anguiano family, is now a doctor who lives in Mexico City and doesn't give a flip about the family feud he has inherited. His rival, however, Rómulo Menchaca, still lives in the village and is very much a macho. He visits Gerardo to assure him that when he recovers he, Rómulo, will be waiting for him. In what is one of the darker jokes of the film, Rómulo apologizes for insulting Gerardo while he is recuperating. "What I did was not manly. I will kill you, but when we're equals" (film dialogue).

Buñuel makes clear that the young males of San Bibiana are not solely responsible for their exaggerated attitudes about their manhood. A kindly little grandmother discovers her son working in his shop without his gun and admonishes him: "I wear the skirts, you wear the gun." The town priest reinforces this state of mind by accepting it. Only one man in the village, Don Nemesio Anguiano, has transcended the *machista* syndrome. A village elder respected by all, Don Nemesio abhors violence and laments the level to which village life has sunk. Every quarrel ends with a mortal threat. At a card game Don Nemesio turns to the priest, saying, "Padre, I'll bet you and I are the only men in this town who are not wearing guns." "No," replies the clergyman in another of Buñuel's jokes on the church, "You are the only one. I wear a gun."

The town officials, like the women and the priest, uphold the fatal code of machismo. Don Nemesio, now desperate at threats against his grandson Felipe, seeks the aid of the town constable. The old man invites the constable to sit down and discuss what can be done to halt the endless bloodshed. "We cannot permit these crimes to go on," asserts Don Nemesio. In perhaps the best gag line of the film, the constable replies, "No, these people are not committing crimes. They are defending their honor." The irony of this line is chilling, for the constable justifies homicide with all the gravity of a man who truly believes what he is doing is just. It is with equal logic that the Menchaca males reason that they must kill Felipe. "With Felipe dead we won't have to kill anymore." And so the killing continues.

Buñuel never allows his public to forget the wide dimensions of machismo. The scenes of village fiestas seem to be clips from an anthropological documentary such as *Las Hurdes* in which the male display of aggression appears to be part of the folklore along with the dances, music, and fireworks. These rural fiestas are flashbacks that contrast sharply with the present plight of Gerardo, now fully recuperated and strolling down a walkway at the university with his new girl friend, a nurse. He tells her that his mother, who has not visited him during his confinement in the hospital, now expects him to return to the village and avenge the family's honor.

In a circular structure, the film's final sequence begins, as in the opening shots, on market day, accompanied by the usual fiesta and evening dance. Forced by his mother's expectations and memories—her husband was a victim of the feud—Gerardo unwillingly confronts his rival. The young doctor in suit and tie—the twentieth-century man—is in stark contrast to Rómulo, dressed in the white cotton garb and gunbelt of provincial Mexico, an embodiment of tribal attitudes. The film culminates in genuine suspense when Gerardo, knocking the gun from his rival's hand, lectures him about the futility of the feud and walks off, daring Rómulo to use the one bullet left in the pistol.

The final scene is unexpected. Rómulo, accompanied by a group of friends and supporters, visits Gerardo but confesses to his enemy he does not know why he came. Sensing the inarticulate Rómulo's frustration at trying to save face, Gerardo tries to lend his rival a self-image he can respect. "You taught me a lesson, Rómulo. You came to look for me in front of everyone, with the village watching. I should have done that." Rómulo's face slowly registers his understanding that, even though he wasn't killed, he is worthy of respect, even gratitude. A century-old pattern of violence is broken when Rómulo blurts out, "To hell with the town," and embraces Gerardo. As light is reflected on the river, the spectator wonders if enlightenment has seeped into the village at last.

In spite of *River*'s didactic slant, Buñuel's insight into the causes of machismo is profound. Its accomplices, women as well as men, pass it on in insidious forms to their children in infancy. It is as a baby in his mother's arms that Rómulo attends his father's funeral. A coffin-bearer turns to the child, as if to an adult, and warns him sternly, "I hope you never forget your father's death." The courage to combat this disease that spreads from generation to generation comes from the perspective provided by education. It is to Buñuel's credit that *River* conveys this perspective without a trace of condescension or superiority. Those critics who dwell on Buñuel's cruelty have not seen *River*. It is as accurate a study of social pathology as *He* is of individual psychosis, and it is just as worthy of careful study.

Character Studies

Robinson Crusoe (1952)

In his first color film, Buñuel enhances the island setting of the story based on Daniel Defoe's eighteenth-century novel. In spite of the yellowish cast, the colors are rich, the deep blue of the sea in strong contrast to the lighter sky. Color also stresses the racial difference between the blue-eyed Crusoe and the dark islander, Friday. The contrast of skin color helps to emphasize the difference in attitudes between the two men. And it is these attitudes rather than the luxuriant tropical surroundings that interest Buñuel in *Robinson Crusoe*.

The first third of the film introduces details of Crusoe's shipwreck, his encounter with the natural world, and his efforts at mastering his environment. After he has managed physical survival by building a house, planting seeds for food, and baking bread, he must still struggle with the emotional hazards of shipwreck—loneliness, sexual frustration, spiritual drift, and the sense of futility of one who sees, as Buñuel himself did, his mature years slip by while his best talents go unchallenged.

Isolation begins to take its toll on Crusoe, who suffers hallucinations. The skirt of the scarecrow in his cornpatch awakens his sexual longing. He falls ill with fever and envisions his father denying him water to quench his thirst. Although he recovers from the fever, it is clear that he is deteriorating as a human being. He seems more like a great bird as he trots down the beach in a jerky gait holding his hide umbrella to shield him from the sun. When Crusoe finds Friday, he feels exaltation at the prospect of human companionship, although the first thing he does is to chain the man to a stockade.

Though Crusoe's encounter with nature and his ingenuity in surviving closely follow Defoe's novel, the latter part of the film, in which Crusoe debates theology with the wise pagan islander, is pure Buñuel. Raymond Durgnat notes the irony that, of an epic of solitude, Buñuel makes a study of social relationships.[7] What happens when Crusoe meets Friday is what happens in most of Buñuel's portrayals of capitalist society: Defoe's paean of individualism ceases and Crusoe becomes not the clever survivor but the *conquistador*, who acts as the Spaniards did when they set foot on New World shores. In accordance with the mandates of their social institutions, they enslaved the Indians, set themselves up as masters, and promptly began to proselytize.

Before Friday's arrival, Crusoe had tried to read the old Bible he found in the sea-chest he had salvaged from the ship, but the Scriptures seemed remote and meaningless. Now he reads to Friday, eager to convert him. While in solitude, Crusoe shouted aloud the Twenty-third Psalm. The only answer was an echo rolling the syllables back to him over the landscape. His faith, at that moment, left him alone and unsatisfied, yet he now plays the priest to Friday.

Friday, however, is a man of considerable wit. While his responses are often comic and make Crusoe appear the straight man in a series of amusing dialogues, Friday is no mere clown. His good sense and human dignity are evident from the moment Crusoe handcuffs him and decides to deny him knowledge of guns. As Crusoe grows to trust Friday, it is clear that it is Crusoe, not Friday, who is growing in humanity. Friday learns to shoot and saves Crusoe from a band of marauders. But while Friday learns technical skills, Crusoe is learning how to trust and to survive as a human being. He also relearns the limits of religion when he is unable to counter Friday's point that if God is all powerful, he must be the source of sin and suffering.

Robinson Crusoe is a good example of how Buñuel accepted the demands of commercial film and adapted them to his own purposes. Into a tale of adventure and solitude, Buñuel finds a way to insert his own themes of exploitation, inhumanity, and hypocrisy. The film is one of his more optimistic, for Crusoe, after the trials of isolation, has been forced to shed hypocrisies in order to survive. He learns to respect Friday and the two achieve mutual trust and harmony. Yet the ending is, in typical Buñuel fashion, left open. As they return to civilization, Crusoe, dressed in sea captain's regalia, will go back to a society whose institutions are founded upon the shallow and exploitative principles he has learned to discard. The question remains whether or not his friendship with Friday will survive reentry into Christian society. The fact that Friday is clothed as a sailor, an enlisted man, hardly suggests that the two take with them the equality they had achieved apart from Christian culture. Crusoe, like Nazarín, is taught by the one whom he tries to educate. Whether Crusoe has learned his lesson of brotherhood and will continue to observe Friday's full equality is left for the viewer to ponder.

The Young One (La joven) (1960)

No region offers a richer field for the study of violence than the American South, as the writings of its native authors—Faulkner, Tennessee Williams, Carson McCullers—attest. Buñuel was one of the legion of creative artists who sought work in America during the 1930s and 1940s. While living in Los Angeles and New York, he had an opportunity to observe America's racial attitudes. Thus it is that this thoroughly Spanish director became familiar enough with the American cultural context to "go to the heart of bigotry" in *The Young One*,[8] based on a short story by Peter Matthiessen, in which sexual and racial violence are discovered thriving, under the most tenuous control.

Although filmed in Acapulco, the action of *The Young One* is set on an island off the shore of an undetermined Southern state in the United States where a gamekeeper, Miller, lives with his senile helper, Pee Wee. As the film opens, Pee Wee dies, leaving his only survivor, his adolescent granddaughter, Evie, alone on the island with Miller. The island setting affords the director the "unity of place," according to Giorgio Tinazzi, in which action may develop out of reach of civilization.[9] Humanizing influences, however, are not entirely lacking. Due to Reverend Fleetwood, a visitor to the island, the murder of a fugitive black, Travers, is narrowly averted. Falsely accused on the mainland of raping a white woman, Travers flees to the island. Here he is confronted by Miller, whose racist vengeance is restrained only by a swamp into which Travers must flee to seek further refuge.

Because of Evie, Miller's pursuit of his unseen enemy, whom he calls "the nigger," ends not in slaughter but in a stand-off. Evie, another of Buñuel's innocents, is not racist and does not hesitate to sell the black man gasoline for his motor boat. Travers also takes one of Miller's guns, so that he is not defenseless when finally he encounters his pursuer. Self-preservation rather than leniency forces Miller to bargain with Travers. It is, however, a white man's bargain, in which Miller makes Travers his "boy" and expects him to do his bidding in return for truce. This is the only kind of relationship racism allows with a black man, that of master to servant. When Travers moves into Pee Wee's shack, Evie must sleep in Miller's house, an event introducing a secondary, no less intriguing theme into *The Young One*.

The relationship between a young woman and an older man that preoccupies Buñuel throughout much of his career is not the

"Lolitisme" some critics glibly assume.[10] Far from the bored and sexually sophisticated urbanite who amuses herself with the inept Humbert Humbert, Evie is an orphan relying on a man with whom she has been raised. As Tristana, by her mother's decree, finds herself in the clutches of her lecherous guardian, Evie, after her grandfather's death, is at the mercy of the gamekeeper. Like Tristana, Evie is unaware of her sexual attraction and does not flirt, as does Lolita. Her acquiescence to Miller is, like Tristana's to Don Lope, the result of her passive, unself-conscious, and willing character, uncomplicated by either desire or knowledge. Freddy Buache, eager to avoid "priestly language," cannot describe Miller's actions as "taking advantage of Evie." Miller can best be understood as behaving in the manner of Don Lope when he finds himself alone with an attractive young woman who does not protest—he seduces her. When Buache calls the seduction "an act of love," he does not specify by whom affection is felt, for Evie can hardly be described as a woman in love.

The arrival of Reverend Fleetwood complicates, then resolves, the increasingly tense relationships on the island. Reverend Fleetwood is drawn with quick, brilliant strokes that define his character as being everything he claims not to be. Amazed to find Evie still not baptized, he persuades her to undergo the spiritual rite of rebirth by referring to it in material terms, as "the golden key that will open the gates of Paradise."[11] Evie's innocence underlines the fatuousness of the cleric when, still dripping from baptismal waters, she reminds him that he promised her a golden key. The Reverend proclaims, in the best liberal tradition, that he is above racism and thus can be trusted by all, a truly Godlike priest. Yet he betrays his own perhaps unconscious racial fears when he turns over the mattress Travers slept on before lying on it himself.

If Reverend Fleetwood is the unknowing agent of a repressive, racist society, he manages to play the two sides against each other. Learning of the priest's arrival, Travers has escaped into the swamp. Miller and an animaloid ferryman, Jackson, pick up their guns, eager to hunt down Travers, whom they can justify killing this time because they have learned he is accused of a crime. But Reverend Fleetwood knows of Miller's seduction of Evie and persuades him to allow the black man to escape in return for keeping silent about Miller's activities with the girl.

It can hardly be said that justice triumphs in *The Young One*.

Rather, one sort of violence is exchanged for another and a kind of uneasy peace is achieved. Miller allows his black prey to leave not because he has suddenly been struck with compassion but because his own safety is threatened. If Miller, however, is checkmated, there remains Jackson, the ferryman, representing the die-hard racists still evident in American culture—the Ku Klux Klan, the White Citizens' Councils—who dedicate themselves to persecution of dark-skinned people.

Studies of Criminal Passion

Los olvidados (1950)

After eighteen years, Buñuel picked up, in *Los olvidados,* where he had left off with *Las Hurdes.* Like that early documentary, *Los olvidados* is based on facts gathered, this time, from reformatory files. In *Los olvidados,* Buñuel again films a devastating account of outcasts doomed by a society too naive and indifferent to meet the needs of the wretched of the earth.

Although *Los olvidados* is set in Mexico City, Buñuel stresses the film's universality in the opening shots tilting over the Eiffel Tower and focusing on Big Ben on the Thames. Finally zooming in on a street in Mexico City, the camera centers upon a group of boys playing at bullfighting on what is described as "a piece of waste ground,"[12] that is, a slum. It is quickly established that the metropolis proudly erected by Western technology consists of a cluster of squalid pits where human life is devoured. This view of the modern city as a kind of maw parallels that reflected in the terrible poems of New York written by Buñuel's colleague, García Lorca.

The outcasts or "forgotten ones" to whom Buñuel refers in the title of this film are a group of juvenile delinquents whose leader, Jaibo (the crab), is a recent escapee from reform school. Jaibo's protégés include six or seven teenagers who relish the older lad's tales of survival in the reformatory. Jaibo wastes no time in reestablishing himself as their leader. He is no sooner out of the reformatory than he leads the pack of juveniles in a raid. The brutality of the film becomes immediately apparent when the hoodlums attack a blind man, whom they torment and try to rob while he plays his guitar.

Not all the youths of *Los olvidados* are delinquents. In an early scene a small boy—one of the few innocents in the film—sits alone, crying in a market place. We learn that the boy, Ojitos (Little

Eyes), is looking for his father, who brought him from a neighboring village and has abandoned him there. The blind man bumps into Ojitos, who helps him across the street, and the boy agrees to serve the blind man as a guide in order to earn his living. J. Rubia Barcia, in his critique of *Los olvidados*, suggests that Ojitos, dressed in a straw hat and poncho and deserted by his father, symbolizes Mexico searching for its heritage.[13]

Among the central characters is Pedro, who, characteristically, is neither entirely good nor bad. A member of the street gang, he finds Ojitos still waiting for his father after dark and brings him a sandwich. Overcoming his inclination to spend the night waiting for his father, Ojitos decides to go with Pedro, who takes him to Meche's house, where they both take refuge.

Pedro's innocence is soon compromised when he becomes implicated in Jaibo's murder of Julián. Pedro is also made to appear guilty when Jaibo wanders into the cutlery shop where Pedro works and steals a knife. Pedro wants to be good, he confesses to his mother, but, he complains, he doesn't know how. Because his fate is uncertain, he becomes the primary interest of the film.

Pedro's mother agrees to allow a judge who suspects the lad of stealing to send him to a juvenile work-farm. Feeling the injustice of being falsely accused, Pedro, in a fit of anger, kills some chickens at the farm. The warden, trying to prove his faith in Pedro, gives the boy fifty pesos and tells him to go out and buy cigarettes. Pedro, amazed at his sudden freedom, steps out to do the warden's bidding, but his good intentions are never realized. Outside, Jaibo lies in wait. He steals the money, so that Pedro, fearing the warden's disbelief, runs away. It is, of course, only a matter of time until the hardened criminal Jaibo fights with his unlucky protégé and kills him. Not unexpectedly, Jaibo himself is gunned down soon after by the police.

André Bazin insists upon the "objective," impersonal character of the cruelty in *Los olvidados* and maintains that Buñuel makes no value judgments of his characters.[14] The structure of the film, however, does not sustain this comment. While the slum is a predatory world whose laws of survival are nonselective, Buñuel by no means leaves the impression that this is "natural," or "God's will," without cause or solution. Scenes of the gang's brutality are inevitably followed by views of their home life, which are no less violent. Indeed, the causes of Pedro's behavior can be traced to his mother, who is

Evils of the slums in Buñuel's Mexican masterpiece, *Las Olvidados:* (above) Jaibo and his gang attack the blind exploiter Carmelo; (below) "Little Eyes" is propositioned in the famous pantomime scene shot through a restaurant window.

herself delinquent. With several children to feed, she rejects Pedro not only physically but emotionally as well. She confesses to Jaibo, who seduces her, that she was only fourteen when Pedro was born. One night she grabs a broom and beats with a vengeance a rooster that tries to mate with a hen. This act is only a link in a chain of violence reaching to her son, who later beats to death the chickens at the work-farm.

Pedro's mother is only one of the exploitative and hostile adults of *Los olvidados*. Sympathy for Carmelo, the blind man, is undercut when he sings the praises of Porfirio Díaz, one of Mexico's most ruthless dictators. Carmelo also abuses Ojitos, fondles the gentle Meche, strokes the coins he hoards in a wall, and rejoices at Jaibo's death. Carmelo, like most of the rest of the adults of *Los olvidados*, is as vicious and as predatory as the youngsters. One exception is the warden at the farm, a prototype of Nazarín, Simon of the desert, and other sympathetic but ineffectual priests who populate Buñuel's cinematic world. The warden, however well meaning, is responsible for Pedro's demise through ignorance of his milieu. Not realizing that the boy lives in a jungle in which he not only preys but is preyed upon, the warden innocently offers the lad money and sends him into the streets. Pedro becomes an instant target. Far from absolving the adult world, Buñuel indicts it for cruelty. Like the warden, who may represent the best of us, society at large is concerned but too incompetent and shortsighted to meet the needs of its forgotten and outcast.

In its almost total condemnation, *Los olvidados* is a bleak film. The warning in the opening shots that the work is "based on reality . . . is not optimistic" (script, p. 217) is an understantement, for the reality it depicts is as grim as the neo-realist films made in Italy after World War II, by directors like Visconti, Rossellini, and Luigi Zampa, who made strong social statements conveyed in unrelenting and austere film images. Parallels between their films and *Los olvidados* are too numerous to be coincidental. Their preference for episodic plots, authentic locations, natural lighting, and nonprofessional actors are all clearly shared by Buñuel in *Los olvidados*. Buñuel's restraint of his cameraman's lyrical fancy is legendary. The restless Figueroa began to wonder why he, rather than a newsreel photographer, had been employed to shoot *Los olvidados* (script, p. 108). The actors had professional experience but were unknown. The film's inescapable horror is enhanced by the incorporation into it of documentary techniques by which neo-realist directors hoped to increase an impression of the veracity of the statements they were trying to make.

Yet Buñuel rejects neo-realism. *Los olvidados* shares, but goes beyond, its aesthetic principles. Acknowledging the contributions of neo-realism, Buñuel points out that it is incomplete, "official, above all reasonable, but poetry, mystery . . . are completely nonexistent."[15] The lyrical quality of *Los olvidados* is conveyed not by neo-realist devices but by nightmares and visions. These scenes depart from the documentation of exterior reality and record instead the inner desires that surrealists believed determine human behavior. For example, one night after Pedro's mother refuses him some meat she has prepared for dinner, Pedro has a dream. In it he sees a white chicken floating about, then his mother who, floating like an angel through the air, perches affectionately on his bed. Pedro looks under the bed and finds Julián, Jaibo's victim, his bloody face smiling. As Pedro stares, white feathers fall over Julián. Pedro protests to his mother that he is innocent of Julián's death. The mother kisses him and hands him a large piece of raw meat. As Pedro reaches out to take it, Jaibo appears from under the bed and grabs the dripping lump of meat from Pedro's hands. The mother recedes into the background as Jaibo disappears with his stolen prize. This dream sequence, expressing Pedro's physical hunger, at the same time alludes to a complex array of emotions that are evoked but undeveloped in the narrative. Pedro's guilt and fear, his need for maternal affection, and, perhaps, a premonition of Jaibo's stealing from him his mother's affection and, indeed, his very life, are all suggested in this provocative scene.

At the film's end, when Jaibo lies dying of a police bullet, Buñuel repeats an image which has appeared throughout—that of the stray dogs—and converts it into a harbinger of death. One of the dogs that has followed Jaibo's street gang like a silent, forlorn shadow of the homeless youths trots toward the viewer. When Jaibo is shot, the dog's superimposed image crosses Jaibo's face. The mangy cur seems also near death. The final scene of the film takes place at night as Meche and her grandfather carry Pedro's body on a donkey to a rubbish heap to dump it. On the way they pass Pedro's mother, who walks the dark streets searching for her son, unaware that he and Jaibo have died the anonymous death of stray dogs.

Buñuel had in mind another surrealist image, but was prohibited from using it by his producer. In the scene of Julián's murder by Jaibo, a multi-story building still under construction rises in the background. Buñuel admits to André Bazin that "I would have liked to put a big orchestra of a hundred musicians in it. One would have seen it just in passing, indistinctly. I wanted to put in a lot of things like that, but they were absolutely prohibited"[16]. The image of musicians might have been intended, like the Brahms music accompanying *Las Hurdes*, as a counterpoint to emphasize the abyss between a society that enjoys symphonies and one which exists in city slums. If Buñuel had had complete freedom, *Los olvidados* might resemble neo-realism less and more nearly parallel his own documentary, *Las Hurdes*.

As in *Las Hurdes*, Buñuel does not overtly reveal remedies to the social problems he portrays but, as the voice in the early frames of *Los olvidados* states, "leaves the solution . . . to the progressive forces of our times (script, p. 217). Buñuel, however, does not attempt to avoid being specific. The strongest statement of how to meet the needs of society's strays is the film itself, which reveals their remarkable lack of the most basic necessities of life. Lack of education is also focused upon when Pedro's illiterate mother cannot sign her name before the judge. The misery of overcrowded and filthy quarters is visually conveyed by the cinematography, which captures the squalid interiors, shared with animals, as well as the slumland cluttered with detritus where Jaibo and the blind beggar take refuge.

In its description of deprivation, *Los olvidados* is a visual contradiction to the conventional views of Mexico's abundant tropical flora. But perhaps it is Ojitos who most strongly suggests what Buñuel considers the primary origin of the outcast. Ojitos, waiting in vain, repeats the phrase, "I'm looking for my father." He is much like Samuel Beckett's two tramps who are waiting for Godot. Neither Buñuel's outcasts nor Beckett's tramps find what they so desperately seek.

Susana (1950)

After *Los olvidados*, Buñuel continued his study of the relationship of the criminal to society. In his next film, the delinquent's crime is adultery, which society considers a form of stealing and punishes with equal fervor. Eroticism in *Susana* is seen as a means to power, an instrument by which established social order is challenged. As in the case of any other crime, the police are called, the delinquent is arrested, and order is restored.

The opening scenes of *Susana* echo the sentiments Buñuel portrayed toward reform institutions in *Los olvidados*. "You'll learn to be good here," one of Susana's wardens assures her as he locks her in a cell (film dialogue). But another warden comes closer to the truth when he reminds his friend that their prisoner has been there two years and is, if anything, behaving worse. Susana's promiscuity is seen as a force that can only be contained, not eradicated.

The film's introductory jail sequence ends with one of Buñuel's most effective images. A flash of lightning casts the shadow of a cross through the bars of Susana's cell. As the frightened prisoner is about to kiss the cross, a spider crawls from the spot where the shadow falls. The body of the film confirms the suspicion, suggested in these frames, that surreptitiously, like a spider, eroticism disturbs the calm exterior of Christian morality.

Susana miraculously escapes through the bars of her cell and finds refuge at a farm owned by a family proud of its Christian behavior. Christian values at the farm, however, have been manipulated so that they are the basis for a feudal system in which labor serves management in a rigid capitalistic hierarchy. Susana, fresh from prison and eager to get on in the world, aspires, like the rest, to be rich. Though she is employed as a maid, she knows there is a shortcut to the top and sets out to get there as quickly as possible. Doing what she does best, she seduces the hierarchy one by one, beginning with the foreman, passing on to the farmer's son, and finally progressing to the farmer himself.

It is not long before Susana runs into an obstacle—the farmer's wife, indignant and armed with the righteous fury of Christian morality. This moral code has, in the face of Susana's forthright eroticism, crumbled three times without a fight in the case of the men at the farm. Without striking a single blow or taking a single life, Susana now threatens the very seat of power, the cold and loveless wife. Susana's triumph, however, is spoiled by the foreman, who, jealous of her success, calls the police to arrest her for licentious behavior. Harmony resumes, the power balance is restored, and the film ends as it began, with Susana back in prison.

Buñuel's respectful treatment of his characters is actually a display of high comic deceit; for, with its conventional, even folksy dialogue, *Susana* treads a delicate path between praise and ridicule of Christian values. The seductive young woman goes beyond the bounds of propriety in luring the men of the farm, yet they fall all too willingly into her trap. It is their moral principles—which allow them to enjoy, then condemn, her advances—that seem false. Finally, Susana's punishment is far too harsh, for hers, in current terminology, is a victimless crime. The audience is left to ponder which system of values, Susana's or her Christian employers', is the more hypocritical and unjust.

The Catholic Film Censors, not wishing to raise such doubts in the minds of their faithful, gave *Susana* an "Adults Only" rating.[17] The French film historian and critic Jacques Brochier finds it one of Buñuel's finest films.[18] It is important not only for its surgeon's touch with sharp satire, but as a treatment of the outcast theme, with which Buñuel is preoccupied throughout most of his career.

Wuthering Heights (Cumbres borrascosas) (1953)

Buñuel's attraction to Emily Brontë's tortured novel was shared by his fellow surrealists, who delighted in the ease with which the novel's perversity, sadism, infanticide, and reincarnation made a mockery of respectability and reason. In the first *Surrealist Manifesto,* André Breton expressed disdain for novels of psychological analysis as neat, logical exercises that failed to penetrate the surface of reason. He preferred instead such tales as Lewis's *The Monk* for its lack of restraint and for the defiance implicit in its attitude that "nothing is impossible to those who dare."[19] Buñuel wrote a scenario of *The Monk* but never filmed it. *Wuthering Heights,* too, languished in the director's files for years. He was ready to shoot it after *L'Age d'or,* but lost interest in the project when no producer would accept it. When Oscar Dancigers approached Buñuel twenty-four years later, the director dug out his original script which was, by 1953, an authentic relic of his surrealist years.

In adapting *Wuthering Heights* for the screen, Buñuel had to simplify one of the most complex novels in literature. What is left in Buñuel's version is precisely what surrealists considered of value in transcending conformity and social dicta. The rebellious spirit of Alejandro (Heathcliff), who avenges himself against those who mistreated him as a poor foundling, and the demonic hero's often cruel and destructive behavior figure prominently in *Wuthering Heights.* Central to the tale is the haunted love between Catalina (Cathy) and Alejandro, a love that inspired the surrealists as a prime example of *l'amour fou.*

Buñuel films two classic British novels that inspired surrealists: (above) Dan O'Herlihy and James Fernandez as Crusoe and Friday in *The Adventures of Robinson Crusoe;* (below) Irasema Dilian and Jorge Mistral as Heathcliff (Alejandro) and Cathy in *Wuthering Heights (Abismos de Pasión).*

Catalina is married to a cold conformist, Eduardo, a man incapable of passion. Alejandro begs her to leave her lifeless marriage, but Catalina is about to have a child and refuses to abandon Eduardo. Furious at her refusal, Alejandro marries Isabel, Eduardo's sister, whom Catalina scorns. Alejandro's marriage turns out even worse than Catalina's. It is, in fact, full of hatred, for Isabel soon learns that Alejandro detests her. These characters live in an entirely negative world ruled by aggression, fear, and vengeance. They are people who are clearly out of reason's range. Even the love between Catalina and Alejandro is torn by fury and spite. Each of the lovers seems to enjoy the capacity to destroy the other.

The culminating scenes, the most powerful in the film, deal with the curious relationship between love and death that has always fascinated Buñuel. It is not until Alejandro discovers Catalina lying ill in her room that sustained expression of his love for her flows from him. In her death scene Catalina, too, confesses to Alejandro she has never loved anyone but him, then falls unconscious. She soon dies in childbirth. Her death seems to call forth depths of love that, in life, Alejandro could dismiss from time to time. Desperate with grief, he visits her newly filled grave one night, unearths it, and embraces the cadaver in its white shroud.

Though the novel continues, Buñuel brings an end to *Wuthering Heights* at Catalina's graveside. When a figure approaches, Heathcliff looks up and sees a vision of Catalina. But the vision of his beloved is in reality Catalina's brother, Ricardo (Hindley), who fires a shot at the grief-stricken Alejandro. The hero falls dead on Catalina's grave, finally united with her in death.

A full range of visual and auditory detail helps to make *Wuthering Heights* a film which, in Claude Beylie's view, is entirely worthy of its director.[20] Gnarled and barren tree limbs are repeated background reminders of the tortured lovers. The English moors become, in Buñuel's version, a stripped, volcanic landscape that appears as uninhabitable as the emotional wasteland the protagonists share. To Buñuel's chagrin, music from Wagner's *Tristan und Isolde* accompanies the entire film. The director had intended to use the music only in the final scenes; however, in his absence from the final phases of production, the complete sound track was filled with Wagner's ponderous tones.

Buñuel's version of *Wuthering Heights (Abismos de pasión* was a commercial tag added later) stands as an attempt to record the ferocity, anguish, torment, and hate that, as the surrealists knew, defy reason. They discovered these emotions described in astounding detail in the novel, which distressed the Victorians who were the first to read it. Not only a horror tale, but an account of passion that transcends time, sex, and social repression, Buñuel's *Wuthering Heights* is stark, repellent, abrasive, and thus faithful to surrealist principles. Buñuel insists that his film is also closer to its awesome model than Hollywood's more polite version (p. 163). (Made in 1939 and starring Laurence Olivier and Merle Oberon, it too presents only Heathcliff's ill-fated love for Cathy.)[21] The excesses of *Wuthering Heights* can also be observed in the couple madly in love in *L'Age d'or.* Aberrations deriving from love still preoccupy Buñuel twenty-three years after *Wuthering Heights*, when the obsessed lovers in *Phantom of Liberty* pursue their passion beyond the grave.

The Brute (El bruto) (1953)

Criminality as the product of corruption and indifference is treated in the context of juveniles in *Los olvidados* and again with a feminine delinquent in *Susana.* It also provides the theme of *The Brute,* a pivotal work in which Buñuel's preoccupation with power and sex both echoes his past films and announces some later ones.

The plot of *The Brute* centers around Pedro the slaughterhouse worker. As the brute of the title, he is unaware not only of his own strength, but of the exploitative power of his boss, the landowner Cabrera. Pedro is Cabrera's paid henchman who evicts tenants late with their rent. As the willing collaborator of an oppressive system, Pedro accidentally kills Carmelo, a fellow worker who protests Cabrera's ruthlessness. A member of the corrupt power structure, Paloma, the landowner's wife, is attracted by the brute's unconscious force. She lures him to her and he becomes her lover. But the workers, aroused by Carmelo's death, organize a hunt for Pedro, who flees and finds refuge in the house of Meche. Taken directly from *Los olvidados*, the character of Meche has the same innocence as the adolescent girl of the earlier film, except that she is now mature. Like the child in *Mexican Busride,* who is the only one capable of harnessing the power of a pair of wayward oxen, Meche is the only character to humanize the strongman of *El bruto.* It is her civilizing influence that finally leads Pedro to understand himself as a tool of exploitation. His awareness, however, comes too late. The jealous Paloma, observing his conversion, alerts her husband. Together they call the police and Pedro is finished. He is not shot, however, before he takes his last revenge by choking Cabrera to death.

Although Buñuel expressed disappointment at what he considered an interesting script diluted by concession to commercial needs, Claude Beylie considers *El bruto* the quintessential "black film."[22] The image of the workers' world as a slaughterhouse, passively observed by the Virgin Mary, whose statue sits peacefully in a niche over the slaughterhouse gates, conveys forcefully the calculated and repeated violence that not only prevails but indeed attracts such creatures as Paloma, the jealous wife. The role of the cold, predatory, capitalist wife is repeated in both *Susana* and *Diary of a Chambermaid.* The only force to counter corruption in *El bruto* is the innocent Meche, who, like most of Buñuel's priests, wardens, and other do-gooders, arrives too late or does too little to arrest the rising tide of violence that engulfs both the corrupt boss and his henchman. Lust for power, together with erotic desire, form a vortex in which the weak perish with the powerful.

He (El) (1953)

This remarkable film, one of the high points of Buñuel's career, has been identified as a study of a pathological case of paranoia.[23] Buñuel himself sanctioned the documentary nature of the film when he confided to André Bazin that "the hero of *El* is a type that interests me like a beetle or a mosquito. . . . I am something of an entomologist" (p. 110). Yet Buñuel adds a dimension to the case history that goes beyond psychological analysis.

The inexorable development of the personality of Francisco might easily be drawn from the notes of a psychiatrist. The respectable upper-class bourgeois bachelor is considered, as one of his dinner guests puts it, "to be a normal guy." Francisco's only apparent difficulty is a lawsuit against someone trying to steal funds from him. So when Gloria, whom he meets in church, deserts his best friend, Raúl, to marry Francisco, she would seem to have made a splendid catch. But, as suggested in a scene of the pair kissing, followed by a jump-cut to an explosion at a dam site, the volatile Francisco soon begins to fly apart.

Another jump-cut to a view of Raúl, who nearly runs over the distraught Gloria in the street, leads to a flashback in which she reveals the horrors of their honeymoon in Guanajuato. Francisco becomes so jealous when Gloria greets a male acquaintance that he demands they leave the hotel dining room and finish their meal in private. Convinced the man is spying, Francisco resorts to the antique practice of sticking a pin through the keyhole. The trip concludes dismally when Francisco meets the man in a hotel corridor and punches him in the nose.

Francisco appears improved upon their return from the honeymoon. The couple entertain friends and Francisco asks Gloria to be nice to his young lawyer. But after she dances with the young man, Francisco, in a violent personality reversal, locks her in her room, accusing her of loving the lawyer. Later we hear Gloria screaming upstairs. The following morning she seeks advice from her mother. But the mother, like the priest from whom she also seeks help, shrugs off the incident, counseling her, "When a man is jealous, you have to love him." This indifference to cruelty in marriage is underlined when Gloria returns home. Francisco suddenly fires a pistol and Gloria falls to the floor. The scientific study seems to have become a horror film until another jump-cut to Gloria and Raúl assures the viewer that the bullets were blanks.

Francisco's threats alternate with moments of repentance, but one night as the clock chimes twelve horror strikes again. The desperate Francisco sneaks into the wife's room carrying a terrible collection of supplies—cotton, a razor blade, string, scissors, and a rope. As he slips Gloria's hands into the rope, she wakes screaming. Now fully recovered from her previous passivity and indecision, she is gone by morning.

Francisco, in an hallucinatory frenzy, pursues her with a loaded pistol from her mother's house to Raúl's office, down the streets, and finally into the church where the film began. There, in flash cuts, laughing faces and signs of the cuckold appear to Francisco's tormented mind. Even Father Velasco laughs, pointing to the top of his head to indicate the invisible cuckold's horns as the police drag off the mad Francisco.

In spite of Buñuel's interest in the pathology of his central character, it is doubtful that the director is primarily concerned with presenting a clinical case. The entomologist that Buñuel recognizes as part of his nature is also a surrealist. Since Buñuel found neorealism incomplete, without room for chance or for the unknown, it is unlikely that he thought of himself as the cinematic equivalent to Zola, preparing an experiment with film as his laboratory.

The mystifying final scene of *El* attests to the fact that Buñuel transcends case history. Now married happily, Gloria and Raúl, with their son, pay an unannounced visit to Francisco, who has entered a monastery. Surprise is compounded when we learn that their young son is named for the once-mad Francisco. "And is this your son?" the amazed prior inquires of the couple. Without answering they ask about Francisco and, finding that he is well, leave. When the visitors are gone, Francisco repeats the same question to the prior, who gives an affirmative reply. "Then I wasn't as mixed up as I thought. Peace is here," pronounces the now-calm madman who turns and walks zig-zag down a garden path. In the final scene the case history of *El* dissolves into a surrealist riddle, remote from the analytical tone of the body of the film. This concluding sequence seems more consistent with the work as a whole if the film is considered in the light of the Spanish theater of Calderón, from which it derives.

To those familiar with Spanish literature of the seventeenth century, *El* can only seem a contemporary version of one of the most important themes in Spanish drama, the theme of honor. In Calderón's plays, love conflicts with honor, resulting in raging jealousy on the part of the husband, who, with social sanction, often kills his wife without proof of her guilt. In *A secreto agravio secreta venganza (To Secret Insult, Secret Revenge)* Don Lope kills a man he only suspects of being his wife's lover. He also sets fire to his wife's bedroom, not because he believes her to be guilty, but because he must go to war and fears what she will do while he is away! The king, apprised of Don Lope's actions, approves of them.

In Calderón's dramatizations of the theme of jealousy, the furious male guards his wife because he considers her a rather risky piece of property capable of damaging his honor at any time. All the dramatic elements of the honor tragedies—the raging husband, the innocent wife, the talk of murder, the duel between males—are reflected in *El*. Francisco's fearsome collection of supplies recalls to French critics the scene in de Sade's *Philosophy in the Bedroom.*[24] It also parallels Calderón's *The Physician of his Honor (El médico de su honra)*, in which Don Gutierre, hoping to make his wife's death seem an accident, calls in a bloodletter and orders him to open the vein of Doña Mencia, who lies not sleeping but drugged on her bed.

The complicity of society with the husband in the torment of his wife, seen in Calderón's honor plays, is also clearly apparent in *El*.

As in his earlier films Buñuel's conception of character implicates society as the matrix in which patterns of human behavior develop. Just as the head of state in *To Secret Insult, Secret Revenge* approves of his subject's murder of his wife, so Gloria's mother and the priest justify Francisco's treatment of her.

The role of the Church as a contributor to Francisco's confusion of erotic desire with religious devotion is made clear in the opening scene of the film, in which Francisco aids a priest in washing the feet of the faithful. In the ceremony, traditionally celebrated on Holy Thursday, an old priest is kissing a woman's bare foot. As the bare feet and legs of other worshipers are brought into view, the scene resembles Gerald Brenan's description of the famous polychrome religious statues, "a kind of pornography dedicated to religious ends."[25] It is no coincidence that, as Francisco's mania progresses to its final, hallucinatory phase, he pursues Gloria into the church where his passion, mingled with religious fervor, was first awakened. Association of religious adoration with erotic desire, a characteristic of such major Spanish writers as San Juan de la Cruz, is one of the most consistent ingredients of Buñuel's portrayals of eroticism.

The final scene, in which Francisco, after seeing the young son of Gloria and Raúl, seems convinced that his suspicions were justified and declares his peace of mind, echoes Calderón's Don Gutierre, who boasts in the last scene of *El médico de su honra* of his courage and of the deft manner with which he has avenged himself. Thus *El* is a psychological study of a typical Spanish *caballero* whose values are untouched by three centuries of social thought and who is able, without remorse, to exonerate himself for attempted murder of his wife. The final shot of Francisco weaving down the path is Buñuel's final joke, for the broken path taken by the disturbed man is a visual contradiction of his assertion that he is at peace. His winding steps instead convey dislocation and alienation.

The Spanish heritage of *El* is confirmed by its documentary character. The film is based on the memoirs of a nineteenth-century woman of the Mexican upper class, Doña Mercedes Pinto, whose husband served as the model for Francisco. The behavior of the Mexican husband follows the pattern provided for male behavior by Spanish culture. The director's goal, as he stated to André Bazin, was to make a study of love and jealousy. Drawing upon the three sources that nourish his art—documented fact, surrealist principles, and Spanish tradition, Buñuel clearly demonstrated in *El* that his creative imagination was in no way diminished by either years of silence or commercial demands. Film critics have pronounced it a masterpiece,[26] and a professor at the Hospital of St. Anne in Paris used it as an example to his students of pathological behavior.

Essay of a Crime: The Criminal Life of Archibaldo de la Cruz (Ensayo de un crimen: La vida criminal de Archibaldo de la Cruz) (1955)

This horror comedy is a key work in Buñuel's study of pathological behavior. Echoing themes of *l'amour fou* that have preoccupied the director since *L'Age d'or*, *Archibaldo* picks up where *El* leaves off and suggests a mischievous parallel between sainthood and criminality, a juxtaposition which is repeated in *Nazarín*. While the happy resolution of *Archibaldo* ends the film in a lighter mood than in *El*, it is both more disturbing and more daring than its predecessor.

Archibaldo is the spoiled son of rich parents who leave his upbringing to a governess. Archi feels neglected when his mother leaves him for an evening at the theater, but he stops pouting when she gives him a music box decorated with a ballerina on the top. While the music plays, the ballerina spins mechanically. As Archi's mother shows the lad the music box, shots ring out. The matron is indignant to learn that the revolution has begun. As a member of the upper bourgeoisie, she views social disturbances as a colossal inconvenience. "They've ruined our evening; they should be hanged," she declares at this interruption of her plans.

While his parents are out for the evening, the governess tells Archi the story of a king who could eliminate his enemies just by opening a music box. As Archi takes the box and opens it, more shots are heard. The governess, killed by a revolutionary's stray bullet, falls dead. Little Archi assumes that he, like the king, caused the governess's death. At first he is horrified, but he is also fascinated by the sight of the woman's shapely legs lying uncovered on the floor before him.

A jump-cut to a hospital room reveals the childhood scene to have been a flashback. The connection, however, between Archi's past and his present confinement in the hospital is clear. The incident has left him emotionally confused. He confesses to the nun who now tends him that he felt the pure pleasure of power at the governess's death. Remembering that crucial moment from his childhood, Archi transfers the governess's identity to the nurse and suddenly approaches her with a razor. The terrified nun runs out of the room, makes a wrong turn, and falls to her death down an elevator shaft.

Archi's childhood experience with the music box causes him as an adult to equate sexual pleasure with death. Recognizing the danger of this notion, he turns himself in to the police and confesses to having caused the nun's fatal fall. Like the guests who represent society's opinion in *El*, the police are not alarmed. In fact, a hospital official has just testified that, although Archi is a "bit quiet," he is normal. But Archi knows that his behavior, for all its apparent normalcy, is potentially dangerous. He insists to the police that the nun is not his first victim, and flashbacks illustrate his past deeds as Archi confesses to the police.

An abrupt cut takes the viewer from the police interview to an antique shop where Archi is browsing. He spies the very music box of his childhood among the precious objects now for sale. A man and a woman are also inspecting the box, but Archi is so eager to buy it that he almost takes it out of their hands. Thrilled at finding his childhood treasure, he cradles it on his way home. The box with its ballerina has become an image of power that triggers Archi's sexual behavior. While he is shaving, he cuts his ear and, at the sight of blood, a vision of the governess appears to him, her bloodied legs sharply focused in his fevered mind.

In spite of its logical narrative and realistic characters, *Archibaldo* is one of the most surreal of Buñuel's films, not only because of its presentation of madness as indistinguishable from sanity, but because of the prominent role given to chance, *le hasard.* It is only through chance that Archi manages to avoid murdering the women he encounters, but his victims perish anyway, without his intervention. Before he can rid himself of the clinging Patricia, she commits suicide. He asks his ideal, Carlotta, to marry him, begging her to decide quickly because, he complains desperately, "You're leaving me to my obsessions." But Carlotta hesitates, puzzled by Archi's confession to her that sometimes he wants to be a great saint and at other times, a great criminal. This surreal joke, based upon the juxtaposition of two states that society considers opposed, becomes one of the central ironies of *Nazarín.* Carlotta does not understand this strange statement from the charming bachelor who appears, as did Francisco in *El,* attractive and innocent in the eyes of society. While she hesitates, Archi's obsessions run their course unrestrained.

Archi, who seems determined to become a future Jack the Ripper or Boston Strangler, meets his match in the undaunted Lavinia. At a restaurant to which she has escorted some American tourists, Lavinia spies Archi at another table. She recognizes him as the man who bought a music box almost out of her hands while she and a male friend were admiring it. She leaves her tourists to join Archi and introduces herself to him. As Lavinia leaves, Archi asks to see her again. She tells him she works as a model in a dress shop and gives him the shop's address. The next day, Archi visits the shop and asks for Lavinia. No one at the shop knows her. Puzzled, Archi turns to go and sees a mannequin which looks like Lavinia. Archi now understands that he has been outwitted by the clever Lavinia, whose likeness is the model in the shop. But Archi is persistent. He goes to the factory where Lavinia works as a live model for wooden mannequins. As Lavinia leaves the factory after work, Archi greets her and invites her to visit him. Always correct, he assures her that he does not live alone but with his female cousin.

When Lavinia arrives at Archi's house, she discovers to her surprise that Archi's cousin is a mannequin that he bought at the factory. Lavinia is both amused and irritated to find herself alone with Archi. But she is not easily intimidated and has a surprise for him in return. When Archi leaves the room to bring drinks, she changes clothes with the mannequin whom the charming bachelor has introduced as his cousin. The plastic figure resembles Lavinia so closely that, when Archi returns, he cannot distinguish between the real woman and the fake. He hands the mannequin a drink and receives an icy stare.

Laughing at him, Lavinia tells Archi that he must choose between her and the mannequin. This crafty woman's tricks are beginning to frustrate Archi. While Lavinia gets dressed in her own clothes, Archi goes to the basement kiln (he is a potter) and stokes the fire in which he plans to incinerate his guest. But Lavinia has still another trick for him. The best of all the surprises in this surprising film is sprung at the moment Archi is ready to grab Lavinia. As he reaches for her, the doorbell rings. Furious, Archi opens the door and a horde of tourists, invited by Lavinia to the house, file in. The noisy visitors, complete with cameras and loud shirts, are eager to see a

Laviani (Miroslava Stern) faces her mannequin-double in the apartment of Archibaldo Cruz (Ernesto Alonso) in *The Story of a Crime.*

typical Mexican home. As they leave, Lavinia delivers Archi the sharpest jolt of all. Following her charges out the door, she announces to him that she is getting married.

With the driven look of a man who, sexually aroused, suddenly finds himself abandoned by his lover, Archi grabs the mannequin. Determined to seek revenge, Archi lugs the wooden figure to the basement. On the way, one of the legs falls off the female form. This artificial leg is given the same careful scrutiny by the camera as in *Tristana* fifteen years later. Archi is undeterred. He sticks the leg under his arm and continues down the stairs to the basement, where he places the female form in the fire and glows with satisfaction while the painted face melts into the flames. But poor Archi cannot even enjoy his simulated moment of triumph. With the suspenseful timing of a horror film, the doorbell rings again. This time Archi's success is not contrived by his obsession. Accompanied by her mother, the eminently respectable Carlotta enters and announces that she has decided to marry this madman.

Suspense mounts as Archi, learning Carlotta has a lover, is seized by a vision in which he shoots his bride as she kneels to say her prayers. Again, however, chance intervenes and Carlotta is killed, not by Archi, but by her jealous lover. A sudden jump-cut brings the action back to Archi chatting with the police. The police chief steadfastly refuses to find Archi guilty. "We have enough to do as it is. . . . To imagine is no crime. If I arrested everyone who thinks of murder the jails would be overflowing." This statement, based on the soundest common sense, links Archi's state of mind with that of most human beings, who, at one time or another, experience desires considered to be criminal.

One day in a moment of resolve, Archi decides to break the link with his childhood association of sexual pleasure and death. He goes to a park and dumps the music box with its tiny ballerina into a lake. Sinking slowly to the bottom, the symbol of his fatal association disappears forever; and it is not the experience of fulfilling his dreams, as J. H. Matthews assumes,[27] but the destruction of this symbolic object that liberates him from his obsession. Archi's desires are not satisfied by his victims' demise, as is clear from his continuing need for still another victim. The chain of murder can only be broken by the destruction of his sex-death association, symbolized by the music box, the instrument that Archi as a child had found to cause both sexual pleasure and death. It is most likely the police chief's suggestion, half in jest, that Archi use an electric razor when shaving, that, as the French film critic Marie-Cécile Estève points out, gives Archi the idea of breaking the chain of violence which torments him.[28]

With the music box gone, Archi appears relieved of his obsessions and walks briskly away from the lake into which his music box has sunk like a bad memory into the deep recesses of the unconscious. He seems to have finally liberated himself from his fatal mental trap. He spies a grasshopper on a tree trunk and pokes it with his cane. As proof of his cure, he walks on, without any inclination to harm it. Who is the woman headed toward him? By another coincidence, Lavinia! He greets her, inquiring about her husband. There is no husband. And her tourists, her "gringuitos"? Lavinia informs Archi that "like fruit, they're not in season now." As if cured of a crippling disease, Archi leaves his cane and walks off arm in arm with Lavinia.

Although the hero is cured, *Archibaldo de la Cruz* is a more disturbing film than its predecessor, *El.* Unlike Gloria, who abandons her pursuer only after her worst suspicions are confirmed, Archi's female victims face their potential killer unaware. In the manipulation of comic horror and suspense, *Archibaldo de la Cruz* is one of Buñuel's most gripping and most representative films. It is a playful but chilling mixture that, rare in the Buñuel canon, presents a satisfactory resolution of a criminal obsession.

A Trilogy of Love and Revolution

Its Name Is Dawn (Cela s'appelle l'aurore) (1956)

Despite unfavorable reviews, *Its Name Is Dawn* is important not only as the first of Buñuel's three portrayals of political morality but because it deals with a theme close to Buñuel's own past—that of the role of the intellectual in social revolution. It was the question of how the intellectual was to serve revolutionary goals that split the surrealist group in Paris in 1930. While Louis Aragon praised revolutionary purpose in his famous long poem, "Red Front," André Breton wrote a detailed critique of it and set himself against blind obedience to any cause other than surrealism, including communism. It is with that sad chapter of surrealist schism in mind that *Its Name Is Dawn* becomes not just another melodrama with undeveloped characters but a political morality play in which hard choices must be made.

The unidentified island in the Mediterranean where the action of *Dawn* unfolds is an outpost of capitalism. It is isolated, its government exploitative and hopelessly static. The characters of *Dawn* are stereotypes of social classes: the capitalist boss, Gorzone, the humanitarian intellectual, Doctor Valerio, and the worker, Sandro. Yet Buñuel complicates these stereotypes with unexpected ambiguities. The agent of capitalism, the police chief, appreciates art and the boss himself allows Valerio to convince him that the gardener, Sandro, need not be fired. It is too late to revoke his prior decision, however. Sandro's replacement has already arrived at Gorzone's estate with his entire family in tow.

Valerio's position is also ambiguous. He is an educated man married to Angela, who begs him to accept her rich father's offer of a lucrative practice and sheltered life in Nice. But when Angela leaves for her vacation on the mainland, Valerio meets Clara, a rich widow who lives on the island. Clara encourages the doctor's nobler desires to remain and tend the poor. Nor is her advice based on self-interest, for, while she and Valerio have fallen in love, she refuses to intervene in his now empty marriage.

The worker Sandro and his wife, Magda, are the victims in this capitalist paradise. Magda suffers from tuberculosis and her cure requires the kind of relaxed life that workers cannot afford. As a direct result of Sandro's loss of his job and their change of lodgings, which requires a taxing trek through crowded streets of the town, Magda dies. Sandro retaliates by crashing one of Gorzone's plush soirees and assassinating the capitalist boss. The hunted criminal finds refuge at Valerio's, but, when cornered by his pursuers, he kills himself.

The last scene confirms Valerio's choice. He has been tempted by the insulated life of a rich physician in Nice, which his wife is eager to assume. His role as minister to the poor takes on sharp contrast to his wife's ideals when he becomes dedicated to helping the workers and begins hiding Sandro, now a fugitive from the law. Angela's father equates Valerio's present action with that of the criminal. He refuses to allow his daughter to live with a man who also harbors murderers under his roof. But Valerio prefers to remain on the island although it means that he must abandon his wife and the social class that was his own. The final shots are of Valerio, accompanied by Clara, strolling along the waterfront. Not far behind, three workers—Sandro and his friends—follow along the beach.

The political sentiment is enlivened throughout by Buñuel's inimitable imagination. Valerio meets Clara when he goes to examine a little girl raped by her grandfather. This harsh detail foreshadows the rape of the young girl, Claire, who frequents the estate in *Diary of a Chambermaid.* The children of the poor, the victims on this exploited island, play war games and shoot each other down in mock firing squads. The desperate Sandro, before breaking into Gorzone's palace, picks up a kitten. Perhaps an emblem of his own fragility, the kitten is in Sandro's hand while he pumps bullets into the boss's stomach. By making certain that life on the island is seen in all its dark reality, Buñuel indicates that Valerio's choice is not romantic idealism but a search for commitment in his life at the expense of idle comfort. What distinguishes him from Buñuel's priests and other futile missionaries is that Valerio chooses to serve not God but man. This triumph of nobility is echoed by the title of the novel by Emmanuel Robles, on which the film is based. Robles, in turn, takes the title from the final words of Jean Giraudoux's play *Electra:* "What do you call it when the day breaks, like today, and everything has been spoiled . . . when innocent people kill each other, but when the guilty are in their death throes, in some corner of the daybreak? It has a very beautiful name. . . . It is called the dawn!"

Death in This Garden (La Mort en ce jardin) (1956)

Buñuel's recurring theme of outcasts in a hostile environment is again the subject of this violent parable of love and anarchy in the "garden," the abundant, malevolent New World jungle of Brazil. The color that enriched the island setting in *Robinson Crusoe* is accompanied here by a sound track of jungle noises. With screeches of birds and monkeys, the hum of insects, and the drone of tropical rainfall, the director succeeds in creating the illusion of an exotic, ferocious planet from which only two survivors escape.

The main characters are, like Buñuel's own father, European fortune-seekers and a priest who all become enmeshed in a common postcolonial dispute between local and foreign developers of the country's resources. Among those who have come to exploit the "garden" are Castin, the old prospector, Chenko, the trader, and Chark, the adventurer. The more passive inhabitants of the "garden" are Djin, the prostitute, María, the deaf-mute daughter of Castin, and Father Lizzardi, the typical ineffectual priest of the Buñuel canon. While none of these figures is particularly sympathetic, they form an interesting array, especially in the second half of the film when, like the Nobile gathering marooned in the upper-class drawing room in *The Exterminating Angel*, they find themselves struggling for survival in the "garden" and reveal personality traits that have so far remained hidden.

The opening shots are of a team of miners hunting diamonds in a mine near the border of Brazil. A troop of cavalry bursts across the clearing, informing the team that mining is prohibited and that they must abandon their work. The angry miners march to town to protest the interruption. The government's response is a volley of gunfire over their heads.

From this expository sequence of confrontation, a quick cut is made to a bar where angry miners discuss their course of action. It is in this raucous gathering that the somewhat precious Father Lizzardi emerges, decked out elegantly in a white linen suit and contrasting black shirt. Although a missionary to the Volente Indians, he is no mendicant and wears a fine watch, a gift from "Northern Refineries." Warning the miners that "he who lives by the sword dies by the sword," Father Lizzardi appears to be a capitalist collaborator beneath his missionary chic.

The man of action is introduced, appropriately, in a long scene with sparse dialogue. Chark, the adventurer, strides in, takes a hotel room, undresses, and goes to bed. A cat enters his room and he throws a boot at it. His next visitor is Djin, the prostitute, whom he receives more cordially. She slips into his bed and, quickly, it is morning. As she sits on his bed sewing, army goons roust Chark out of bed and march him off to jail. He escapes by trickery. Begging Lizzardi to have the guards bring him pen and ink to write to his aging mother, Chark gouges the priest with the pen, throws the ink at the jailer, and flees.

The rest of the first half of the film is taken up by gun battles, the imprisonment of miners, and firing squads. Among the enemies of the government is Casin, the old prospector who seeks refuge with Djin, whom he hopes to marry and take back to France. His dream is to open a restaurant and live a peaceful family life. Now fugitives from the army, the old man, his mute daughter, and the prostitute escape in the night to a boat owned by the trader Chenko. They are joined by the priest, who has decided things have gotten too hot and that he must get back to his Indians. They leave for the border but are taken by surprise when Chark, who has climbed aboard secretly, takes control of the boat. Pursued by the army, they decide to leave the boat and hide in the jungle. Chenko drops them off and steams away, leaving the fugitives in even more danger than before. Abruptly the little bands fid itself in the alien world of reptiles and insects where the first worry is no longer avoiding the police but merely surviving.

Hunger, exhaustion, and despair soon begin to take their toll. Chark kills a python for them to eat. They find another snake, but ants have already begun to demolish it. Casin's survival instinct fails and he gives up, his hope of returning to France shattered. In despair he tears up his only reminder of sanity, a postcard picturing the Arch of Triumph. Lizzardi's mind, too, begins to wander as he reminisces about seminary days and his mother, whose name, he informs his friends, was Mary. Realizing that their lives are at stake, Lizzardi, in his finest hour, begins to tear a few pages from his Bible to start a fire.

As madness threatens beneath the surface of despair, Buñuel's surreal imagination begins to disturb the realism of the film. The fugitives discover an air liner wrecked in the jungle, the result of a technological disaster, in which there were no survivors. The fugitives bury the dead, with Lizzardi remembering to wear his clerical collar for the ceremony. Refreshed from eating the plane's rations, the fugitives set up housekeeping in the wreck. Suddenly a jump-cut reveals the film's most incongruous image. An elegant woman dressed in a black strapless evening gown and jewels sits in a clearing surrounded by lianas. It is Djin, dressed in a dead passenger's finery. Now safe, her passion returns and she tells Chark she loves him and wants to flee with him from their jungle prison. An alluring figure, she stands while speaking, as if in a French drawing room. But without warning a shot rings out and Djin falls dead, a victim of the now mad Casin, who, seeing his last dream collapse, takes his revenge. Before Chark can load his remaining charge, María, onto one of the plane's inflatable life-rafts, the old man claims another victim, Lizzardi. Chark, losing no time in shooting the old man, jumps into the boat and paddles off with María. Like Djin, she has raided the dead passengers' luggage and sits in the life-raft dressed in a low-cut white gown.

The New World "garden" as seen by Buñuel is a savage place, whether it is the town where an oppressive military dictatorship imprisons and kills miners or the alien jungle where the fugitives, weakened to the point of madness, kill each other. Greed, exploitation, cruelty, and official repression find their natural equivalents in the insects, unexpected quagmires, and leafy labyrinths that convert the "garden" into a maw where violence, manmade or insectile, seems inevitable. The only escapees are Chark, the vigorous man of action with a strong instinct for self-preservation, and the innocent María, whose survival from the evil of the garden seems accidental, if not miraculous. The director, however, characteristically prevents us from knowing their future. A sad trumpet note signals their departure as their life-raft sets out to sea in the open ending so frequent in the films of Buñuel.

Fever Mounts on El Pao (La Fièvre monte à El Pao) (1959)

Irony and antithesis are two of Buñuel's most characteristic patterns of thought. As Luc Moullet cogently points out, "Truth for Buñuel is the juxtaposition of an opinion with its opposite, of an action with its opposite, of an attitude with its opposite."[29] André Breton announces, in the *Second Surrealist Manifesto,* his intention to "expose . . . the factitious character of the old contradictions . . . calculated to hinder every unusual agitation on the part of man."[30] Thus, if Buñuel goes to great lengths in his films to show that justice is often unjust, that criminality often passes as normalcy, and that charity approaches exploitation when practiced by the Church, he is not attempting to prove, as some would have it, that everything is one and the same. The play of opposites that Buñuel learned from surrealism is not an ideal metaphysical game but a challenge, in Breton's words, or, as Luc Moullet explains, "a search for a higher truth,"[31] an attempt to reveal reality as a combination of known factors which must be transcended if a new reality is to be attained.

Fever Mounts on El Pao is a study of revolt and compromise, an entirely characteristic Buñuelian exercise in the resolution of opposites in which revolt takes on the appearance of compromise. A cerebral account of a dialectical process, *El Pao* achieves its purpose. Buñuel's best films, however, are much more than intellectual études. The director had, from the first, misgivings about this film, based on a novel by Henri Castillou, "because the subject lacks humor. Actually it is close to melodrama. It will be tough going, but maybe we will pull it through."[32] Buñuel's reservations were not unfounded, for spontaneity, the gift of his special humor, becomes lost in melodrama.

Using a setting similar to *Its Name Is Dawn, El Pao* opens with a documentary exposé of the island of the title in the New World tropics. The camera gives a quick visual tour of its important landmarks—a colonial palace, a monastery, and the governor's country estate. Also included is the labor camp where political prisoners harvest copra, the island's major export, according to the textbook tone of the narrator. From panoramic shots, Buñuel zooms in, as in *The River and Death,* to focus on a fiesta. The festival scenes are interspersed with views of the governor in his office. That all is not well with his marriage is apparent when he slaps his wife for being unfaithful. At a public rally at which the governor is to speak, he is suddenly assassinated, and pandemonium breaks out. The poor peasants begin to steal sides of meat from a butcher's cart. Perhaps representing the corruption and violence to come, a whole animal carcass is carried off, its legs bobbing stiffly in the air.

In the ensuing power struggle, the villain, Alejandro Gual, gains control by imprisoning his enemies, and the idealistic young Ramón Vásquez becomes his rival. Vásquez, who is in love with the governor's widow, the clever, power-hungry Inés Vargas, finds himself immediately compromised. Views of torture at the workcamp, where Vásquez's old teacher Cárdenas toils as a political prisoner, are interspersed with scenes of Inés urging Vásquez to challenge

Gual. Inés visits Gual herself and offers him sexual favors in exchange for his allowing Vásquez, whom Gual has accused of aiding the governor's assassin, to remain free. There is a memorable strip scene in which Inés, in black underwear, is viewed through a philodendron in Gual's office. Power and sex are again mingled when Inés tries to shoot Gual, but misses. Suddenly she switches her attack from attempted murder to seduction, and regains control by pulling the dictator down and kissing him.

Gathering his courage, Vásquez incites a prisoner uprising and takes control of the island. He is too late, however, to save the tired old Cárdenas, who has died. Gual is taken prisoner, summarily robbed by the guards, and executed. This death without a trial troubles Vásquez, who explains to the unscrupulous widow that they, too, have become assassins.

Inés is unmoved by Gual's defenseless death. But she is infuriated when Vásquez is willing to compromise her reputation in order to be named governor. Reminding Vásquez of all she has done for him, she remarks bitterly, "You've come a long way, Ramón," insinuating that he has replaced Gual not with nobility but with equal self-abasement.

Finally, Vásquez is overwhelmed by events. Freeing the political prisoners, he tries to end tyranny, but the final commentary informs the viewer that his refusal to sign a document curtailing the people's liberty "is the harbinger of his own death and the sign that he is a free man." Free, but hopelessly inept, Vásquez swings from betraying his friends to playing into his enemies' hands. Seriously compromised, the conscientious rebel, like Nazarín, becomes hopelessly enmeshed in a system beyond his capacity to control.

Ado Kyrou, the surrealist critic and one of Buñuel's admirers, apologizes for this trilogy of films, explaining that the director made them hoping to convince a French public that he was capable of more than visionary incoherence.[33] But after *Las Hurdes* and *Los olvidados*, why would Buñuel feel bound to prove his commitment to social revolution? A remark by another well-known film critic, Andrew Sarris, may reveal why. More receptive to Buñuel's work than most American critics, Sarris observes that, "for a leftist, Buñuel shows no interest in the mechanics of reform or revolution."[34] Since only a viewer who knows Buñuel by his best-known films could make this statement, it is possible that Buñuel, fearing such a remark, felt the need to express himself concretely on such political topics as reform, collaboration, and social commitment. Thus he made these three films, generally considered among his worst. They are, however, not any worse than the many other melodramas of film history; indeed, their moral integrity sets them apart from the sentimental conventions of most of the cinema of the 1950s.

They are not, however, among Buñuel's best. It is not only that his well-known humor, irony, and surreal imagination are lacking. Outrage, insult, and surprise are reduced to a minimum as the pioneer surrealist tries to convince a new, existential, and very serious generation of intellectuals that they have something to learn from him. As if answering Sartre's allegation that the surrealists, after having sat out the war, were not interested in revolution but in magic, Buñuel responds not in his own surreal terms but in the vocabulary of political reform. Putting aside his comic heritage, he makes three insightful and honest, but dull comments on revolutionary action. Only when he drops the grave, often-pompous, predictable style of political rebuttal and takes up again his own film vocabulary inherited from slapstick and surrealism, does Buñuel regain his strength and spontaneity.

4

Masterworks: Character Studies

Nazarin (1958)

THE PERSONALITIES BUÑUEL CHOSE to analyze closely during the 1950s include two psychopaths—Archibaldo de la Cruz, who recovers from his obsession, and Francisco of *El,* who does not. Another, Robinson Crusoe, is a shipwreck victim finally rescued from his involuntary isolation. Nazarín, a priest, is in a sense also shipwrecked. His emotional isolation is voluntary and is caused by pure idealism. Determined to pattern his life on the life of Christ, Nazarín is also finally rescued. The priest at last realizes that he can only serve his cause by joining the human community and by learning from others rather than by confronting them as an outsider.

Nazarín is unlike most of Buñuel's characters in that he is not merely a product of his environment but is in revolt against it. As a rebel, Nazarín is endowed with a degree of nobility not often present in Buñuelian protagonists. He disdains the religious and secular establishment and prides himself on his independence from material needs. When he is robbed of food and clothing, he shrugs it off: "It really wasn't worth keeping under lock and key."[1] Property, in his view, should belong to those who need it. In his practice of religion, Nazarín is again unorthodox. He refers to himself as a Roman Catholic Apostolic who does not preach but who says Mass for the poor. He refuses to don the collar and cassock, which might afford him special treatment by those who respect the clergy. In all, Nazarín's views, revealed in an introductory question-and-answer sequence between Nazarín and two electricians, contradict established views of property, social status, and religion.

Parallels between Nazarín and Christ are numerous and frequently noted by critics who see Nazarín's two followers, Andara

Francisco Rabal receives a disciple's tribute in Nazarín *(1959).*

and Beatriz, as equivalents of Mary and Mary Magdalene. The protagonist's name seems to confirm the supposition that he is indeed a twentieth-century Mexican Christ, yet Buñuel's Nazarín seems even more tormented than Jesus. Well-intentioned but inept, he causes an uprising in a railroad gang whose members feel threatened by his willingness to work not for wages but only for food. Though he cures a child, he simply annoys a woman who only wants to be alone with her lover in the last few moments before she dies. Nazarín stands up to an abusive colonel who insults a peasant, but is beaten to a pulp by two thieves when he is arrested and jailed as an accomplice to Andara's crime of setting fire to a house early in the film. That Nazarín's failures outnumber his triumphs is emphasized in the culminating scene in the jail, where he is closely questioned by his defender, one of the thieves who shares his cell. When the priest asks the thief if he would like to be good and change his life, the thief returns the question: "Would you like to change your life?" Nazarín is surprised when the thief measures Nazarín's contribution by his own: "You're on the side of good, I'm on the side of evil . . . and neither of us is any use for anything" (script, p. 200). The surrealist technique of juxtaposition of two opposites—saintlinesss and criminality—creates a new awareness of the futility, if not the actual danger, of the kind of purity Nazarín attempts to practice.

Emotionally jolted by the thief's analogy and physically exhausted by the beating he received in jail, Nazarín appears to achieve a fresh understanding of himself and his role in the final scene. Escorted by church guards sent to protect him, Nazarín waits for the other prisoners to file by on the march to the capital they must undertake. A peasant woman who is pushing a cart-load of fruit along the road offers the priest a pineapple. Confused, distracted, and unhappy, the priest walks on a few steps, ignoring the gift. But the old woman insists, disappointed by his rejection. In the background at this moment is heard the sound of drums rolling. This is actually a replaying of "Rhythm of Holy Week in Calanda," a series of drum rolls which accompanies processions during Holy Week in Buñuel's native town of Calanda.[2] They are solemn and insistent, announcing impending death. As the drum rolls reach a crescendo, Nazarín appears to have a sudden change of mind. He turns to the old woman, takes the fruit, and thanks her. As he cradles the pineapple, his tear-streaked face reflects what the script describes as "a mixture of gratitude and hope" (script, p. 205).

The Spanish film director José Antonio Bardem considers this final scene the most profound and disquieting in the history of film. "From now on, Nazarín will doubt."[3] Whether the drum rolls indicate the death of Nazarín's faith, as some critics assert,[4] or whether he simply accepts membership in the human community rather than remaining an ineffectual nomad is characteristically left open by Buñuel. Indeed, as André Labarthe maintains, it does not matter.[5] For Nazarín's decision to receive the woman's gift is a symbolic gesture of his humanity which transcends the question of whether or not he is a Christian.

That both the Communist *L'Humanité* and the Catholic *La Croix* claim *Nazarín* as a voice of their own points of view attests to the film's great success in attracting a widely divergent public. Buñuel's ambiguity irritates some who, looking for solutions, declare the film weak because it "doesn't fall into place as it goes along."[6] Yet acclaim by opposing schools of thought is rare and registers a universal appeal not easily achieved.

Stylistically *Nazarín* represents Buñuel's most impeccable realism. Based on Benito Pérez Galdós's novel of the same title, Buñuel remains faithful to his model until the last scene where, ironically, Buñuel, master of dreams and visions, eliminates the vision of Jesus which appears to Galdós's hero. Buñuel's use of the sound of drums, however, has a symbolic purpose and suggests the priest's agonizing ordeal. Since there is no other music throughout the film, the sound of drums builds tension at the awesome conclusion.

If Buñuel restrains his proclivity for hallucinatory images in *Nazarín*, the film is not entirely lacking in surrealist inspiration. In the introductory sequence, Andara is recuperating from a wound while hiding in Nazarín's apartment. As she gazes at a traditionally tragic painting of Christ on the wall, the face, surrounded by its halo, begins to laugh. This mocking image is the first hint of Buñuel's prevailing notion, which he develops throughout the film, that comfort is to be found with humanity itself, rather than in religious devotion. Buñuel's love of the grotesque, as deeply rooted in Spanish art as in surrealism, is expressed in the figure of Ujo the dwarf. This deformed creature, found dangling from a tree from which children have suspended him in one cruel scene, develops love and loyalty so genuine as to surprise those unable to see beyond the gnarled form that houses them. Andara cracks jokes at him, saying, "Ujo, my little dumpling! But you've only brought your head to see me, where did you leave your body?" (script, p. 181). But Ujo's emotions are, in spite of his body, well balanced and fully human, in contrast to Nazarín's more abstract fixation on goodness and self-denial. When Beatriz rests her head on Nazarín's shoulder, the priest in turn becomes engrossed with a snail he has placed on the back of his hand. Ujo's concern for humanity seems more genuine, as he tells Andara, "Even though you're a whore I like you" (script, p. 175). Human passions are clearly not within Nazarín's emotional range.

Stark contrasts also dominate the visual impression created by *Nazarín*. Dark objects are almost black, while the light is the intense, washed-out white of a parched and arid land. It was in *Nazarín* that the cinematographer, Gabriel Figueroa, claimed to have found the secret to filming Buñuel's style. "All you have to do," he said, "is plant the camera in front of a superb piece of scenery, with magnificent clouds, marvellous flowers, and when you're ready, you turn your back on these beauties and film a stony track or a lot of bare rocks."[7] Buñuel's stringent restriction of visual pleasantry, together with the painfully slow but functional pace of the action, results in an authentic, often-dramatic commentary on the failure of pure idealism.

Viridiana (1961)

Viridiana is one of the few full-length portraits of a female Christ figure in Western art. She can also be compared to a modern Joan of Arc[8] as well as to Nazarín, the worker-priest who tries to pattern his life after Christ's. Like the priest, Viridiana is an orphan, an outcast who decides to abandon the sheltered convent and minister to the poor. She meets with the same failure as Nazarín and is subjected, as he was, to cruel physical abuse. In spite of the priest's disastrous career, however, *Nazarín* ends with a glimmer of hope as the protagonist accepts a gift from a passerby. But, perhaps because she is a woman, or because of the rather dull, materialistic partner available to her, Viridiana's future holds less promise. Although Buñuel claimed that he wanted only to make a "funny film,"[9] *Viridiana* is not only one of his best, but one of his darkest works as well.

Because of its faster pace, *Viridiana* does not sink into dismal and lugubrious stretches as does *Nazarín*. The introductory sequence, although lengthy, efficiently establishes the motivations of the central character. As the film opens, Viridiana, about to take her vows to become a nun, makes a final, obligatory visit to her only relative, Don Jaime, who lives alone on his estate. The old man is delighted by her visit and is overcome by Viridiana's resemblance to his wife, Doña Elvira, who died on their wedding night. Viridiana's feelings, however, are not so warm. They are expressed unconsciously one night when she sleepwalks into her uncle's room. Carrying a wicker sewing basket, she takes ashes from the hearth and scatters them on Don Jaime's bed. The next morning when he informs her of her actions, she is embarrassed, understanding full well the death wish intended. When the old man commits suicide, Viridiana feels so guilty she informs the Mother Superior that she has changed her mind and will serve God outside the convent.

With great economy and little psychological examination, Buñuel develops the narrative and introduces new characters in the main segment of the film. Don Jaime leaves his estate to his illegitimate son, Jorge, who comes to claim his inheritance and to modernize the estate. Viridiana sets up a kind of communal home for the poor and installs on the estate a memorable collection of beggars, including a blind man and a leper, in a building away from the main house. The contrast between two opposing modes of life is rich in comic potential. The devout Viridiana leading her beggars in odd jobs and in prayer inevitably conflicts with Jorge, the determined materialist who begins renovating the place without delay. Viridiana's ultimately disastrous missionary zeal collides with Jorge's cold efficiency in the violent juxtaposition of a view of the beggars reciting the Angelus as shots and sounds of a nearby dump truck drown out their prayer.

The action is brought to its grotesque culmination with the natural lust of the poor for the finery of the rich. While the owners go into town one day, the beggars are left to their own devices, and they lose no time in taking over the house. Comic tension builds within the context of a dinner that the beggars prepare and consume with the family's heirloom china, linen, and silver. All motion stops for a moment in the famous freeze shot of the beggars in groups of three around the central figure, the blind and arrogant Don Amalio. This by now classic parody of DaVinci's *Last Supper* is followed, as was its biblical source, by disaster. As the drinking of fine wine continues, the atmosphere deteriorates. While the leper, decked out in Doña Elvira's wedding gown, dances to Handel's *Messiah*, the blind Don Amalio discovers a couple fornicating behind a couch.

The beggars' parody of the Last Supper in *Viridiana.*

Enraged, the blind beggar smashes his cane on the table repeatedly, creating what is described in the script as "a battlefield of destruction."[10] When the owners return, destruction escalates into attempted rape and murder as the leper and another beggar tie up Jorge and assault Viridiana. Jorge bribes the leper to kill Viridiana's assailant, as the police arrive at last.

If the technique of rapid pace and jump-cuts in *Viridiana* are borrowed from the American film comedies, Buñuel's humor derives from the kind of surrealist gags that often carry indirect punchlines. When the beggars learn that the "good news" Viridiana brings them one day is that "everyone will have some work to do" (script, p. 56), their faces register shock and disgust. Their general opinion of their benefactress was formed early on and expressed by Enedina: "She's very good but a bit of a simpleton" (script, p. 48). The heroine's naiveté is also ridiculed during Viridiana's visit with her uncle. She observes a servant milking a cow and discovers she cannot bear to hold the cow's udder in her hand. She recoils in a gesture revealing how out of touch she is with the physical side of human experience.

Buñuel's humor also underlines some of the important themes of the film. The contrast between the figures kneeling for the Angelus and the practical tools of industry illustrates that Viridiana's efforts, however sincere, are profoundly ineffectual. This joke derives from the surrealists, in particular from Dalí, for whom Millet's painting of farmers in *The Angelus* embodies sexual impotence as well as general resignation. The cross containing blades that, when opened, become a knife, suggests that the religious dogma which drives Viridiana's ministry can easily become a dangerous weapon.

The beggars function in the film as a troupe of clowns dressed outlandishly in ill-fitting clothes, insulting each other and resisting Viridiana's attempts to keep them from quarreling. One of them, Poca, confesses to being a clown when he admits to Viridiana, "I'm only good at making people laugh" (p. 57). Their antics range from the slapstick to the sinister and their dialogue is a constant stream of complaints, insults, and accusations. Some of their jokes, however, reveal deeper truths. The leper's remark to Viridiana that "if all women were as bad as the priests say, you wouldn't take care of me," pinpoints the misogyny that runs deep within the priesthood. On his way off the "battleground of destruction" that he helped create, Don Amalio improvises a mock beatitude: "Blessed are the generous, master, who take into their respectable house a poor, defenseless blind man . . ." (p. 99), he mumbles as he rapidly exits past the aghast Jorge.

The beggars' undercurrent of comic action finally erupts in an explosion of violence. Until the denouement, however, Buñuel develops his central character against a background of zany antics. The protagonist is not a comic role, but Silvia Pinal, whom Buñuel chose to play it, is known in Mexico as a fine comedienne, and the choice indicates the unsentimental manner in which Buñuel portrays his heroine. For Buñuel is not a romantic but an entomologist, and he studies not his characters' sentiments, but the actions they take to adapt to the stress they undergo. Thus Buñuel's purposes of character portrayal are best served not by an actress trained in the expression of grandeur and weeping but by one who understands the exquisite sense of timing required for subtle visual jokes. The choice of Silvia Pinal was highly perceptive, for she creates precisely the right amount of tension between Viridiana's foolish, often ridiculous naiveté and her excruciating process of self-discovery.

Buñuel's techniques of character development are cinematic rather than literary. The surrealists' disdain of psychological analysis is well suited to the cinema, for they considered visual symbols to be often more concise and eloquent than words. Thus, while the narrative of *Viridiana* is, like that of *Nazarín*, straightforward and realistic, it is punctuated and advanced by the skillful use of visual imagery. One of the most important symbols in *Viridiana* is the jump-rope, which appears throughout the film.

The first image after the opening sequence in the cloister is of the maid's child, Rita, skipping rope as Viridiana arrives at her uncle's estate. The dialogue further establishes the jump-rope as one of the central motifs of the film. We learn that the rope is a gift from Don Jaime, who enjoys watching the little girl's legs as she skips. As Viridiana approaches, the old man takes the rope from Rita and hangs it on a tree. After greeting the visitor, Rita climbs the tree from which she can view the exchange below. When Don Jaime admits to his niece that he hardly ever leaves the house, Rita, unseen in the tree branches, announces that when he does go out, "He makes me jump rope" (script, p. 7). The importance of the jump-rope, which provides pleasure both to Rita and to the old man who watches her, is evident early in the film.

The following sequence is a quick series of shots alternating from Viridiana's bedroom, where she undresses to go to bed, to Don Jaime playing the small organ in his sitting room. The connection between these two disparate scenes is established by the maid, Ramona. Spying through the keyhole, the maid views the objects—a rough crucifix, a crown of thorns, a hammer, nails, and sponge—which Viridiana carries with her. The puzzled maid reports her findings to her employer. The next shot is a jump-cut to a close-up of a cow's udder. It is the next morning, and we are suddenly in the barn where Viridiana watches the milking. This sequence of rapidly juxtaposed images establishes the visual relationship that is the key to Viridiana's character and inner conflict. The jump-rope handle is equated with the cow's udder, which has a similar shape. The child, given the rope by the old man, grasps it, eager to play, but Viridiana, encouraged by the servant to try milking the cow, cannot bring herself to grasp the udder. Rita watches Viridiana's squeamish withdrawal with mocking derision. The udder, suggesting a phallus, disgusts the novice, who prefers instead the dead religious objects whose potentially harmful uses recall the instruments of torture that Francisco carries furtively to his wife's bedside in *El*.

The jump-rope handle, introduced as an integral part of the narrative, thus serves to identify Viridiana's ignorance of, and refusal to acknowledge, carnal desire. With the surrealists' fondness for changing one image into another, as often happens in dreams, Buñuel puts the jump-rope to several uses. When Don Jaime hangs himself with it, the suggestion is strong that his erotic desires have led him, through guilt, to final self-punishment. But Rita begins skipping rope soon after Don Jaime is found suspended by it from a tree, which reminds us that the rope is, first of all, a toy. Later, one of the beggars uses it for a trouser belt. When the beggar assaults Viridiana, the rope assumes its phallic meaning and her hand freezes as she feels the rope handle. The appearance of the jump-rope in various guises, a device that establishes visual and thematic unity throughout the film, derives from the surrealists' enjoyment of surprise in the discovery of objects used outside their ordinary context.

The jump-rope is not the only symbolic key to Viridiana's character. The actions of little Rita also seem to provide a kind of commentary on the behavior of the older woman. As if implying that Viridiana is in some ways as immature as Rita, Buñuel includes a shot of the two jumping rope together shortly after the sleepwalking scene. Like the other innocents in Buñuel's world, Rita occupies a special place and can be counted upon to register true, spontaneous action unaffected by adult pretension. From the moment Viridiana arrives at the estate, Rita observes, often from a safe hideaway, the woman's actions. Rita does not, however, hide her disgust for the beggars and warns them not to touch her. As Viridiana drinks the drug her uncle has prepared to put her to sleep, the scene cuts to Rita announcing to Moncho that she was frightened by a black bull which came into her room, a vision that foreshadows Don Jaime's attempt to seduce Viridiana. After she observes the old man embracing Viridiana's inert body on the bed, Rita repeats to her mother that "a black bull came into my room" (script, p. 31), echoing the display of erotic desire she has just witnessed. Finally, it is Rita who provides the clue to how Viridiana comes to terms with religion. As the little girl pricks her finger on Viridiana's crown of thorns, she tosses it into a fire. Flames surge up in the evening darkness, making clear that Viridiana herself must alter a perilous course which has literally led her to the brink of destruction.

If the protagonist of this dark-comic film is not a comic character, neither are the two secondary roles, both male. Don Jaime, the aging uncle, is a poignant figure whose sexual obsessions and desperation to possess his niece are the toll exacted by years of loneliness and sexual repression. Like Viridiana, however, Don Jaime is often seen in a comic light. Just as Viridiana carries her holy objects in her suitcase, taking them out only to say her prayers in the privacy of her room, Don Jaime, too, stores his treasures—Doña Elvira's wedding attire—in a chest and takes them out during his own silent ritual in which he stares at them fondly. Yet he looks ridiculous as he puts the crown of orange blossoms on his head and tries on the corset and a dainty shoe. Again like Viridiana, who hides her objects when Jorge enters her room unannounced, Don Jaime realizes his masquerade may appear foolish and quickly puts the wedding garb away when he hears a noise.

The preposterous scene in which the old man requests Viridiana to wear the wedding attire, drugs her, arranges her body on the bed as if she were a corpse, and finally begins unbuttoning her dress, suggesting necrophilia, borders on the horrible. But a quick shot of Rita curiously observing it all restores perspective. The shock of how this scene appears from the point of view of an onlooker—including not only Rita but the film-viewer as well—makes it a complex comic masquerade. Order is restored when Don Jaime gains control of himself and rushes from the room.

The role of Jorge is the most puzzling of the film, yet this secondary character holds the key to Viridiana's future. Like the heroine and her uncle, Jorge is largely a sympathetic figure. He sees himself as Viridiana's protector, disliking her collection of monsters—"You ought to let me kick them out" (script, p. 70)—but restraining himself from interfering in her ministry to them. In the final scene, he exerts his full strength to save Viridiana from being raped. For all his methodical planning, Jorge is also capable of generosity. When he sees a cart with a dog tied to it trotting, fatigued, behind it, he admonishes the driver for inhuman treatment to an animal and buys the dog forthwith to spare it further misery. As he turns to leave, another cart rolls by, with its dog also trotting breathlessly behind. The joke is on the individual's sporadic, monumentally insufficient need to do good and serves, in the view of Claude Gauteur,[11] to ridicule Jorge's efforts to restore the farm. Like Don Jaime's earlier rescue of a bee from drowning in a bucket, this incident reveals a capacity for tenderheartedness that softens a complacent character.

Don Jaime's bastard heir, however, is far from heroic. Lacking in sensitivity and angered by Viridiana's indifference to him, he barges into her private sanctum as she is saying her prayers. Nor does he try to hide his preference for his new farm over his girl friend, Lucia, who accompanied him to claim the estate. He seems relieved by her departure and finds a ready substitute in Ramona, the maid. When the two are taking inventory in the attic, he becomes aware of Ramona's adoration of him. He turns toward her as the camera focuses upon a cat pouncing upon a helpless rat. If this scene is any indication of Jorge's true nature, his relationship with Viridiana will repeat the cat-rat pattern. In the final scene, Viridiana joins him and Ramona in a card game. Jorge smugly states that "the first time I met you I said to myself, 'My cousin Viridiana will end up playing cards with me' " (script, p. 108). Indeed, in the original version of the final scene, Ramona slips out of Jorge's bed to be replaced by Viridiana. But Buñuel changed this action at the censor's request, a change which, he admits, improved the film.[12]

Like all works of art, *Viridiana* can be appreciated on many different levels, and it is not surprising to find widely ranging interpretations of it. Perhaps the most frequent is that *Viridiana* is an allegory of modern Spain, with the heroine representing the Spanish people who have been sleepwalking through almost half of the twentieth century.[13] This interpretation seems justified by the setting Buñuel devises for *Viridiana*. Frederic J. Hoffman admits his amazement at the suggestion that Buñuel should be offering us modern Spain. "Were it not for automobiles and electricity . . . we might have been watching a timeless world."[14] The first picture Buñuel had made in Spain in over thirty years, *Viridiana* was filmed near Madrid and Toledo. The story of how Buñuel changed the last scene for the censors and of the film's prohibition in Spain after it was whisked to Paris by the director, enhances, along with "l'affaire *L'Age d'or*" the aura of scandal surrounding Buñuel's career.[15]

For Stanley Kauffman, the film is a "baroque parable," while for Raymond Durgnat it is "a study in the Games People Play."[16] Each of these interpretations touches upon themes suggested in the film and offers avenues of exploration into its many possibilities of meaning. Yet, if *Viridiana* endures as a lasting work of art, it will not be due solely to its handling of themes of social and religious decay which Buñuel has examined elsewhere, but to the memorable creation of a character whose harrowing experiences lead her to reject an untenable, lonely way of life to join in a game of cards, a metaphor for her decision to take her chances with her peers in the game of life.

In this portrait, considered by many to be Buñuel's best film, the director has achieved mastery through humor. His subtle insights into human nature are revealed not only through realistic exposition, as in *Nazarín*, but indirectly by way of parody, dark comic irony, and surreal gags. In portraying the beggars, Buñuel treads a fine line between the creation of character and caricature. It is primarily through comic disillusionment that Buñuel manages to bring the protagonist, whom he both ridicules and respects, to an ending which offers no escape.

The final scene of *Viridiana* is ambiguous. All indications are, however, that whether she joins Jorge in a *ménage à trois*, goes back to the cloister, or decides to resume her ministry, Viridiana faces a "closed world"[17] in which there is no hint of love. If Viridiana feels gratitude toward Jorge and her glance seems to ask his pardon, her blank face and limp hand as she joins in the card game do not convey the hope with which Buñuel illuminates the tearful face of Nazarín. As Jean Sémolué remarks, "One does not have the impression that Jorge will give Viridiana joy and exaltation."[18] The comedy of errors that has been Viridiana's ministry contrasts starkly with the sealed existence she now faces as mistress of an estate. Her only alternatives offer no exit and recall the final frames of *Un Chien andalou*, in which the couple sinks waist-deep into the sand. Viridiana's future seems to suggest that of another Spanish female protagonist in *Tristana*, wherein laughter again falls silent in the face of resignation and futility.

Diary of a Chambermaid *(Le Journal d'une femme de chambre)* (1964)

In *Diary of a Chambermaid*, Buñuel again narrates a tale of a young woman who travels from her world to a latter-day feudal manor, struggles for a time to exist there on her own terms, and is finally swallowed up by a sterile, neurotic, but implacable social order. While providing a glimpse, as Ado Kyrou points out, of the private life of provincial fascists,[19] Buñuel does not, as in *Exterminating Angel*, offer a panoramic social view. Instead, he focuses, like a diary, upon intimate details of the process by which a shrewd, compassionate outsider capitulates to a system she deplores.

The heroine's relentless fate is established from the first when she

Monsieur Rebour (Jean Ozenne) indulges his shoe fetish with the title character (Jeanne Moreau in *Diary of a Chambermaid*).

leaves her job in Paris to establish herself in the decadent, isolated environment of an estate in rural France. That this closed world represents not Celestine's past but her future, prefigures the desperation which is fulfilled at the conclusion of the film. Just as Viridiana arrives at a farm no longer productive, Celestine passes through what the script describes as the "sad countryside"[20] of the provinces. Her first encounter with her employer, Mme. Monteil, includes a tour of the family's fragile treasures—the Chinese vase, the Savonnerie carpet, the silver snuff box, the Sèvres figurines. This inventory makes clear that Celestine has entered a static world inhabited by people as inert as their costly objets d'art.

Heirlooms themselves, the family members are a precious lot. The patriarch, Monsieur Rebour, is, like Don Jaime of *Viridiana*, an aging neurotic whose fetish for female shoes and feet testifies to his long years of isolation and repression. He seems harmless enough when he suggests to his son-in-law that animals may be more beautiful alive than dead. His remark, however, is ironic, since it is made while the two are out hunting. The statement becomes entirely hollow when, in a surprise shot, the old man raises his gun and shatters his target—a butterfly hovering over some blossoms.

Rebour's daughter, Mme. Monteil, appears to be made in her father's mold. She supresses her own desires to the extent of dreading her husband's twice-a-week sexual advances. Her friend the priest, agreeing that such demands are excessive, advises her to refuse to enjoy them. Mme. Monteil assures the priest that she feels no pleasure at all. Like her father, and Don Jaime before him, Mme. Monteil indulges her fantasies in secret rituals behind locked doors. Retiring to her bathroom, which is off-limits to Celestine, Mme. Monteil prepares undescribed solutions in a variety of tubes and bottles. Peter Harcourt supposes that this mysterious activity manifests a fetish for cleanliness.[21] But Buñuel refuses to be specific, always preferring mystery to facile explanation.

However repressed she may be, it is the exacting, competent Mme. Monteil who handles the family finances. Control of the family affairs has passed from the patriarch to his daughter rather than to his son-in-law, Monsieur Monteil, a parasite who can find nothing to do with his life. He seems entirely predatory, for his only activities are hunting and seducing the female servants. Representing more than any other character the enormous waste in human terms of bourgeois capitalism, he consumes without replenishing the considerable resources at his disposal as the heiress's consort.

The upstairs hierarchy, composed of Mme. Monteil, her father, and her petulant husband, has its downstairs counterpart in the servants. If Mme. Monteil rules upstairs, Joseph is the unquestioned master of the servants. In his prejudices, his respect for traditional institutions, and his fondness for discipline, Joseph is a rough copy of his superiors, whose minimal civility masks cruel and sinister passions. But while his masters release their sexual energy in promiscuity and fetishism, Joseph on a dark night rapes and murders the innocent orphan girl Claire who frequents the estate. The little girl is gathering snails in the forest when Joseph passes her in his cart. The child greets him, then offers him a snail which he brusquely refuses. He continues on his way as night falls quickly. It only when the moon comes out, illuminating the forest creatures on their nightly forays, that we see through the brush the child's legs, bloodied and stiff, three snails attached to her calf and crawling toward her knee.

For all its horror, Claire's murder is not entirely unexpected. When Buñuel's other innocents—Meche of *Los olvidados* and Rita of *Viridiana*—escape unharmed, it is their survival that continues to surprise the viewer, who awaits their imminent sacrifice in the ferocious world they inhabit. The guileless Claire roams alone through the forest like Little Red Riding Hood of folk tradition. When she meets the surly Joseph, who holds anti-Semitic views and who once tortured a goose before killing it because "the more it suffers the better it is" (script, p. 44), the fatal outcome is surprising only in its visual detail. The dead child's body is discovered after the director first focuses on a squirrel and two rabbits. The brutalized corpse is described as being "like one animal among others" (script, p. 77); thus Claire joins the goose in Joseph's string of tortured victims.

Buñuel's intuitive grasp of Joseph's pathological character is one of the many considerable achievements of his dramatic skill. Joseph's complacent racism, his sadistic bent, and his self-righteous satisfaction in reporting to his superior that he observed Celestine talking to the neighbors are indications of the violence that lies barely restrained beneath his calm exterior. When alone with Claire one day, he grabs her around the neck, turns her face to him, and demands of the little girl, "Look at me. Look in my eyes. . . . What do you see?" The amazed, slightly terrified Claire replies, "I see myself." Joseph quickly reassures her, "That proves I'm fond of you" (script, p. 14). Celestine, who has just arrived, stares with concern at Joseph's hands around the child's neck. Confronted with innocence in the person of Claire, Joseph's ruthlessness begins to surface. When he meets the child in the forest, he seems to warn her that he is losing control of his dark emotions. As he moves on in his cart, he calls over his shoulder to the little red riding hood figure behind him, "Watch out for the wolf" (script, p. 76). The renowned psychoanalyst Eric Berne defines a fascist as a "person who has no respect for living tissue and regards it as his prey."[22] In light of Berne's description, Buñuel's meticulous portrayal of Joseph's predatory, fascistic instincts is uncannily accurate, even to the objects in his room—the crucifix, a portrait of a military officer, a length of rope, an alarm clock—which, as Giorgio Tinazzi reminds us, are keys to his personality.[23]

During the first half of the film, Celestine is the perfect domestic servant who, passive and correct, navigates safely through a "household of personal shipwrecks."[24] But Claire's murder so angers Celestine that throughout the second half of the film she becomes quietly but stealthily more aggressive. Determined to find Claire's killer, she stalks her prime suspect, Joseph. She goes to the gardener's room prepared to seduce him as a detective might research clues to a murder case. When she asks him to confess to killing Claire, Joseph, so far disinterested in making love, suddenly becomes amorous. "Claire does not concern us now," he replies in a tone described ambiguously in the script as "convincing or seductive" (script, p. 98). One day Celestine visits the city hall to discuss Claire's death with the police. Soon after, two officers visit Joseph. In a suspenseful scene of controlled tension and understatement, Celestine silently sews while she listens to the police, using data she has provided, present evidence against Joseph, arrest him, and take him away.

For the perceptive critic Tom Milne, the disparity between Celestine's passivity in the first half of *Diary* and her active second half is too pronounced and leaves the film, he complains, "broken-backed."[25] Yet, just as Buñuel suggests in *Viridiana*, through continuous juxtaposition of Rita and the heroine, that the child is somehow a reflection of the innocence of the mature woman, in *Diary* there is a similar association between Claire and Celestine. Like a mother hawk, Celestine watches Joseph's every move when he puts his hands around Claire's neck one evening at dinner. She sits by Claire and caresses her when the sleepy child puts her head down. When the sacristan visits Joseph and discusses with him the slaughter of Jews in Romania, Celestine, disgusted with such talk, gathers Claire in her arms and puts her to bed as if to protect her from sinister forces. Having had enough of the Monteil household, Celestine informs her employers that she is quitting. She is already at the train station when she overhears two officers discussing the brutal assault on the child. At once Celestine begins putting information together in her mind and returns to the estate with a new sense of resolution.

On her return, Celestine finds her neighbors discussing the murder in front of the villa of Captain Mauger. Mauger is a retired army officer still interested in women despite his seventy years. In his anti-Semitism and love of discipline, he is a kind of upper-class equivalent of Joseph. Mauger, too, has fascist attitudes and exploits those around him, including Rose, his servant and mistress. Yet his ridiculous bearing when he sticks out his chest, his costume of cast-off army garb, and his delight in annoying his neighbors the Monteils, mark him as a gruff clown, the kind of comic character that W. C. Fields became famous for creating in his early comedies.

Mauger's favorite pastime is dumping trash over the wall onto the Monteil property. His only motive seems to be the criticism Monteil has aimed at him for allowing Rose to share his table at meals.

Unlike Monteil, who seduces servants on the sly, Mauger is at least open and direct, and he invites Celestine to visit him. Celestine appears to have only one goal. She admits to Mauger and the other villagers who discuss the rape-murder, "All I know is that I loved that little girl . . . innocent and so sweet. . . . If I get hold of whoever struck her . . ." (script, p. 83). Soon after, Celestine, returning from delivering evidence against Joseph, meets Mauger. She is stupefied to learn that the old soldier has dismissed Rose. Why? She was jealous of Mauger's conversation with Celestine. What will he do now? "Let's talk squarely, like soldiers. Celestine, do you want me to marry you?" (script, p. 104). To visually enforce this amazing turn of events, Buñuel jolts the viewer by cutting from the scene of Joseph's arrest to a village wedding in which Celestine is the bride of the paunchy Mauger.

The surprise wedding is not as astounding in the film as it was in the novel by Octave Mirbeau, on which Buñuel's *Diary* is based. Mirbeau's Celestine marries Joseph the murderer. Buñuel's solution seems more credible, since the dream of most servants is to improve their lot by marrying money, not murderers. Even Jean Renoir, who filmed a less violent version of *Diary* (1946) in Hollywood, had Celestine marry the scion of the wealthy family. But in trying to advance herself, Celestine has succumbed to the kind of life she scorns her employers for leading. Celestine the clever worker has no friends to join in combat against capitalistic exploitation and greed. She has, instead, joined the bourgeoisie, though with a sense of resignation that has haunted her since Claire's murder, an event symbolizing the death of innocence.

Diary of a Chambermaid is unique in Buñuel's canon, for it ends not with an ambiguous scene of potentially contradictory meaning but with an unequivocal statement. A sullen Celestine has her coffee in bed in a room hung with the guns and military mementos dear to the heart of her new husband, Mauger, who stands at her bedside in suspenders, an aging, overinflated martinet. He brings Celestine the news that Joseph has been acquitted for lack of evidence. At this mention of Joseph, the scene cuts to a demonstration of right-wing patriots marching with banners proclaiming "France for the French" and "Down with Foreigners."

In the final frames, Joseph, his arm around his new wife, steps out of his café to applaud the marchers and to join in shouting, "Vive Chiappe!" (script, p. 131). If, in remembering thirty-three years later the chief of police who censured *L'Age d'or*, Buñuel displays a long and bitter memory, his sense of the future is even more disturbing. For the thunder and lightning accompanying the fascist march announce scenes enacted throughout Europe in the war that followed within a decade the events of *Diary of a Chambermaid*, set in the mid-1920s.

Response to *Diary of a Chambermaid* ranges from acclaim to censure. Buñuel's tenacious adherence to his traditional, realistic portrayal of a past era made his new film seem an instant antique in the 1960s, when most serious directors were experimenting with the latest film style, the *nouvelle vague*. Michel Mohrt writes that Buñuel's anarchism appears dated; for Tom Milne, the work does not live up to standards of *Viridiana*.[26] When considered from its several levels, however, *Diary of a Chambermaid* seems as rich, if not as ambiguous, as any of Buñuel's films. The central character is as intriguing, complex, and contradictory as any living person. Her actions are treated in such a way that it is not her sellout that stuns, but the inexorable power of the bourgeoisie, against which individual protest is futile.

Simon of the Desert (Simón del desierto) (1965)

In *Simon of the Desert*, Buñuel continues the study of the ascetic character that he began in *Nazarín*. Simon's existence is an even more austere ordeal of self-denial and endurance than the priest's. Yet *Simon* is much livelier than the earlier character study. The absentminded Simon and his preposterous situation are richly comic, and Buñuel takes full advantage of their hilarious potential. Much of the film's delight lies in the temptations that Simon undergoes. A series of surrealist gags, these tests of his devotion are the result of a virtuoso performance of Buñuel's extraordinary imagination. *Simon of the Desert* is not, however, merely an entertaining farce. The tender treatment of the protagonist, the multi-level symbolism of the jokes, the sense of history, and the surprise ending with its moral warning make this short surrealist comedy one of the most robust and fluent achievements of Buñuel's career.

As in *Diary of a Chambermaid*, whose mournful countryside in the opening frames signals the emotional setting of the film, the

The crowd visits Simon Stylites' column in *Simon of the Desert*.

inhospitable environment of *Simon* is established in the script's first paragraph: "The burning sunlight falls upon a cracked and uneven landscape: there are no trees, only thorn bushes and other small desert plants" (p. 199). The Spanish viewers of *Las Hurdes* who complained because Buñuel did not include some of the region's more scenic attractions did not understand that Buñuel's harsh landscapes serve to underscore the fact that his characters are outcasts. Their hostile habitat indicates their physical and emotional distance from the world. Thus the desert horizon, uninterrupted by architectural detail, identifies Simon as another of Buñuel's outcasts. Simon, however, has withdrawn to his isolated perch by choice.[27]

The film's opening shot is of desert landscape crossed by a line of people walking and chanting Psalms. Like the line of children marching across the cloister courtyard in *Viridiana*, the line of figures is a striking visual lead into the frame and thus into the action of the film. The religious chanting and the view of monks and a bishop heading the procession of pilgrims appear to announce the beginning of a serious religious film. But when the procession stops at the foot of two columns and Simon comes into view, standing in a Christlike pose, arms outstretched, palms up, atop one of the pillars, the comic possibilities of the pose are irresistible, and the farce begins.

Simon, the bishop announces, has stood for six years atop a column. His example of penitence has attracted wonder and admiration. Praxedes, a rich man, expresses his respect for Simon in the only way he knows how, by providing him with a new and taller column. The bishop acknowledges Simon's devotion by offering to make him a priest. But, like Nazarín, Simon refuses tribute of any sort and is annoyed by those who would interrupt his duties, which consist of standing on the pillar, praying, and fasting. But there is a constant stream of visitors at the foot of the column, each of whom reveals aspects of Simon's character.

Though Simon refuses the bishop's blessing, he gently receives a cripple whose hands were amputated as punishment for theft. The cripple's wife implores Simon to help, and he kneels and prays with them. When the cripple's hands are miraculously restored, the man does not pause to thank Simon but begins chatting with his wife, hits his daughter for asking to see his hands, and walks away. This curious incident seems to suggest that human nature is fundamentally indifferent to miracles and sacrifice and that, as Peter Schillaci observes, "People remain morally unchanged."[28]

If Simon tolerates the presence of the unfortunate, he is generally impatient with everyone else, especially women. His mother wishes to live at the foot of his column to be near him, but Simon, warning her that his love for her "cannot come between the Lord and His servant," bids her farewell: "When we meet again it will be in His presence" (script, p. 205). Another woman carrying a pitcher on her shoulder catches Simon's eye. He insists she has a squint. When the other monks assure him that she does not, Simon becomes adamant. Reflecting the fear of women characteristic of Christian priesthoods, Simon intimidates the monks by reminding them of the commands, " 'Do not look upon any woman,' and 'Neither let her take you with her eyelids,' and above all, 'Do not permit yourself to burn in the fire of vain contemplation' " (script, p. 211). That the woman carrying the pitcher is the same woman who later turns into the devil and tempts him indicates that Simon sees all women as being the same, that is, corrupt.

Nor does Simon tolerate any sort of frivolity. Matias, the youngest of the monks, is a carefree lad who wears no beard and who, childlike, expresses his exuberance by jumping and skipping. He is immature, and, like Viridiana, blushes when the goatherd touches one of his goat's udders. Though it is Matias who brings Simon food, the ascetic is displeased by the young monk. Weak from hunger, Simon grumbles to himself, "I had managed to forget my body, but that wretched child has reminded me of it" (script, p. 217). Later, Simon tells the head monk, Zeno, to get rid of Matias. "It is not wise for him to live in the monastery, because of the devil's temptation." Simon advises that Matias not return "until his beard has covered his cheeks" (script, p. 230).

If Simon is reminded of unholy thoughts in the presence of Matias, he is bombarded with erotic provocation from a female character appearing in various guises. The famous comedienne Silvia Pinal makes full use in this role of her considerable comic talent, singing abusive verses and tormenting poor Simon with comic obscenity. She appears from nowhere dressed in a dark hat and sailor suit, rolling a hoop. But this schoolgirl garb is ironic, for her intent is far from innocent. She displays her body and sticks her tongue out in Simon's face. Since one of the commonplaces of Christian literature is that Satan takes female form, Simon easily recognizes his tormentor. When the ascetic announces to Satan that he is not afraid, the girl gallops away naked on a huge white pig, vowing to return.

Simon's concupiscent visions are all presented with the utmost clarity and realism. There is nothing vague or misty about them, but since they represent what is going on in Simon's fevered mind, they have the force of surreal or hallucinatory images. His second vision is another juxtaposition of opposite values. A character identified as the "Good Shepherd" appears carrying a lamb. But, like the face of the laughing Christ in *Nazarín,* this image is surprising. On closer observation, the "Good Shepherd" is revealed to be a female Christ with golden curls and beard. At first, Simon is deeply moved, but when the apparition tells him that he must change, the poor hermit becomes suspicious. "Get down off this column," the Shepherd orders him, "and sink yourself in pleasure until its very name makes you sick. . . . Then I say to you . . . you shall be close to me" (script, p. 233). Simon now knows that he is not in the presence of Christ but of the devil. "I'll see that that fat-assed father of yours pays for my wasted journey," Satan complains, and angrily throws down the lamb. The lamb promptly turns into a frog, the traditional symbol of evil, and Satan's identity is confirmed.

While not battling the devil, Simon chants hymns or takes out a piece of lettuce from the bag of food the monks provide him and nibbles it. He tries to eat as little as possible, showing his disdain for physical needs, but when he spies a rabbit chewing a lettuce leaf he has dropped, Simon forgets himself for a moment and, following the animal's example, eats with pleasure. He catches himself enjoying a physical act and pours out the last drops of his water, but not, the script notes, "without regret" (script, p. 221). At one point he is about to bless a shred of lettuce he finds between his teeth, but realizes what he is doing and tosses it away. He finds a grasshopper on the column's capital and blesses it. He also blesses the goatherd's goat, Pelagia, at the goatherd's request, for the animal is pregnant.

The goatherd, however, is annoyed when Simon adds another blessing for him: "Don't you go blessing me and my goats in the same breath." The malformed dwarf, played by the same actor who took the role of Ujo in *Nazarín,* is irritated by Simon's absentmindedness. However lowly and grotesque, the goatherd is sensitive and compassionate. He is also a sensible fellow who feels rebuffed when Simon takes no notice of his generosity. The dwarf complains that "yesterday I took him a bowl of curds and a slice of bread only three days old, and damned if he didn't ignore me, the . . ." (script, p. 212). Ironically, this ugly dwarf is the most spontaneous voice of sanity in the film. "I respect and love you, and tomorrow I'll bring you a bowl of milk straight from the goat," he tells Simon; but, he adds, "I don't think you're quite right up there," and taps his head (script, p. 236).

The goatherd is correct, for Simon has allowed himself to become indifferent to humanity, caring only for his own saintliness. Echoing the criminal who tells Nazarín that neither of them is of any use to anyone, Buñuel again suggests an analogy between an exclusive desire for religious purity and outright evil. Satan tells Simon that "there is really very little difference between us" (script, p. 241). Simon attempts to withdraw into prayer, but the devil has other plans. A jet airliner appears in the sky. Suddenly the time and place are transformed. Simon has become a twentieth-century intellectual—complete with tweed coat and pipe—and Satan is a young woman. They are conversing in a bar where young people dance frantically to "Radio-active Flesh" played by a rock group who call themselves the "Sinners." She wants to dance. But Simon refuses and tells her he's going back. "You can't," she states flatly. "There's another tenant. You'll just have to get used to it, Simon."

This ending, which departs radically from the script, has been widely criticized and often misinterpreted. It is, of course, abrupt, caused by the sudden drying-up of funds for the film, which was planned as the first of two short features to be shown on a single program. But this final scene is neither inconclusive, as A. H. Weiler decides, nor a negative comment on today's youth.[29] Rather it is a visual suggestion that Simon's behavior, found in Christian culture since its earliest days, has its contemporary counterpart that can only be defined as withdrawal. Simon, as Jackson Burgess reminds us, is "wise, humble, and innocent," yet entirely inadequate when faced with the instincts represented by the dance, "Radio-active Flesh."[30] All he can do is retreat to his column, a safe outpost from which he can avoid humanity. The wildly gyrating youths do not represent, as Pauline Kael assumes, "the mad, decaying world in its final orgiastic dance,"[31] but the demands of the flesh, which are so volatile or "radio-active" that they cannot be ignored. Although Simon may dismiss those who disturb him, such as his mother, Matias, and the goatherd, he is subject to the same carnal needs as the rest of humanity. His flaw, ludicrous in its rigidity and naiveté, is his refusal to accept his physical reality and needs.

Buñuel reconstructs the character of Simon Stylites to warn of the absurdities of asceticism and the withdrawal it implies. That Buñuel's character is based on the life of a man who lived in Syria from A.D. 390 to 459 makes this surrealist farce a kind of documentary whose most central preposterous fact—that this individual spent thirty-seven years atop a column in the desert—is true. Not only is the comic situation factual, but Buñuel's symbolism, the devil in female form, for example, is based on Church history. If Buñuel's most fanciful flights of imagination are based on fact and carry the validity of history, this is not to say that *Simon of the Desert* is an historical film, as José Monleón reminds us.[32] As in *Las Hurdes*, Buñuel takes historical fact as a point of departure. Basing his film on historical texts, Buñuel constructs a narrative with surrealist imagery. This is the process by which, as Isak Dinesen once observed, "Art turns fact into Truth."[33]

Belle de jour (1966)

Belle de jour is a surrealist tour-de-force. In it Buñuel portrays the state of mind André Breton predicted in the first *Surrealist Manifesto*. Affirming his conviction that dreams illuminate reality, Breton declares, "I believe in the future resolution of these two states—outwardly so contradictory—which are dream and reality, into a sort of absolute reality, a *surreality*."[34] *Belle de jour* is an example of surreality, for it is a film in which real and imagined action are almost indistinguishable. Yet Buñuel's effort to treat reality and fantasy with equal veracity makes *Belle de jour* one of his most puzzling films. Critics, trying to solve its multiple mysteries, have labeled it "a comedy of manners," "a story of a masochistic housewife," and "a poem."[35] T. J. Ross judges it to be an "overrated film" and takes Buñuel to task for using "fashion-and strip-show" techniques guaranteed to insure box-office success.[36] J. H. Matthews comes closest to understanding *Belle de jour* when he concludes that the film may be "some kind of a fairy tale the heroine is telling herself."[37] Modern psychiatry has for some time held that fairy tales, like myths, are expressions of the collective unconscious which parallel and often symbolize individual acts of irrational behavior.

Belle de jour is the story of an upper-class young Parisian woman who, unable to respond sexually to her handsome, intelligent husband, seeks employment in a brothel where she finds sexual pleasure with crude and often cruel and ugly men. Her actions, unknown to her husband, are not well understood by herself; and she carries them out with a blind, driven determination. Her lack of self-awareness is the viewer's first clue that the heroine is acting out a role or, in terms of transactional analysis, a "script," a sequence of behavior which limits "spontaneous and creative human aspiration."[38] The role Belle de jour has chosen closely parallels that of the young girl in the tale of "The Beauty and the Beast." Carl Jung, in his discussion of "Ancient Myths and Modern Man," summarizes the most important features of this tale[39] (which inspired Jean Cocteau's fantasy film *Beauty and the Beast,* 1946).

Beauty, her father's favorite child, lives with him and her four sisters. Beauty has asked her father for a white rose as a gift and, in an effort to find one for her, he steals a rose from the enchanted garden of Beast. Angry at the theft, Beast demands that the father return to be punished, but allows him three months' reprieve. (Beauty's father notices that Beast seems at once both cruel and kind.) Beauty insists on taking her father's punishment for him and goes in his place to Beast's castle, where she is kept unharmed. Her only worry is Beast, who asks her repeatedly to marry him. Each time she refuses. One day she sees a vision of her father lying ill. She begs Beast to let her visit her father, and he agrees, provided that she return in a week. At home, Beauty is received joyfully and she overstays her allotted time. But a dream in which Beast is dying causes her to return to find him on his deathbed. Beast pleads that he is unable to live without her. Now unaware of his ugliness, Beauty has fallen in love with Beast and promises to marry him if he will not die. Suddenly Beast vanishes. In his place appears a handsome prince who tells Beauty that he had been cursed by a witch and turned into a beast. The curse was to last until a beautiful girl loved him for his goodness in spite of his ugly appearance.

Jung identifies the central theme of the story as that of the young woman who, living in spiritual love with her father, comes to terms with the animal or erotic principle of love. This theme appears to explain much of the action in *Belle de jour*. The equivalents of the Beast are not hard to recognize in the gallery of characters Severine encounters at Mme. Anais's brothel. Monsieur Adolphe, the paunchy bon-bon salesman who wears suspenders and is "always ready to make some stupid remark";[40] the fat Japanese businessman with his inscrutable little box: and Marcel, the arrogant thug with false teeth and a long scar on his back, form an unforgettable array who express their passions with animal lack of restraint.

Severine's first reaction to these monstrous clods is, like Beauty's at her first sight of Beast, repulsion. After her first encounter with M. Adolphe, she goes home and bathes. The scene of her scrubbing vigorously in the shower and then applying perfume concludes when she takes her underclothes to the livingroom fireplace and burns them. As Pierre, her husband, comes in, she pretends to be asleep. When he leaves, she has a dream that attests to her disturbed state of mind and her obsession with filth. In her dream she is dressed in a long white robe. Her hands are tied. Nearby stand Pierre and his friend Husson. A herd of bulls bellows in the background. Husson remarks that the bulls are frequently named Remorse, except for one which is called Expiation. The dream sequence ends when Husson begins slinging mud at her. Husson asks Pierre what time it is and Pierre replies, "Between two and five but not later than five" (script, p. 87). This is a verbatim repetition of Severine's words when, as Belle de jour, she informs Mme. Anais of her working hours at the brothel.

This dream, which clearly expresses Severine's guilt feelings and her need for punishment, parallels Beauty's guilt for having endangered her father's life and her need to be punished in his place. In the fairy tale, Beauty's guilt causes her to go to the castle of the Beast. A similar sequence of action takes place in the film; the dream of mud-slinging is followed by scenes at the brothel. Thus Belle (whose name means "beauty" in French) goes willingly to the brothel, as the Beauty of legend voluntarily surrenders herself to Beast.

The theme of punishment is, of course, central to Buñuel's film. In the opening scene Severine is in a carriage which rolls through the Bois de Boulogne only to be stopped by Pierre, who has her hauled out and whipped, thus defining the terms of her punishment. In this and other scenes punishment is inflicted with Pierre standing by observing, or actively directing it, and with Severine expressing both protest and pleasure. The flogging in the first scene leads to attempted assault by the coachman who, wearing white gloves, lays his hands on Severine's shoulders. Buñuel describes her expression as "a mixture of repugnance and pleasure" (script, p. 39), adding that she both fears and "expects something" from her assailant. This strange mixture of opposing emotions is similar to the fairy-tale heroine's voluntary submission to, and later fondness for, Beast, her supposed tormentor.

If the legend of "The Beauty and the Beast" seems to help clarify some of the mysteries in *Belle de jour*, there appear, at the same time, basic discrepancies between the film and the tale which leave major points in *Belle de jour* unexplained. Why, for example, does Severine reject the advances of her husband, who is the antithesis of bestiality? A surgeon, Pierre has the respect of society and the admiration of even the most cynical of his friends, such as Husson. Pierre's patience with and understanding of his wife are genuine. When she interrupts his work to ask him if he has ever visited a brothel, Pierre, although somewhat surprised at her question, shifts his concentration to the topic that intrigues her and tries to give her honest answers. When his remarks begin to irritate her, she blurts out, "Shut up. . . . Don't talk about it anymore." Instead of being angry, Pierre is only more concerned about her. She excuses her outburst by pleading exhaustion and begs him to stay by her side until she falls asleep. As if comforting a child, Pierre puts his arm around his distraught wife and accompanies her to the bedroom, saying, "Won't you ever grow up?" (script, p. 53).

If Pierre is tolerant of his wife's frigidity toward him, he does not appear to resign himself to it. In the first scene he treats her tenderly, but expresses his desire for her, saying, "So would I like everything to be perfect. . . . For your coldness to go . . ." (script, p. 35). In the next scene, back in their apartment, Pierre is disappointed when his advances toward his wife are refused. When she asks forgiveness he replies brusquely, "It's all right, go to sleep."

Pierre thus appears to be the equivalent of the beautiful prince in fairy tales whom lonely young girls long for. In his wife's fantasies, however, Pierre does indeed turn into a beast. In the opening scene it is he who delivers his wife to her tormentors, the two coachmen who whip her. Pierre directs the flogging; "There's no need to be afraid of hurting her, the little tart" (script, p. 36). When he decides she's had enough, he invites the footman to enjoy her: "She's yours now. Carry on" (script, p. 38). When Pierre and Husson are standing by a herd of bulls, she is seen tied to a tree, her dress torn. The two men stand talking over a pot of steaming soup, which they lift and pour over Severine's head and shoulders. This is followed by another image of Severine tied now in a cattle shed. Pierre watches while Husson insults her and slings mud at her face until she is covered with it. To his wife, then, Pierre has a double, and contradictory character. He is, at one level of her consciousness, which we may call "reality," kind and sympathetic. Yet on another level, no less real but because of its bizarre images more properly called daydream or fantasy, Pierre is bestial.

Again, psychoanalysis of fairy tales provides a useful clue to Pierre's demonic role in the mind of Severine. The fairy-tale lover often appears in the ambivalent guise of both man and beast. In a French legend he is a green snake, a monstrous beast in the Scandinavian *Prince Hat beneath the Earth*, an ugly serpent in a Swiss version of *The Bewitched Prince*. A repulsive frog is accepted by a princess as her beautiful lover and husband in *The Frog King*. Ugliness in these tales appears to represent the erotic aspects of love. The presence of ugliness juxtaposed with the positive emotions of love portrays the "need for synthesis of the physical-biological and the ideological-emotional world."[41]

By analogy with these stories and legends, Pierre's dual character as handsome lover and cruel tormentor may reflect Severine's ambivalent feelings toward erotic passion. She suffers guilt and fear of the erotic while, at the same time, feeling amorous desire. Buñuel, an astute observer of the human psyche, is thorough in his study to the point of suggesting a probable cause for Severine's lack of ability to resolve the contradictory emotions of sensual and spiritual love. Early in the film, there is a flash-back from Severine's childhood. The scene reveals an incident in which a plumber, making repairs in the bathroom, suddenly embraces and kisses the little girl. During the scene, Severine's mother is heard calling her, but the little girl, overcome by the attentions of the plumber, is momentarily unable to answer. When her mother finds her on the bathroom floor, the little girl replies, "I slipped, Mummy, I fell" (script, p. 51). Her ironic reply may be seen as an answer to her mother and also as an expression of guilt.

Severine's introduction to erotic instinct is seen as a negative rather than a positive one in the film. Buñuel's description of the plumber as a man "full of vigor, but greasy and dirty and unshaven" with the "same brutal face as the Footman in the first sequence" (script, p. 50) makes clear that this early incident has to a large extent determined Severine's later sexual response. As an adult, her feelings of sexual pleasure are triggered not by the handsome Pierre but by the brutes who correspond to the plumber from her childhood. Her fantasies of humiliation by Pierre, in which her face reflects both pain and pleasure, are for Severine the result of a process initiated in childhood when she learned that sexual pleasure was aroused by rough, abusive behavior.

Severine's inclination toward sexual abuse leads her to ponder the logical outcome of masochism, that is, death. One of her escapades is with an aristocratic necrophiliac whom she meets one day, by chance, of course, while sitting in a café near the Bois de Boulogne. At the sound of bells, which signal her visions, the familiar coach pulls up and a distinguished man gets out. He asks Belle her name and tells her he once had a cat called "Belle de l'Ombre," a name that corresponds to his liking for the "autumn sun, the dark sun." The Duke, as he is called, confesses to be a man of another era . . . in which people still had a feeling for death" (script, p. 102). His special pleasures are indeed concerned with death, and he invites Belle to his house to participate in what he calls a "kind of religious ceremony." This calls for Belle to lie draped in black negligée in a coffin, while the Duke recalls the sweet moments of what sounds like a ritual sado-masochistic murder. The Duke leans over her in remorse. "I hope you have forgiven me. . . . It wasn't my fault.

Belle de jour: The masochistic desire of Severine (Catherine Deneuve) for sexual abuse is fulfilled at a brothel (above) by her hoodlum lover (Pierre Clementi). (below) By an Oriental customer.

. . . I loved you too much" (script, p. 114). After telling the butler to "beat it" with his cats, the Duke disappears under the catafalque, which begins to shake as a clap of thunder resounds. Curious, Belle leans over the edge of the coffin to observe what is going on below. What she sees is not shared with the viewer, but the script describes her as being rather disgusted.

Severine's visits to the brothel, where she encounters abusive treatment, provide her with sexual fulfillment until she is discovered by her husband's best friend, Husson. Husson's visit to Mme. Anais's and his meeting there with Severine is one of those chance encounters that surrealists believed determine the course of human destiny. When Husson wanders into Mme. Anais's one afternoon and finds that it is his friend's wife who is offered to him, the fantasy of Belle de jour, part-time prostitute, collides with the reality of Severine, respectable wife of Pierre. In her shock at the unexpected intrusion of her public identity upon her erotic life, Severine begs Husson not to reveal her activities to Pierre. Husson, realizing his sudden power over her, tries to calm her but cannot resist enjoying his new discovery: "I have friends who would be delighted to know you're here. I could send you some customers" (script, p. 14). Having lost interest in the afternoon's activities, Husson turns to go. On his way out he leaves money on the table as a final insult, instructing her, "These are not for you. You can buy Pierre some chocolates, from me . . ." (script, p. 142).

The shock of discovery is traumatic for Severine, and her tormented mind produces another and final fantasy. After Husson leaves, Severine sinks into a chair. A vision of the Bois de Boulogne appears. There is a dueling scene in which Pierre and Husson are rivals. The two men draw their pistols and fire, but it is Severine who is hit. Her body, again tied to a tree, is lifeless, and blood trickles from a bullet wound in her temple. Pierre comes up and kisses her, but she is clearly dead. Perhaps that part of herself which has demanded abuse and defilement may be seen in this final vision as having been killed by Pierre and Husson.

Severine's two lives are brought into violent conflict with each other by Husson's discovery of her at the brothel. Her erotic escapade finally threatens the very existence of her life with Pierre. Marcel, the thug enamored of her at Mme. Anais's, presents himself at her flat and lies in wait to shoot Pierre. It is at this point, when Pierre's life is endangered by one of her more vicious lovers, that

Severine's fantasies fade from her mind and she becomes a devoted, attentive wife caring for her husband, severely wounded by Marcel. Yet it is Husson who erases the last veil between Severine's two lives. Unable to resist inflicting a final punishment, Husson reveals Severine's affairs to Pierre, who sits helpless in a wheelchair. After Husson leaves, Severine returns to Pierre and finds him motionless, a tear running down his cheek.

The final scene of *Belle de jour* has been described as "the most surprising in all of cinema."[42] The fusion of fantasy with reality produces here a surreality, or a new level of truth. As if concluding that the revelation of her secret achieves the needed synthesis of Severine's antithetical lives, Buñuel delivers the final shock to his audience. Pierre suddenly arises healthy and whole again from his wheelchair and asks Severine what she is thinking. The couple seems to have achieved blissful harmony. Their discussion of an upcoming vacation appears to portray the resolution of conflict, the equivalent of the traditional "they lived happily ever after" ending of fairy tales. The sound of bells, the motif which throughout the film has signaled the passing carriage of Severine's fantasies, is heard mingling with the traffic sounds from the street below. The meowing of cats, symbolizing Severine's sexual fears, is also heard.[43] But the carriage, familiar conveyor of Severine's tormentors, the two coachmen, now passes by empty.

A series of fortuitous events brings about the shocks that serve to jolt Severine out of her repetitive, compulsive behavior. Confronted with Pierre's knowledge of her escapades and his possible death at the hands of the preposterous, swaggering thug, Severine realizes that Pierre is not a beast after all. Fear of losing him is sufficiently threatening to allow her to discard that part of her life script which demands submission to destructive eroticism. Only now is she able to complete the process, begun in youth and symbolized in "The Beauty and the Beast," of realizing Eros to be not an "animal monster, not a diabolical force . . . , but a beautiful being. True chastity," Julius Heuscher concludes, "may well require the prior recognition of this."[44]

André Breton, defining the surrealists' attempt to reach new perspectives on human life, wondered, in 1924, "Could not dreams as well be applied to the solution of life's fundamental problems?" Buñuel's answer in *Belle de jour*, coming forty-four years after the first *Surrealist Manifesto*, is clearly affirmative. True to his surrealist principles, Buñuel shares Breton's belief that dreams exercise on the human mind a force at least as important as the events of daily, or waking, existence. Dreams, fantasies, and hallucinations, or waking dreams, occur frequently in his films and have special, often revelatory significance in the actions of such Buñuelian characters as Tristana, Viridiana, and Simon of the Desert.

Myths and fairy tales are no less revelatory than dreams and have in common with them, as Breton remarks, the capacity to "portray preconscious apprehensions, longings, and aspirations."[45] *Belle de jour* can easily be interpreted as a series of masochistic daydreams. When understood as a fairy tale, however, the full range of Buñuel's study comes into view. The film is not merely a vision of an individual's torment but an expression of established patterns of behavior reflecting the myths and legends of Western culture. The analogy of this film with a fairy tale also dispels the notion that *Belle de jour* is a piece of pornography. Buñuel's remark that *Belle de jour* "is a pornographic film" may have helped to convince critics that his primary intention was to titillate a middle-class audience so as to gain box-office success. Yet Buñuel qualified his description, saying, "By that I mean *chaste* eroticism."[46] This remark underscores the tension between the heroine's opposing notions of love, which is the source of conflict in the film, rather than the bedroom scenes themselves. The surrealist narrative of *Belle de jour* is illogical and absurd, yet it contains, like traditional fairy tales, clues to human growth and development. Comparison of it with the tale of "The Beauty and the Beast" indicates that Buñuel's work is not a frivolous, sensational piece of entertainment, but a cinematic inquiry into problems of the human psyche that are universal in scope.

Tristana (1970)

Buñuel's last character study, *Tristana*, is his most savage, equaling Goya's *Caprichos* in the merciless rendering of hypocrisy and corruption. The soft, muted colors that begin this beautiful, flowing film gradually grow harsh, illustrating the process of destruction which is, as Arnau Oliver points out, the central theme of *Tristana*.[47] Like a laboratory technician carefully staining diseased tissue for microscopic examination, Buñuel chooses a setting in which the process is most apparent, Spain. The action develops from 1929 to 1935, the years of the director's own young manhood. During this period, Spanish men freely pursued careers; women, however, were still bound by archaic codes of honor to remain at home. Thus, if *Belle de jour* belongs among Buñuel's pathological studies, *Tristana* documents the process by which a healthy, innocent young girl snared in the chivalric double standard becomes a murderess.

Tristana is set in Toledo, the capital of medieval Spain sometimes referred to as the "Mirror of Spain." Buñuel had known Toledo well. The poet Rafael Alberti, recalling college escapades, remembers Buñuel as one of a group who called themselves "The Order of the Brothers of Toledo," whose principal activity was wandering through Toledo at night. Initiates into the group were draped in a sheet and turned loose to find their way through the labyrinthine, unfamiliar routes.[48] In the opening frames of *Tristana*, Buñuel remembers Toledo's back streets. But he converts El Greco's dramatic view of Toledo into a parched panorama of ochre spires and towers. Giorgio Tinazzi notes the sense of a closed, archaic society conveyed by this dry portrayal.[49]

The impression of a closed society is further supported by the first sequence of the film, which takes place at a school for the deaf. A group of boys is playing soccer, but, strangely, there are no sounds. No human voice is heard. Protest is silent even when a fight breaks out, as if Buñuel were equating Spain with the deaf players. Only furious gestures and clenched fists register the boys' anger. The offender is Saturno, the young deaf lad whose mother, Saturna, has brought Tristana to the soccer game. Saturna, maid of Tristana's guardian, explains to the soccer coach that the young woman hasn't been out of the house in two weeks. "I brought her here to get a breath of fresh air" (script, p. 17).

This opening scene implies a subtle analogy between the deaf Saturno and Tristana, who has sequestered herself in mourning for her recently deceased mother. With a gesture often laden with meaning by Buñuel, Tristana offers a piece of fruit to Saturno. Unlike Nazarín, who hesitates before accepting a pineapple, the deaf mute eagerly bites into the apple Tristana hands him. Buñuel suggests a parallel between these two young people.

The role of Saturna is enacted with consummate skill by Lola Gaos, who not only has, as the script requires, "the air of a servant" (script, p. 15) but also displays silent reserves of her own inner strength. In the novel by Benito Pérez Galdós on which Buñuel bases his film, Saturna is described as the orphan Tristana's teacher, instructing her in the realities of woman's lot. Galdós has her advising Tristana that "if you want to keep a little reputation, you've got to take twice as much slavery."[50] And Buñuel's Saturna seems to know what slavery is when she mentions her husband, then adds that her son is just like his father, "God rot his soul" (script, p. 19). It is no coincidence that the meaning of the adjective "Saturna" in Spanish means the same as "triste," from which comes the name Tristana, that is, melancholy, sad.

Thus from the outset Tristana is equated with servants. The two servants, Saturna and her son, are important in the film not only as contrast to but as reflections of the central character. The fact that the two servants are named for Saturn, god of agriculture, identifies them as earthy types in close touch with their instincts. But Saturno is mute, unable to express himself. He is, as Tristana becomes, handicapped; isolated, he turns his repressed desires inward. The Roman god of agriculture was honored by orgies, or Saturnalia, but Buñuel's mute Saturno locks himself into bathrooms to release his sexual energy in solitude.

The two servants provide clues to the central figures in Buñuel's group portrait. Sharing center focus is Don Lope Garrido, the personification of Spanish society in *Tristana*. He is an arrogant, autocratic seventy-year-old Don Juan whose strict adherence to an antique code of honor and hatred of work are historically accurate character traits of the Spanish male. He is a complex personality, deeply contradictory, yet his contradictions are typical of the hypocrite who accepts from social dogma only what justifies his own biases. Don Lope is staunchly anticlerical and opposes marriage. "As far as love affairs and women are concerned," he states, "I consider that sin just doesn't come into it" (script, p. 44). If he has no use for religion, Don Lope is not without his own ethics. Woman is fair game only if she consents—"and it is up to us to make her so . . . but with two obvious exceptions . . . the wife of one's friend and that strange flower, so rare these days, which is born of perfect innocence" (script, p. 44). Shortly after announcing this principle to his friends whom he meets regularly at his café, Don Lope seduces Tristana, his ward, placed in his care by her mother before she died.

Don Lope's attitudes toward women are rather like those held toward servants, that is, they are to be dominated at all times, for they are not equals. He discourages Tristana from working, telling her, "You haven't come into this household to be a maid. You're the mistress here, and Saturna is here to serve you" (script, p. 24). He boasts of defending the underdog when he sees a thief chased by the police. But he claims domination of women as an inalienable right and cites a Spanish proverb which gives him this right. At dinner he announces, as if to challenge Tristana, the maxim by which he intends to treat her, "If you want an honest woman, break her leg and keep her at home. Have you got anything to say?" Thoroughly intimidated, the young woman shakes her head. "Me? No, sir" (script, p. 48).

After Tristana rebels and finds a lover, Lope attempts to assert his domination by requesting small favors of her, such as cleaning his hatband, thus replacing her in the servant role from which he had earlier absolved her. In confrontation with his ward, he reminds her of his unlimited rights over her body as well as to her loyalty: "I am your father and your husband, and I can be one or the other as and when it suits me" (script, p. 76). Such pronouncements undermine the lovable-old-codger image which Don Lope assumes from time to time. There are, in fact, moments in which he appears diabolical. When Tristana awakes one night after having the vision of Don Lope's severed head that torments her throughout the film, the old man comforts her, but his ironic remark helps explain her nightmare, "Calm yourself. . . . You screamed as if you'd seen the devil himself" (script, p. 41). The next day, Don Lope goes to his café decked out in an "elegant black cape with red lining" (script, p. 42) which gives him a mephistophelian air. The satanic image Buñuel attributes to Don Lope is taken directly from the novel, in which Galdós refers to the old man's "satanic shadow," and Saturna calls him "Don Lepe," a nickname for the devil. But Don Lope is not evil; he is merely predatory. When Tristana returns to his house as an invalid, Buñuel describes him as being overjoyed, as he exclaims to Saturna, "This time she won't escape. . . . If she comes into my house, she will never leave it again" (script, p. 113).

Don Lope, of course, did not invent his conception of women as servile creatures, but absorbed it from Spanish culture, the psychological framework for both his own character and that of Tristana. Forced to live with Don Lope, Tristana has no other home. She soon becomes a virtual prisoner of his exaggerated notion of honor. When Saturna tells Lope that Tristana is stifled, he responds by asking, "Doesn't she go to Mass?" (script, p. 48). Buñuel alludes to the sterile vacuum that is Tristana's life in repeated scenes in which the young woman plays a game of choice. First with chick-peas on a plate, then, with church columns, and later, deciding which street to take on walks with Saturna, Tristana takes special delight in choosing between two alternatives. Critics have speculated on the possible meaning of this game of choice. One of its most obvious features is its triviality. Nowhere else in her life does Tristana have such a range of options as in questions of no consequence.

Like most women in Spain, Tristana's choices of what to do with her life are much fewer than men have. Galdós's Saturna advises her that there are only three: matrimony, the theater, and the other, unmentionable. Tristana has already eliminated all three. That Tristana lacks choice where it counts seems confirmed by Don Lope's boredom with Tristana's slightest exercise of preference. When she asks him which column he prefers, he brusquely requests she change the subject (script, p. 52).

Don Lope, in his arrogance, is confident of Tristana's continued subservience. Glimpses into her mind by means of surreal images, however, reveal that resentment has already begun to take root. Her recurring vision of Don Lope's severed head swinging like the clapper of a bell is the central motif of the film. Another surreal image provides a further clue to Tristana's feeling. Wandering in a church with Don Lope, Tristana climbs upon the tomb of an archbishop and peers into the sculpted marble face, examining the sightless eyes. When her guardian notices her lying on the sarcophagus, he asks her what she is doing, to which the young woman replies, "I was thinking that you need another pair of slippers" (script, p. 53). Shortly after this scene, Tristana begins sharing Don Lope's bed.

Tristana's character develops with the passage of three two-year segments that serve as the chronological structure of the narrative. The first begins in 1929 with her adoption and ends with her seduction by Don Lope. Her rebellion, beginning in 1931, continues until the final segment, starting in 1935, when she takes vengeance upon the old man for the years of abuse imposed upon her. Her disgust begins shortly after her seduction, and she soon confesses to Saturna that she cannot stand Don Lope any longer. Her chance meeting with Horacio the artist, and her ensuing love affair with him, allow her temporary escape. But another, equally fortuitous event, a tumor on her leg, requiring amputation of the limb, eventually destroys her struggle for independence.

By the time she meets Horacio, Tristana is a young woman who has already absorbed her upbringing. So when Horacio mentions marriage to her, she recoils, remembering early warnings from Lope against matrimony as a killer of true love. "Love is finished for them," Lope had remarked when a married couple passed by on one of their walks. "Dear little Tristana, don't ever get married. . . . Passion should be free" (script, p. 52). Desiring above all to keep the passion she now feels, Tristana hedges with Horacio, "I will live with you as long as you love me. If one day you've had enough of me . . . then it's bye-bye sweetheart without any fuss" (script, p. 95). Horacio and Tristana go away together and are happy for a time. But when she becomes ill she thinks, because of her pain, that she is going to die. Helpless in the face of Tristana's refusal to marry, Horacio takes her back to Don Lope, explaining that she wants to die at home and that "she still thinks of you as her father" (script, p. 104).

Tristana reacts to the amputation of her leg as any woman reacts to, say, a mastectomy—with horror and the sinking conviction that with the amputated member goes her sexual attraction. Such fears are so universal that today postoperative counselors aid depressed amputees. Confirmation of the universality of such fears seems necessary when critical imagination goes no further than that of Peter Harcourt, who cannot understand why Tristana returns to Don Lope. Nor does the critic understand the fierce pride, horror, and self-loathing that cause an independent young woman like Tristana to reject Horacio. He wonders at her hostility: "While the loss of her leg is obviously central to it, the intensity of her anger is hard to understand."[51] Such comments only echo Horacio's own well-meaning ignorance when he tells Tristana, "You seem to have changed" (script, p. 123). Furious, the young woman retorts, "Naturally . . . I have changed," and exposes the stump which not only mars her physical beauty but also robs her of her independence. For Tristana's fate is doubly crippling. When, at a time she felt near death, she reached out for a father, she was also, unavoidably, delivering herself to her captor. As Buñuel makes horribly clear, they are one and the same.

In the final segment the roles of Don Lope and his ward are to some degree reversed. It is now he, helpless and senile, who is her dependent. Not surprisingly, he receives the same arrogance, domination, and double-dealing with which he raised his charge. Amazement from critics such as Peter Harcourt at Tristana's behavior may be because it is enacted now by a woman, generally expected to remain forever passive and submissive. Tristana, however, only reflects the manner in which she has been brought up. And she is an exact replica of the old tyrant. The cane she now carries not only helps her walk, but, like Lope's, serves as a symbol of domination. She even assumes his diabolical air. The priest, Don Ambrosio, warns her, "Take care, my child. . . . There is something satanic in this resentment of yours" (script, p. 130).

The final segment of the film reveals the destruction of all Tristana's hopes. Her goals, to be free and to work (script, p. 88), are now remote. Having, in her fury, driven off her lover, she is marooned with Lope, whom she hates. Tristana realizes that her hatred is excessive, but after years of submission she can no longer repress her resentment. When Don Ambrosio suggests a doctor, Tristana seems to understand that her resentment is due to the repression of physical desires which she now appears doomed to suppress forever. "Don't talk to me about doctors. I need something else . . ." (script, p. 129).

Tristana's final illusions are shattered when Don Ambrosio, in the interest of respectability, counsels her to marry Don Lope. She does so, but becoming a bride only intensifies her anger. She refuses to allow the old man to kiss her at the wedding, for which she is dressed, as befits her mood, in black. The pleased old man prepares for his wedding night, primping and perfuming himself, as Tristana laughs openly at his vanity. Using the insulting innuendo of the diminutive form, she bids him goodnight calling him Lopito, and stumps off to her room on her crutch, slamming the door on the humiliated Don Lope.

All the kindness and attention that Lope showers upon Tristana after the amputation of her leg have come ten years too late. "If he treated me differently, I would like him" (script, p. 85), Tristana once complained to Saturna before leaving with Horacio. But her passions have long been programmed by her own upbringing in which Lope protected or exploited her as he wished. His old age is the hour of retribution.

It is now Lope who lies ill and in pain. He calls for her, as she had earlier reached out in her suffering for him. And with some of the same relief Lope expressed in claiming his prey, vowing that the crippled woman would never escape him again, Tristana now claims him. Pretending to telephone the doctor, Tristana goes to the adjoining room, picks up the receiver, and begs Dr. Miquis to come quickly. Satisfied that Lope has heard her, she hangs up the receiver without making the call. The script describes her as calm and deliberate: "The opportunity has arisen and she is taking advantage of it. That is all" (p. 142). Certain that he is comatose, Tristana shakes Lope, then goes to the window and opens it. The snow falling outside blows in. Just as the rat and scorpions destroy each other in the introductory scenes of *L'Age d'or*, *Tristana* ends with each predator vanquishing its prey.

Francisco Aranda complains that *Tristana* is a gray film without "a single scene of brilliance" (p. 241). But in spite of its rigorous and faithful realism, *Tristana* is punctuated by surreal and haunting images. The central motif of Lope's severed head, which, according to Pascal Bonitzer, expresses the heroine's desire to castrate the aging Don Juan,[52] is frightening and surges forth directly from Tristana's unconscious mind. Julian Jebb notes the singular shot, taken from under the piano, of Tristana's one leg pumping the pedal. Such a point of view would not have occurred to a director without the surrealists' eye for objects in unexpected circumstances.[53] The theme of mutilation, central to both *Tristana* and to surrealist art in general, is emphasized as Buñuel focuses upon the young woman's artificial leg. Lying on the bed surrounded by sheets and underclothes, it is, like Don Lope's head, a symbol of the brutal destruction of sexual life.[54]

There is one scene, however, which, in its complexity and surprise, is brilliant. Before Tristana marries, Saturno enters her room as she undresses. He indicates he wants to sleep with her and Tristana orders him out. He goes outside, but stands beneath her window and throws a pebble at the door to her balcony. Tristana steps out and the camera views her from a low angle. With her hardened expression, strange smile, and the strong red tint of her makeup, she closely resembles the famous polychrome religious statues which became an art-form in Spain. Watching from below, Saturno gestures for her to open her robe. Surprisingly, she does so. The sight of her exposed breasts so staggers the poor mute that, almost in terror, he runs into the protective foliage of nearby bushes. In Tristana's smile there is both cruelty, poignancy, and amusement, at the perversion of sexual energy suffered by these two lonely sexual cripples.

The images that flick rapidly on the screen as the film ends, scenes from Tristana's life, recall the director's penchant for documentary. The wedding ceremony and the statue of the virgin closely resembling Tristana are all links in a chain of images stressing that the film itself is a record of a hideous series of circumstances. Donald I. Grossvogel finds that "Buñuel uses his camera as a psychoanalyst might use his couch."[55] But Buñuel goes beyond the function of a psychiatrist. As historian, he records in *Tristana* an individual's reactions to a decadent social order so distorted that it is revealed by Buñuel to be fatal, leading from hypocrisy and exploitation to annihilation.

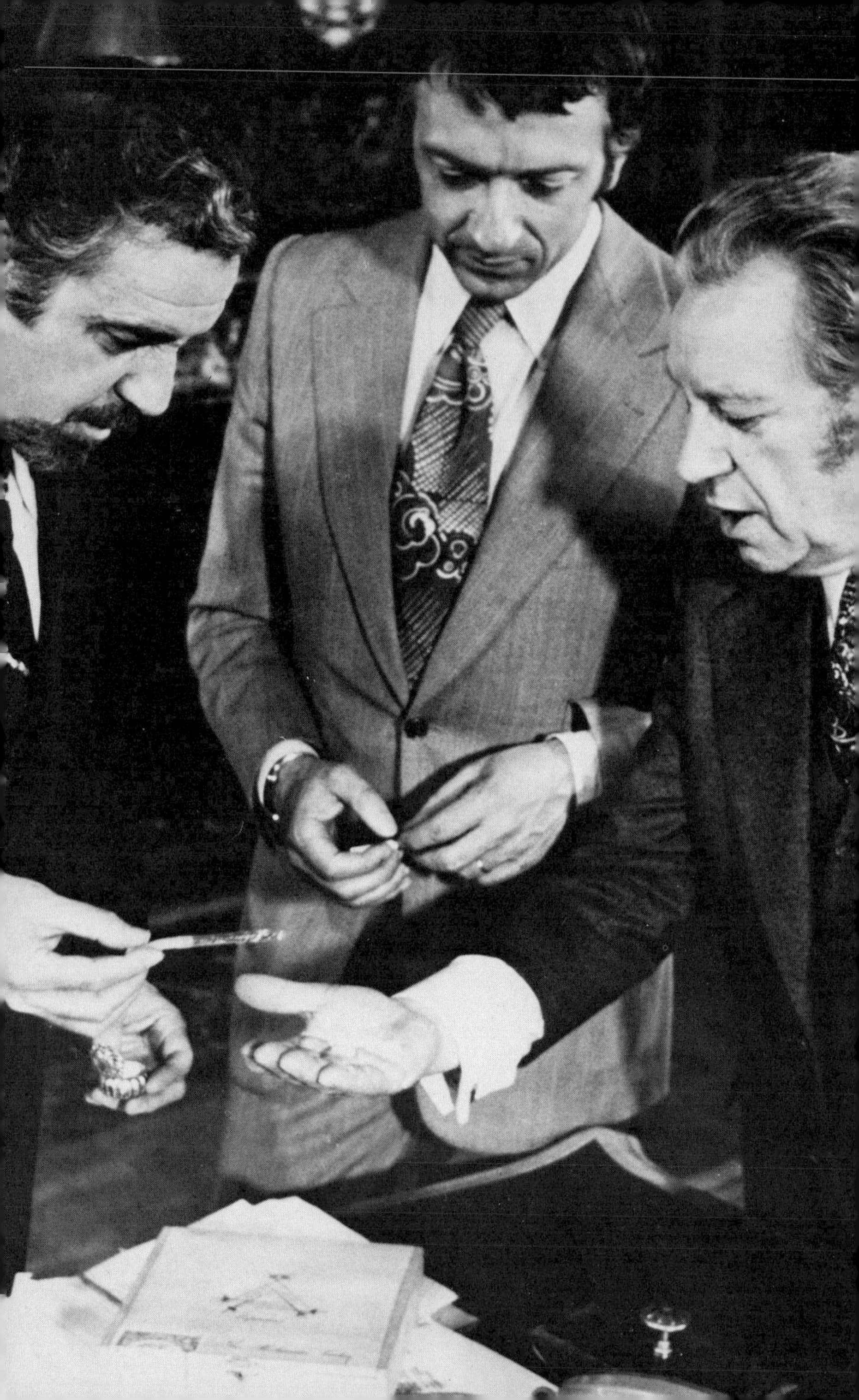

5

Masterworks: Social Satires

The Exterminating Angel (1962)

BUÑUEL'S LIFELONG PREOCCUPATION with outcasts *(Susana, Death in This Garden,)* outsiders *(Las Hurdes, Los olvidados,* and *Nazarín),* and shipwrecks *(Robinson Crusoe)* culminates in *The Exterminating Angel.* This provocative and surreal film, one of Buñuel's most profound, is compared by critics with two of the most compelling dramas of our century which also deal with isolation, *Waiting for Godot*[1] and *No Exit.*[2] As in Beckett's play, references to the Christian tradition are of central importance in *Exterminating Angel,* as its title denotes. Along with Sartre's Garcin, Buñuel's group of haute bourgeois characters discovers that hell consists primarily of other people—specifically, one's friends and associates. Yet Buñuel does not take refuge in the absurd. The secondary theme of disease that underlies the characters' isolation suggests quite clearly that their alienation is not an abstract meaninglessness but is rather what Marie Von Franz has called "a collective infection."[3] This infection is conformity, and it is lethal. The yellow flag that flies throughout the film warns us that it is also highly contagious. Since one of its most toxic forms is religion, particularly the Catholic dogma, Buñuel refers to the infection as the traditional Christian harbinger of death, *The Exterminating Angel.*

That conformity is the carrier of death is clear from the preposterous situation in which a group of aristocratic guests are, for some unexplained reason, trapped in the drawing room of their hosts and cannot leave. The action of the film is thus limited to what can happen within the space of one room. The restlessness, frustration, and ennui the group suffers is, to a large extent, shared by the viewer. Buñuel's genius in the creation of cinematic images and

The respectable partners in heroin smuggling examine a new shipment from South America in The Discreet Charm of the Bourgeoisie *(l. to r., Fernando Rey as the Ambassador from Miranda, Jean-Pierre Cassel and Paul Frankeur as French businessmen).*

manipulation of visual symbols overcomes the absence of narrative to create suspense and mystery. In spite of its uncinematic situation, the rather more literary than visual reliance upon dialogue, and its deliberate cultivation of confusion, *Exterminating Angel* is a carefully structured film that builds, as Ado Kyrou notes, precisely and inexorably[4] to its devastating conclusion.

The introductory segment of the film, in which the servants begin to desert the Nobile mansion just as the Nobiles return with guests from the opera, serves as a warning of disaster. The butler, a willing agent of his wealthy lords, is aghast: "We've got twenty people coming to dinner," he protests to a servant, "and you're going for a stroll?" (script, p. 19). The servants' departure is as unexplained as the predicament in which the guests soon find themselves. One guest describes the servants as "rats leaving a sinking ship" (script, p. 53). Later, a servant, Pablo, comments that the house is quarantined "Just as if there were an epidemic" (script, p. 93). Indeed, the situation resembles a ship attacked by plague and abandoned by its crew.

The uneasy, imprecise awareness of danger does not, however, prevent the dinner from being served. But the party is often interrupted by surprising and unexplained events. The servant who brings out the first course, an exotic Maltese ragout, trips with the tray and falls in an explosion of dishes, food, and gravy which hit the floor near the seated guests. Some are surprised by the spectacular spill. Others are entertained. Raúl, the unflappable bourgeois who refuses to be surprised by anything, congratulates the hostess, "Delightful, Lucía. And totally unexpected." Another guest, Russell, is not amused, but Blanca, sitting next to him, is impressed: "Lucía has a flair for surprises like that." When the next surprise, a small brown bear, wanders into the room, Lucía, always in control, gives a familiar order: "Don't let it out" (script, p. 27). Like Severine, who begs Pierre not to let the cats out in *Belle de jour*, Lucía wishes to restrain the bear as well as a trio of sheep that suddenly appears huddled under a table.

The surrealists viewed animals as creatures who live by instincts, forces that society prefers to repress at all costs. Only one or two members of the Nobile party are in touch with their instincts and can behave with anything resembling spontaneity. One of them is Letitia, called the Valkyrie because, Ana explains, "She's a savage" (script, p. 25). Ana and Leandro discuss Letitia's supposed virginity, a topic reflected in Norse legends in which Valkyries were virgins who brought the souls of the dead to Valhalla. Letitia is the catalyst who precipitates events in the film. As if to confirm her reputation for savagery, she hurls an ashtray through a window in an unexplained moment of passion. This display of free will begins the third segment of the film, the guests' after-dinner conversations.

These conversations provide a closer view of the characters. The arts are conspicuously represented among them: Eduardo is an architect, Mr. Roc, a conductor, and Silvia, an opera singer whose performance in *Lucia di Lammermoor* was attended before dinner by the group. Russell, the eccentric, the colonel, and the doctor are other easily identifiable guests. Blanca's rendition of a Paradisi sonata sets the polite, correct tone of the after-dinner talk. Yet unexpected things happen among this cultured group that belie their gentility. Ana, hunting in her purse for a handkerchief, instead pulls out a pair of chicken feet. The fussy eccentric quickly becomes annoyed at being introduced to another guest. A conversation between Leandro and Christian is a comic non sequitur. A discussion of such topics as the fauna of Rumania typifies the exotic interests of the sophisticated guests. Out of range of the general conversation, however, more important transactions take place. In the exchange between the hostess, Lucia, and the colonel, he is revealed as her lover as they plan to meet secretly after the party. The impatient colonel's remark about the lateness of the hour is, in fact, the first clue as to what is happening, or more accurately, what is not happening. For the anxious hosts, and soon the guests as well, begin to realize that no one is leaving.

Imperceptibly, voluntary action becomes involuntary. Always the perfect host, Nobile remains unperturbed. "I like the unexpectedness of this situation," he affirms cheerfully as he offers to find beds for his guests (script, p. 38). But they do not wish to stay. Silvia and Christian both have early appointments. Russell insists they all leave immediately. Others, however, are less concerned and shock Lucía by taking off their jackets. Excusing Leandro of this breach of etiquette, Nobile reminds his wife that, after all, Leandro "lives in the United States" (script, p. 39). But the doctor, the voice of reason throughout the film, is worried. While protesting that they must leave, the guests pass back and forth in front of the open double doors of the drawing room. Not one attempts to leave. On the contrary, they prepare to sleep. Lights are extinguished, two lovers

Bourgeois Response to Crisis: the sleeping guests trapped in the Nobiles' drawing room in *The Exterminating Angel*.

embrace, Eduardo remarks that "life is amusing . . . and strange" (script, p. 40). As the voluntary after-dinner socializing turns into involuntary confinement, an outside view of the street and the Nobile residence flashes on the screen, a reminder that the Nobiles and their guests are now enclosed and isolated.

Although the reason the guests are confined is never overtly explained, there are many clues. "Why didn't you leave . . . last night?" the colonel asks Eduardo. "Well, I don't know. . . . Like everyone else. What about you?" (script, p. 46). Clearly, an individual act that contradicts group action is beyond the capacity of either of these gentlemen. When Russell collapses and needs medical care, Francisco almost dares anyone to leave. "We must make an effort. Which of you dares take him?" Raúl responds as Eduardo did, by returning the question. "Why don't you do it yourself? Then see if we don't all follow you" (script, p. 51). Raúl soon wonders if they are all insane. "We haven't gone mad, have we?" (script, p. 53). But when asked at the beginning of the confinement his opinion of the situation, Raúl responds with the telling remark that "it seems highly improbable. . . . Unless it's all too normal" (script, p. 46).

The predicament of the Nobile guests is easily recognizable. It is, simply, a crisis, and the guests are responding to it the way the bourgeoisie usually responds to crises—by doing nothing. Nobile, instead of demanding that the guests leave, counts on their discretion and hopes they will depart voluntarily (script, p. 42). Some retain their civility: Alicia, asking for spoons, begins, "Excuse me, Lucía, but there aren't any spoons. . . ." Lucía, horrified and confused at what is going on, replies in her best hostess manner, "It is I who should be excused" (script, p. 48). Speaking of the priest whom she has chosen as her children's tutor, Rita explains that Father Samson "has exquisite manners." But the guests are too disturbed to listen to Rita. They are nearing the brink of hysteria. Silvia admits she knows people are behaving badly, but she hasn't said anything, "out of politeness" (script, p. 47).

Clearly, the fear of being the first to act, the terrible inertia imposed by conformity upon the group, has infected Nobile's guests and has rendered them helpless. Herman G. Weinberg asserts that "why they're caught in the room is of no importance."[5] To ignore the cause of their inertia, however, is to miss the point of the film. The talk of manners and the refusal to take action are so central to the film that to dismiss them is to discount half the dialogue. Furthermore, the paralysis caused by conformity does not attack only the upper class, but extends to officialdom as well. One of the first principles of Buñuel's social diagnosis is that the haute bourgeoisie is supported by the police and the Church, thus what is going on outside the mansion closely mirrors the confusion within.

A crowd has gathered at the mansion gates. A priest, probably the Father Samson whom Rita described earlier, has brought her and Christian's children so that "they can see the house where their parents are. . . ." A professor, described as "eccentric looking," tries to convince the police to let him through the gates to aid the victims, but he is pushed away by the police chief, who labels him "another lunatic." When Christian's young son, Yoli, approaches the house, the crowd urges him on. But the lad stops and runs back to the crowd in tears. Father Samson asks him why he stopped and, in an aside to the crowd, advises, "Never trust a child." Throughout Buñuel's work, children are frequently innocents who retain their natural instincts and mysteriously simplify insurmountable tasks, as in *Mexican Bus Ride*. Father Samson, with his "exquisite manners," however, seems to have already infected Yoli with his lack of confidence in children. Conformity is enforced by the priest and the police outside the mansion with the same zeal with which it is observed within. When a lady in the crowd implores Yoli to try again to enter the gates, the priest firmly refuses. "Oh, no. . . . No! Come on, children. . . . It's time to go" (script, p. 83).

Inside the mansion, the infection takes its emotional and physical toll on the guests. They insult each other, threaten violence, and generally lose all their supposed sophistication and perspective. Christian angrily challenges Raúl to a duel; the conductor crawls about on the floor, kissing women; Francisco shaves his legs with an electric razor. All reasonable efforts to find a solution are abandoned as the guests instead seek comfort in drugs. The doctor, as if meeting needs of epidemic proportion, insists that "we need sedatives as much as we need food" (script, p. 71). But since there are not enough drugs to go around, some guests turn to magic and even to death as a way out. The two lovers, Eduardo and Beatriz, commit suicide together. Along with Russell, who dies of a heart attack, they are "buried" in the cupboard, one door of which is decorated with a painting of the exterminating angel. As in an epidemic when the dead cannot be buried fast enough, the smell of death quickly penetrates the room. Lucía is almost overcome by "that terrible smell! It's unbearable" (script, p. 69).

The extent to which the haute bourgeoisie have shed their facade of civilized behavior is indicated when the group decides to make a scapegoat of their host. In a low voice, as if ashamed to speak such feral thoughts, Blanca states that "Raúl says that if Nobile died, this would all come to an end" (script, p. 46). The doctor reminds the group that talk of offering sacrifice is "mad . . . senseless . . . completely irrational." But Francisco freely admits that the group is "not interested in reason. We want to get out of here" (script, p. 74).

The struggle between the rational doctor and his once-elegant and unflappable friends reaches the point of violence when Raúl grabs a knife on the table. Suddenly Letitia the Valkyrie steps forth and orders everyone still. Addressing each guest, Letitia, speaking "like a sleepwalker slowly waking up," seems to have had a revelation of the means of escape. "Or," she wonders, "is it another hallucination?" (script, p. 96).

Thus the twenty victims, locked by conformity into fear and hysteria, are finally rescued by a flash of insight that occurs to the freest spirit among them, Letitia. As if remembering a secret combination, she recalls what each guest was doing the night they became prisoners and urges them all to resume exactly the places they had that night. Repeating the same dialogue as in the early scenes of the film, the guests eagerly reenact the moment they became trapped. Like terminal patients jubilant at the remission of their disease, the group follows Letitia, who pauses a moment at the double door, then joyously leads them through.

Remission, however, is shortlived. That the ordeal was not enough to cure the victims of conformity is apparent when we next see them inside the church, where conformity is required most rigorously. As the priest and the two deacons walk down the aisle after Mass and pause, looking at the open door, we know the congregation is recaptured. People begin milling about inside the church but no one leaves. Church bells toll as the view from outside flashes on the screen. The familiar quarantine flag now flies over the church courtyard. In a final shot that sums up and symbolizes the meaning of the film, a flock of sheep trots up the steps into the church while revolution breaks out in the street. Bullets are fired, "people fall, women scream" (script, p. 104), yet the bourgeoisie, symbolized by the sheep, continue to follow each other into the church, looking straight ahead as if nothing were happening. Perhaps one of them is pleased, as Nobile had been earlier, and is thinking, "I like the excitement of revolution. . . ."

Exterminating Angel thus ends as it began, with its victims again being quarantined for an infection whose existence they do not even suspect. The music of the film underscores its circular structure; the *Te Deum* sung by a choir both opens the film and accompanies the guests' entrance into the church in the concluding scene.

The final juxtaposition of sheep with sounds of revolution, suggesting an analogy between the bourgeoisie and their customary reaction to crisis, is only the last of many jokes in this surreal comedy of manners. One of the funniest is Leonora's promise, if she gets out, to go to Lourdes to pray and to buy a "washable Virgin, made of rubber" (script, p. 71). To those who protest that this is strongly anticlerical, Buñuel responds only by recalling that these items are in fact sold at such shrines. The offering of a synthetic idol to an all-powerful redeemer merely parallels the guests' more ominous suggestion of human sacrifice. The joke also underlines the primitive, almost tribal behavior to which the guests have reverted.

Humor and surprise are so important in *Exterminating Angel* that they are the two principal stylistic devices of the film. From the earliest scenes when the servants mysteriously depart, the ragout crash-lands on the floor, the bear and sheep wander about, and the Valkyrie tosses an ashtray through the window, surprise gags and nonsense bring to mind the ridiculous antics of American silent comedies. Yet the surrealist director uses these devices not for entertainment alone, but to suggest a wider meaning. The view of Ana pulling two chicken legs from her purse is an amusing hint that beneath Christian values lies a deep reservoir of superstition. The talk of good manners throughout the film and the guests' sporadic efforts to be polite contrast ironically with their more spontaneous insults and lack of dignity. At the broken water pipe, some guests knock each other down to get water while Raúl shouts, "Women first" (script, p. 63) in a scene illustrating the comic contrast between bourgeois dignity and the greed of an exhausted and sick society.

Dark irony and surprise lead easily into visions of horror that plague the minds of the guests. Ana, who carries the chicken feet in her purse, is later tormented by the vision of a severed hand which slithers along the floor. The hand dodges the blows she strikes as it reaches for her neck and attempts to encircle it. This whole episode, deriving perhaps from the severed-hand scene in *Un Chien andalou* and from the segment in *The Beast with Five Fingers* that Buñuel contributed, expresses Ana's hysteria. Yet it is so obviously contrived and trite that it parodies cinematic attempts at horror.

Other terrifying images of destruction echo the actions or desires of those locked into conformist isolation. A cello, representing the elegant music cultivated by the bourgeoisie, is broken up and used as firewood. Later, a picture of a cello flashes upon the screen as a saw grinds through its strings. The cello becomes a hand which is in turn sawed through. Next the saw slices a woman's forehead, an updated version of the razor through the eyeball in *Un Chien andalou*. Several guests are disturbed by visions or memories, including Nobile and Letitia, who, perhaps prophetically, see the Pope standing on a mountain top.

Humor, surprise, and irony, are, of course, all surrealist devices whose full use in *Exterminating Angel* make it one of Buñuel's most purely surreal films. The ridiculous yet mysterious situation, the gags, comic horror, and the metamorphosis of visual images in the concluding segment of the film compile a compendium of surrealist techniques. Not since his first two films has Buñuel resorted so freely to hallucinatory images and playful chaos. Yet Ado Kyrou stresses the realism of *Exterminating Angel,* and Peter Schillaci comments upon its detached point of view, "the extreme sangfroid with which the camera records the horrors. . . ."[6] Thus, in one of the three or four most surreal films of his career, Buñuel still treats the bizarre as if it were ordinary.

Generally hailed as a masterpiece by critics, *Exterminating Angel* is a pivotal work that both evolves from Buñuel's earlier themes and announces those to come. The dinner party is a motif deriving, Raymond Durgnat recalls, from the salon sequence of *L'Age d'or.*[7] The orchestra conductor who suddenly becomes possessed by *l'amour fou* in the earlier film reappears in the Nobile salon, now seeking erotic stimulation by crawling about on the floor. The cow that lolls on the heroine's bed in *L'Age d'or* is replaced by the bear and sheep who appear just as inexplicably in the elegant interior of the Nobile mansion. The guests of the Marquis in *L'Age d'or* react to a fire behind a closed door with the same sophisticated indifference with which the Nobile's guests at first ignore their confinement. Just as the Marquis's friends remain seated and chat when the game-keeper's son is killed, the sheep of *Exterminating Angel* trot blithely into the church, oblivious to shots being fired a few steps away in the street.

While *Exterminating Angel* echoes scenes from Buñuel's early films, it also foreshadows works to come, such as *The Discreet Charm of the Bourgeoisie.* If the Nobile's guests are unable to leave the dinner party, the guests of the Sénéchales are doomed to repeat an unending series of dinner parties at which events equally as unexpected occur. Throughout Buñuel's films the bourgeois dining room where elegantly attired guests are sumptuously treated to exotic dishes is a haunting metaphor of the overfed and stagnant ruling class indifferent to a hungry world.

The surreal style of *Exterminating Angel* and its deliberate cultivation of mystery and confusion usually achieve the director's goal of disturbing and puzzling his viewers. When asked for an explanation of this film, Buñuel composed a prefatory statement that does not in any way contradict the apparent confusion of the work itself: "If the film which you are about to see seems to you enigmatic or incongruous, that is how life is also. The film is repetitious, like life, and, like life again, subject to many interpretations. The author declares that it was not his intention to play with symbols, at least not consciously. Perhaps the best explanation for *The Exterminating Angel* is that, rationally, there is none" (script, p. 19).

The Exterminating Angel is a rich visual experience touching upon varied fields of thought. One that comes most readily to mind is the field of social behavior. In *The Lonely Crowd,* David Riesman observes that "utter conformity in behavior may be purchased by the individual at so high a price as to lead to character neurosis and anomie: the anomic person tends to sabotage either himself or his society, probably both."[8] In *The Exterminating Angel,* Buñuel depicts a lonely crowd undergoing the process of social disintegration and individual neurosis. And he even goes so far as to suggest that society is willing to pay this price because the sacrifice of individual autonomy, or conformity, still demands less than the search for freedom.

The Milky Way (La Voie lactée) (1969)

In view of the surrealists' love of paradox, it is fitting that one of the most persistent obsessions of Buñuel the avowed atheist is the Catholic Church. Many viewers may suspect that Buñuel's return to religion for the subject of a fourth film (after *Nazarín, Viridiana,* and *Simon of the Desert*) undermines his atheism. For the central character of *The Milky Way* is no longer an individual struggling with religious principles, but the Church itself wracked by heretical argumentation. Yet Buñuel's fascination with Church dogma is in no way nostalgia for lost faith.[9] It is, rather, that for Buñuel, theology, like anthropology or entomology, is a topic that arouses his curiosity.[10] Applying his meticulous eye to the Scriptures, Buñuel discovers them to be equal to any surrealist text in their respect for and manipulation of irrationality. The heresies forming the outline of *The Milky Way* are, for Buñuel, a rich source of the incongruity, absurdity, and humor which appeal to his surrealist sensibility. In *The Milky Way,* he reworks some of his favorite themes, such as the impotence of reason, the problem of evil, and the denial of physical needs. But *The Milky Way* is most remarkable for its revelation of the arbitrary nature of the Church. Much like the confused Francisco in the last scene of *El,* Catholicism is seen dragging its victims along a zig-zag path of orthodoxy through centuries of Western culture.

This extraordinary journey through Church history begins, as does *Fever Rises on Mount Pao,* with a map, a means of creating the stamp of authenticity that surrealists sought in art. As in Buñuel's earlier "essay in human geography," *Las Hurdes*, the voice of a narrator describes the historical framework of this "theological essay."[11] Since the eleventh century, the Spanish town of Santiago de Compostela has been one of the chief shrines of Christendom, for it is here that the remains of St. James the Apostle are reputed to lie. According to legend, a star guided villagers miraculously to the tomb, hence the name Campo Stella, field of stars. In the fifteenth century, the body was hidden to protect it from desecration in religious wars, and it was lost until the nineteenth century. When relocated, it was only after considerable delay and hesitation that the remains were authenticated by the Pope, their real identity being impossible to verify. From this legend Buñuel takes his title, and from historical fact—a journey to the shrine—the structure of *The Milky Way*.

Buñuel's two travelers are Pierre and his younger companion, Jean. They are twentieth-century hitchhikers who begin their journey from Paris, flagging down rides on the Autobahn. Suddenly they meet a diabolical-looking man in a black hat and cape. But when he begins to speak, we recognize Buñuel's love of paradox. This sinister gentleman is not the devil but God, who, all-knowing, guesses the pilgrims' destination. He repeats to them God's words spoken in the Old Testament to Hosea (chapters 1 and 2) commanding them to have children by a prostitute and to name the offspring "You are not my people" and "No more mercy."[12] With this mysterious command, the stranger turns his back and walks away, accompanied now by a dwarf carrying a dove which flies off from his hand.

The introductory sequence of *The Milky Way* establishes its cinematic style as episodic. Such a style—together with the use of two adventurers as central figures—prompts many critics to describe the film as picaresque. Yet the film is unlike traditional adventures of rogues in that Buñuel's characters come and go inexplicably, time is disjointed, and the two main characters disappear at intervals throughout the narrative. Although likened to a riddle and a dream by Raymond Durgnat, and reduced to "shards and fragments" by another reviewer,[13] *The Milky Way* is a carefully structured film, unified by the theme of the journey through both time and space, and by the prophecy pronounced in the opening frames and fulfilled in the final scenes. The intervening episodes consist of an interrelated dialectic on the six most controversial heresies in church dogma: the Eucharist, (the mad priest), Origin of evil (Rites of Priscillian), Nature of Christ (Restaurant), the Trinity (exhumed bishop), free will (Jansenist-Jesuit duel), and the Immaculate Conception (the Spanish inn).

One of the first stops the two travelers make along their route is at an inn where they ask for handouts to eat. The conversation in progress between a priest and a police officer is an exercise in absurdity. The police officer, described in the script as a vigorous man of "l'esprit rationalist," assures the priest that the miracles of religion are all natural phenomena and that "science explains everything." He has trouble, however, understanding the Eucharist: "You'll never make me believe that the body of Christ is in this piece of bread." The priest confidently explains that "the body of Christ is not *in* the bread. By the sacrament of the Eucharist, it *becomes* the body of Christ." The innkeeper adds his own version of this mystery: "I always say that the body of Christ is contained in the host like the hare in the paté." But the priest rejects this version angrily, accusing the innkeeper of sounding like the heretical Patelier sect of the sixteenth century (script, p. 26).

By now, Pierre and Jean have entered the inn. Barely tolerated by the innkeeper, they listen respectfully to the debate. Pierre turns to the priest and, in sincere tones, asks the question which, in its practicality, destroys the gravity of the topic: "Once in the stomach, what does the body of Christ become?" (script, p. 27). This return to reality and logic offends the police officer. He demands to see the travelers' identification, inspects their papers summarily, and orders them out.

Suddenly, in a moment of insight, the priest decides the Patelier sect was right. The truth was revealed to him as he gazed at the paté on the table. "Yes, I *feel* that the body of Christ is in the host like the hare is in the paté. I'm sure. Absolutely sure" (script, p. 27). When the astounded officer reminds the priest that he had just affirmed the opposite view, the priest becomes angry and throws coffee in the surprised officer's face. It is at this point that two male nurses enter and take charge of the priest, who, they inform us, has escaped from a mental ward. "He was the priest of Chevilly until last year" (script, p. 28), we learn. From priest explaining the Eucharist to lunatic requires, in Buñuel's view, no change of identity. The discovery by one of the nurses of a knife beneath the priest's cassock was not retained in the final version of the film.

Dismissed from the inn, the travelers camp in a nearby forest. Suddenly a group of men appears, speaking Latin. They are the followers of Priscillian, the fourth-century Bishop of Avila who was executed as a heretic for his Gnostic ideas. Elegantly attired, Priscillian himself steps forward and recites his doctrine of evil. To purify the soul, which is divine, the body, which is evil, should be subjected to fleshly delights, so that the soul, after death, may return to its divine state. This extravagant interpretation of the dogma seems to grant permission for an ensuing orgy on the theory that evil cures evil. Women in various states of undress begin wandering about and couples walk off slowly together, with quiet dignity. This Roman orgy, blessed by a bishop, is a religious rite and is carried out in the name of purification of the soul.

The orgy takes place while Pierre and Jean are sleeping in the forest, as if they dreamed it. When they wake, the pair make their way to Tours, a region famous for its cuisine. We are suddenly in a deluxe restaurant. A crew of young waiters busily setting tables, arranging flowers, and building pyramids of fruit, is supervised by a dour headwaiter, Monsieur Richard, who moves among them like a priest among his acolytes. This analogy is almost inescapable when the conversation begins. The topic is religion. To a waiter's question as to whether everyone believes in God, M. Richard answers unequivocally, "Yes." There are, he admits, atheists, but these are either fools or people who merely call themselves atheists and are not. As proof, M. Richard cites Psalms 14:1: "It is a fool who says in his heart 'There is no God.' "

Soon M. Richard is heard declaring to his waiters that "only people with bad manners do not believe in God" (script, p. 34). A cleaning woman now asks the headwaiter about the nature of Christ: How can God be Christ, a man and God at the same time? M. Richard's explanation, interspersed with last-minute orders to see that the cloakroom is clean, is that God becomes man like the devil takes the form of a wolf. A disconcerting analogy, to be sure, but no doubt apt, since satanic wolves are common in folklore. But a young waiter is still puzzled. If Christ was a God, how could he be born and die? Did he eat? Sweat? Cough? M. Richard admits the complexity of the question and cites various opinions: that Christ's human form was a kind of illusion or appearance; that, according to the Monophysites and Nestorians, Christ did not suffer or die. As if to ease the anxious minds of the devout, the scene suddenly changes to another, more modest feast, the Marriage at

Cana, and focuses upon Christ, who asks the apostle Peter what time it is.

Buñuel's view of Christ is that of an ordinary man who gets hungry, becomes irritated with his mother, and enjoys sharing stories with his friends. In *The Milky Way,* Buñuel depicts Christ laughing, a mood in which no other artist has ever dared portray him. Mary, too, is an ordinary mother. She is overheard telling a friend of her surprise at her son's birth: "At first I couldn't believe it. But afterwards, I was very happy" (script, p. 36). When she calls Jesus away from the table to tell him they are out of wine, he is impatient. "Woman, how does that concern us? My hour is not yet come" (script, p. 37). An indulgent mother, Mary humors him.

The scene jumps back to the restaurant where guests have come to dine. The headwaiter wonders aloud to his staff why Christ succeeded when other wise men of his time did not. One of the guests, Mme. Garnier, has the answer. For her, it is quite simple: Christ was the only one who was God. Suddenly this conversation is interrupted when the two travelers appear and ask for food. Charity clearly is not within M. Richard's theological expertise, and he orders them out.

How people become dogmatists such as M. Richard is illustrated in the next sequence, a year-end picnic at the Institut Lamartine, a school for young ladies. Parents watch their daughters perform recitations condemning deviations from Christian dogma. Little Brigitte leads the group in a kind of fearful litany denouncing unorthodoxy: "If someone says Christians may have several wives, . . . let him be cursed." The audience repeats, "Let him be cursed." Each refrain is followed by a cut to a group of marching revolutionaries who form a firing squad. At the command of their female leader, they shoot their prisoner, the Pope. The revolutionary events are dimly perceived by one of the parents at the picnic who asks if there is a shooting-range nearby. Jean, too, heard the sound and confesses he thought someone shot the Pope. The consequences of irrelevant education seem faintly apparent to some, but are dismissed by most as exaggerated fears.

If the fanatical litany of the Institut can lead, as Buñuel suggests, to violent reaction against religion to the extent of killing the Pope, it can also be self-destructive, as in the case of the Convulsionnaires. The next stop that Pierre and Jean make is at a village where a procession of nuns files into a chapel. Once inside, a nun, fully dressed in her habit, is seen outstretched on a huge cross. One of her sisters drives a nail through the nun's hand. The Superior tries to dissuade the young woman from going through with her plan to be crucified, but the nun insists she wants to suffer as our Lord suffered. The young Convulsionnaire has turned inward the desire to denounce and condemn that the Institut Lamartine instilled at an early age in its pupils.

The two travelers, prevented from entering the chapel, are next confronted by two gentlemen dressed in eighteenth-century black costumes. One is the famous Jesuit, Father Buillard, who explains that what is going on in the convent chapel is Jansenist sacrilege, fanaticism. The other man is a count, a Jansenist, who challenges the Jesuit to a duel and enlists the two travelers as witnesses. Appropriately, the duel takes place in front of an abandoned chateau, which, like the Church, has become overgrown and decayed. The duel is accompanied by a verbal battle over the question of free will. The Jansenist declares, in a line from which Buñuel takes the title of his later film *(Le Fântome de la liberté),* that "my thoughts and my will are not in my power! And my freedom is only a phantom" (script, p. 45). The camera focuses on the two travelers, who, after also discussing the problem, turn to find the duelists walking away from their quarrel as friends. Their physical energies exhausted, the heat of their theological dispute also cools.

As Pierre and Jean cross the border from France into Spain, they meet what might be their Spanish counterparts, François and Rodolphe. These two young men, dressed in sixteenth-century garb, become the focus of the narrative. They observe the disinterment of a long-dead bishop who is being pronounced a heretic posthumously for his unorthodox views of the Trinity. They meet a priest at an inn who entertains them with tales of the miracles of the Virgin.

That night at the inn, Rodolphe, who had had a vision of the Virgin, sees another vision. This time it is not the Virgin Mary, but an attractive, unfamiliar young woman who appears in his room. The priest, always monitoring the affairs of others, knocks at the door of Rodolphe's room. But the young man has been warned by the innkeeper not to open the door to anyone. Refused entry, the undaunted priest sits outside Rodolphe's room and continues his discussion of the Virgin: that she remained pure before, during, and after the birth of Jesus, that her purity had been questioned by some, including St. Basile and St. John Chrysostome. Rodolphe asks the priest what he would think if he were to marry the young woman in his room. The priest replies with misogynist quotations from St. Paul and St. Thomas.

Not satisfied with discouraging all contact between Rodolphe and the young woman, the priest now moves on to François's room, where he also begs to be let in and is again refused entry. The priest then says, "At least let your friend out." The camera discovers a young man reading in the other bed in François's room. The scholarly stranger does not wish to leave, but when the priest finally departs, he shuts his book and murmurs a sentence which has been taken as the director's own feelings: "My hatred of science . . . and my horror of technology will finally force me to that absurd belief in God" (script, p. 60). That this statement is construed by some critics as representing the views of Buñuel, whose films are full of anthropological, historical, and entomological allusions, as well as jokes at the expense of the Church, is difficult to explain. Rather it expresses Buñuel's respect for mystery, to which the Church addresses itself but, in Buñuel's works, in an inadequate and often ridiculous way.

The two travelers who serve to unify the film narrative appear in the transition scenes, which are usually planned with the same care as the major segments of action. The narrative advances as they begin or stop their journey. Never perfunctory, the transitions frequently add meaningful details to the fabric of the film. The shift from the inn to the meeting with the prostitute, for example, is a minor scene, yet the unexpected leniency of the guard who catches but does not arrest Jean when he steals a ham is worked in so fluidly and concisely that it underscores Buñuel's respect for *le hasard*, a principle of surrealism which he has always maintained.[14]

The arrival of Pierre and Jean at Santiago brings both surprise and anticlimax. As the city and its church towers finally come into view, the tired travelers are stopped by a young prostitute in high-heeled shoes and tight dress. Learning that the pair is headed for the holy city, she deflates their anticipation by telling them they needn't hurry, for the place is vacant: "No one is there, not even a cat" (script, p. 62). The bones in the sepulcher were found not to be those of the saint after all. Since the head was missing, the cadaver is thought to be that of Priscillian. Heretics, suggests Buñuel slyly, can be found everywhere, even in some of the most prestigious graves.

Christ and his followers hear a petition in *The Milky Way*.

Since the travelers now have no reason for pursuing their journey, they are attracted by the prostitute's suggestion that they father her offspring. What will their names be? Fulfilling God's command issued in the opening sequence, they will be called "You are not my people" and "No more mercy." Not only, Buñuel suggests, has Christianity become empty, its shrines holding fragments of unidentified skeletons, but Everyman has been abandoned by an angry God. Rejected as unrepentant sinners ("You are not my people," "No more mercy"), Pierre and Jean do not hesitate to follow the prostitute into the forest.

No sooner do the pilgrims disappear than two blind men walk rapidly down a path. The camera's view of their feet accompanied by a cane emphasizes their incapacity and uncertain gait. They call upon Christ, whom they know to be nearby. He appears and miraculously cures their sightless eyes. But, if he has restored their vision, his enigmatic and incomplete parables do not provide them or his disciples with understanding. Jesus does not answer their questions but issues one proclamation after another. In their harsh and devisive meaning, Jesus' words echo to his followers God's words to Hosea quoted in the film's first scene. Jesus states, quoting the biblical passage from Matthew, "I am not come on earth to bring peace, but the sword. I am come to set son against father, daughter against mother. . . . Truly I say unto you, a man's foes shall be those of his own household" (script, p. 63). To his followers' pleas for guidance, Jesus responds only with pronouncements that sound much like a call to arms, a license for the violence which historically has followed in the Church's wake.

As bells toll in the distance, the group walks on. The final frames are some of the few close-up shots of the film. They are of the feet, first of Jesus and his disciples, then of the once-blind men who follow a few steps behind. As they come to a small bridge, Jesus and the disciples cross without hesitation. The two men, however, cross haltingly, probing with their canes, as if still without vision. The camera angle clearly leads to the conclusion that Christ's passage through the forest, that is, through the minds of those who follow his teaching, did not bring clarity but confusion, leaving them as hesitant and halting as ever. Certainly the blind men do not follow their leader into the forest with the same eagerness and sure sense of direction that Jean and Pierre followed the prostitute.

The Milky Way is, for non-Catholic viewers in a non-Catholic country, a difficult and often tedious film. Pauline Kael probably best expresses the wonder of most American critics and viewers when she confesses that, for her, Buñuel is, in *The Milky Way*, "the amiable academician whose recondite anecdotes depend on a familiarity with ancient languages."[15] Vincent Canby, less distracted by church history, is more sensible: "Even a non-Catholic can enjoy *The Milky Way* as a Pilgrim's Progress through the Buñuel iconography."[16] Yet it is true that *The Milky Way* is not only a visual but also a scholarly achievement. Every dialogue in which dogma is argued, as well as Christ's words and the incidents upon which the six major heresies are based, are factual and carefully documented in the script. Buñuel's desire to convey the film's authenticity and historical veracity is also expressed in the last few moments of the film in which words appear verifying its accuracy like footnotes to a scholarly tract. The insistence on the truth of the subject matter is, of course, essential to understanding the film fully. For not the least of surrealist philosophical tenets is that the most absurd and bizarre occurrences are those of reality itself.

The Milky Way has been called many things, from a "theological western," in which "sheriffs in mitres impose a return to the scriptures with their authoritarian crosses," to a "shaggy dog story that might be told in a seminary."[17] Yet the true source of *The Milky Way*, in addition to church history, is surrealism. Buñuel's co–script writer, Jean-Claude Carrière, reportedly found among André Breton's papers a work signed by Breton and other surrealists expressing a certain affinity between themselves and religious heretics, both being oppressed by orthodoxy.[18] Carrière also mentions that the director of *The Milky Way* hopes that his film will bring forth still more heresies, which are good for the Church.[19] Thus it is not only as a challenge but also in the spirit of kindred outcasts that Buñuel returns once more to Church history for artistic inspiration.

The Discreet Charm of the Bourgeoisie *(Le Charm discret de la bourgeoisie)* (1972)

This comedy of errors is a direct descendant of the ferocious *L'Age d'or* and the disturbing, allegorical *Exterminating Angel*. Like its predecessors, it is a satire on the bourgeoisie, the clergy, the military, and their trivial, conformist lives. Yet *Discreet Charm* is, for Buñuel, almost mellow. While *L'Age d'or* was banned from public view and *Exterminating Angel* left its audience puzzled and confused, *Discreet Charm* scandalizes no one and has garnered almost unanimous critical acclaim. Missing from it are the corrosive analogies of the de Sade/Christ scene in *L'Age d'or* and the neurotic despair of the guests in *Exterminating Angel*. Buñuel explains his restraint: "I feel less and less inclined toward violence . . . scandal and violence are no longer useful . . . they have lost their punch . . . I now say with humor what I used to say with violence."[20] Buñuel's most reliable arm of attack has always been humor. Since *Discreet Charm* has been described as his funniest film,[21] the most complete understanding of the work may lie in analysis of its comic techniques.

Like the master of American film comedies, Mack Sennett, Buñuel does not focus upon individual comic actors in *Discreet Charm*, but chooses instead a team of six characters who carry the comedy like a troupe of carefully understated clowns. The principals are Don Rafael, the Ambassador of the fictional Republic of Miranda, Mr. Thévenot, a businessman, his wife, Simone, her younger sister, Florence, and another couple, Alice and Henri Sénéchal. All are, like the kids of Peanuts or the Marx Brothers, members of a well-defined group, in this case, the bourgeoisie.

Their understated, always-correct and elegant costuming is the key to one of their characteristics that Buñuel considers central—their impassivity. In the most extraordinary circumstances, these well-mannered people maintain a stiff upper lip. In the opening scene they are not deterred by the fact that a favorite restaurant is darkened and empty. They rouse a waitress, sit down at a table, and begin to pore over the menu with ritual seriousness, debating whether to order melon or caviar. The group is oblivious to everything but the desires of their palates. Only after they have discussed the menu and delivered their orders to the waiter do they become aware of the sound of sobbing in the adjacent room. The three women get up to investigate, to the chagrin of Mr. Thévenot, who warns them not to be indiscreet. They discover that the owner has died and is lying in state in the next room. Mrs. Thévenot prefers not to stay for dinner, but the others are unconcerned. Impassivity closely resembles insensitivity when Florence shrugs, "It's all the same to me" (script, p. 22).

The impassivity of Buñuel's discreet bourgeoisie also emphasizes their social rigidity. The six characters, who apparently have no other acquaintances, seem to live in a social vacuum composed of the same people repeating their only activity of social interchange—eating together. Their gatherings are usually marked by inane dialogue often dedicated to the discussion of their taste in food. Corresponding to the lack of visual close-ups, the characters do not develop but are caught in an endless cycle of dinner parties.

Buñuel does not find the bourgeoisie entirely despicable. He seems to admire the aplomb with which Alice Sénéchal, like Lucía Nobile of *Exterminating Angel*, makes the best of an unexpected situation and produces dinner for a number of uninvited guests. Yet both these hostesses, trained in the bourgeois tradition of good manners, spring into their hospitable action like robots. Alice requests only five minutes to prepare supper for a troop of soldiers and their colonel. She jumps up from the table, leaves her guests, and rushes into the kitchen. The delight with which Buñuel frustrates his characters' plans and submits them to unexpected trials reveals not the sympathy or fondness of the portrayal, for example, of Nazarín or Viridiana, but a kind of entomological curiosity about the habits, under stress, of a curious species of insect.

The action of *Discreet Charm* consists of a series of gags triggered by interruption. This technique is used much like the comic chase, in which the characters are always seeking something that lies just beyond their reach. Of the film's ten major scenes, seven are based on interrupted meals, one is an interrupted rendezvous, and another, an arrest which must be retracted. Yet the scene revealing the ambassador and his friends to be drug pushers is, significantly, not an unfulfilled action.

Buñuel admits that one of the major sources of humor in *Discreet Charm* is irony, explaining, "The contradictions of the bourgeoisie fascinate me. They have a certain charm. In their offices or at their board meetings, they may be ruthless, heartless businessmen. But when they're away from their money-making activities, among their own kind . . . they can be quite delightful."[22] And the bourgeoisie of *Discreet Charm* abound in contradictions. A priest whose parents were murdered years ago discovers the assassin to be the old man to whom he is giving last rites, and he kills the dying man. The priest's nature is best expressed when he attends a party and tries on a hat once worn by Napoleon. Henri Sénéchal laughs, telling the priest, "It seems made for you" (script, p. 90). Some of the characters' contradictions are unexpected; for example, a colonel smokes and defends using marijuana, and a peasant woman tells the priest she hates Jesus.

As in *Exterminating Angel*, brutality lies just under the elegant bourgeois facade. With the blithe disregard of those who praised Mussolini for making trains run on time, the ambassador assures his friend that the Nazi butcher who is hiding in Miranda is a perfect gentleman. The ambassador also explains that Miranda treats student rebels as if they were mosquitoes, "Pam! . . . pam!" (p. 98). Earlier, the ambassador has demonstrated this policy himself. Seeing a girl outside his window selling toy dogs, he declares her a terrorist, grabs his rifle, and shoots one of the dogs.

Brutality toward students, is, of course, not limited to Miranda but is practiced by the police in the unidentified but unmistakably Parisian metropolis in which the six reside. While a pacifist is tortured, the six bourgeois are quickly released. As the detective who toiled to arrest his well-heeled culprits dreams he is forced to free them, the phone rings. It is the Minister of the Interior, who orders their immediate release, for reasons of state which do not concern the detective.

Violence, in fact, is another of the most persistent characteristics of the bourgeois society, and it is repeatedly ascribed to enforce-

Don Rafael, Miranda's Ambassador to France, responds to crises in his characteristic manner: (above) confronting a student revolutionary in his apartment; (below) defending his honor at a social gathering *(Discreet Charm of the Bourgeoisie)*.

ment agencies such as the military and the police. Yet, while their institutions consistently practice violence, the bourgeoisie steadfastly insist they do not condone it. When a young female terrorist breaks into the ambassador's apartment with a revolver in her purse, her intended victim disarms her and assures her that "violence leads to no good" (script, p. 65). But, again with his curious logic, the ambassador admits to the young woman that "the only solution to the problems of hunger and misery is military" (script, p. 67). With a gesture of great generosity, Don Rafael opens the door and allows his would-be killer to leave, apparently without punishment. But no sooner is she out the door than he signals from his window to police waiting below who seize the girl as she enters the street and drag her to their car. The ambassador promptly dismisses the incident, having more important matters on his mind. "I have a dinner tonight. I have to get ready" (script, p. 68).

Violence is punished severely when the perpetrators are young and leftist. When the bourgeoisie traffic in drugs, however, they are immune from punishment. The arrest and jailing of the six is a brief interruption of the nonstop dinner party which is their main activity. From the jail where the detective ponders his prophetic nightmare, the scene cuts to the Sénéchal living room where the six are going through their greeting ritual: "How are you? Are we too late? What a lovely dress you have on" (script, pp. 127–28). They go directly to the table where Henri stands in order to carve a leg of lamb. "It is more correct to stand," he assures his guests (script, p. 131).

The lamb dinner is interrupted, this time by a band of robbers or guerrillas, it isn't clear which. This is the final interruption, for the gang mows down the six, who fall to the floor, their discreet clothing now blood-soaked. As the gunmen shoot at the dishes, the ambassador rises from beneath the table to grab a last handful of lamb before going under for good. This antic is the viewer's clue that the class-murder is only a ghoulish joke, dreamed up by the fearful mind of Don Rafael. The punchline of the joke is the cut to the ambassador's kitchen, where, after waking from his nightmare of the murder, he goes to take a slice of cold lamb from the refrigerator. The film ends with its leitmotif—a view of the six walking, now disheveled and exhausted, down a highway leading nowhere. Any conversation between them is made impossible by the roar of a jet passing overhead like a final insult to the haggard but persistent bourgeoisie.

The leitmotif of the characters heading down a highway seems to stress the importance of motion in the lives of the elite. For Buñuel, their perpetual activity is often mindless and without direction. There are many scenes of the characters being driven in cars. Some motion, accompanied by noise, is actively destructive, as when planes fly over, drowning dialogue. Even the Sénéchals' frantic love-making, in which they climb out a bedroom window and flee to the woods to escape notice by their waiting guests, is an athletic caper. The repeated interruption of ongoing action and its similarity to the chase, together with the leitmotif of walking nowhere, contributes to the rapid comic pace of *Discreet Charm.* The fast action of the film prevents the viewer from stopping long enough to think about the scenes and thus from taking them seriously. This pace is slowed only three times in scenes which are without comic value, suggesting that they are to be considered more carefully. Two of these are dream sequences; the other is a torture scene.

The dreams are each experienced by young soldiers in whose disciplined lives love is linked with death. The first of these dreams is narrated by a lieutenant who recalls his childhood for the three bourgeois ladies whom he approaches in a restaurant. At the age of eleven, he is fitted with a uniform and sent away to military school by his father, who warns him that the discipline will be hard. "But it is for your own good," the father reminds the boy with a justification often used when inflicting punishment (script, p. 54). The boy sees a vision of his beloved mother, now dead, who informs him that the man who claims to be his father actually killed the man she loved, his real parent, in a duel. Following her instructions, the boy poisons the impostor, whose death agony his mother and her lover calmly observe.

In the next dream scene, a young sergeant, one of those on military maneuvers who drops by the Sénéchal home, tells of his dream in which he meets two friends and his former lover, all lost for years. Soon it is apparent that these characters are dead. He leaves them for a moment and returns to find them gone. Tears streaming down his face, the sergeant wanders down the street calling for his mother. In the dream, he tells his listeners, no one answered.

These dreams may suggest that harsh military discipline, represented by the constricting uniform, deprives the boy of the nurturing of the protective parent, for whom the young man continues to search. Clearly, Buñuel views disciplinarian life and education, to which the bourgeoisie often submit their male offspring, as a cruel system that impairs emotional development.

The other noncomic segment in this generally humorous film is the torture of a young pacifist by police officers. One of the most persistent themes of Buñuel's career is that of cruelty. Individual sadism is explored in films like *El,* in which tools of torture are carried stealthily to the innocent victim's bedside. The role of cruelty in a religion that stresses sacrifice is hinted at in the de Sade/Christ scene of *L'Age d'or* and in the brief view of de Sade with a young female victim in *The Milky Way.* Prisoners are whipped by agents of a corrupt regime in *Fever Mounts in El Pao,* while the ascetic inflicts starvation and exposure to the elements upon himself in *Simon of the Desert.* The torture scene of *Discreet Charm,* however, is unmatched by these earlier films in its detailed depiction of refined cruelty. The sadistic brigadier wires the penis of the young pacifist to cords in a piano, which are electrified. The prisoner's body is then dumped into the piano and the electric current released. While muffled screams from inside the piano are heard, cockroaches crawl on the piano keys. The analogy of the torturers with the repulsive insects seems inescapable. The brigadier is, of course, assisted by agents, indicating how individual sadism becomes imperceptibly institutionalized in an oppressive society.

The inclusion of his most brutal torture scene in what critics generally agree is his most pleasant film raises important questions, not only about the style of *Discreet Charm* but also about the final direction of Buñuel's art. Described as the director's "most accessible work" and his "most enjoyable," but also as "slight" and "all for fun," *Discreet Charm* seems to have impressed some observers as a relaxation of long-held attitudes of protest by the old surrealist filmmaker.[23] Buñuel himself seems to give support to this impression in an interview regarding *Discreet Charm:* " 'At the time of *L'Age d'or,*' he has since recalled, 'I took positions. I don't take positions any more. I have no great illusion any more. Art is pleasure. You express yourself and' . . . he lifts his drink . . . 'Thank you very much, I'm finished.' "[24] Is *Discreet Charm* the fading glimmer of former brilliance?

Clearly, the anger in *Discreet Charm* is less intense than in *L'Age d'or* and *Exterminating Angel.* The leitmotif of the six walking down the endless road may suggest the endurance of the bourgeoisie and Buñuel's final acceptance that the middle class will not disappear as

Marx had hoped. There is also a kind of detachment in *Discreet Charm* that defines all political groups either as cruel or irrational. The young female terrorist sounds as violent as her enemies, the military and the police, when she tells Don Rafael, "Mao Tse-tung was right: Shameless ones like you should be eliminated without pity" (script, p. 67). On the other end of the political spectrum, there is Florence, with what Jonathan Rosenbaum describes as her "dopey, indifferent, comic-strip face" issuing a blanket condemnation of everyone: "Do you know the sign of the International Women's Movement? It's this (she holds four fingers out straight, thumb under). It's a ridiculous salute, like all the rest . . . Fascism, Communism, victory, and Christ our Lord" (she makes each salute with her hand as she speaks) (script, p. 70).

The detachment allowing Buñuel to ridicule violence and oppression by any political movement is inherent in the comic style of *Discreet Charm.* Jonathan Rosenbaum considers this comedy of special importance because in it "Buñuel has finally achieved Style . . . the secret of Buñuel's achieved style is balance . . . in which absurdity and elegance, charm and hypocrisy have become indistinguishably fused."[25] Buñuel has always been a master at revealing how reality becomes parody. In *Discreet Charm,* however, he plays his comedy straight so that while his characters' elegance and dignity are beyond question, they seem, at the same time, subtle caricatures of themselves.

At a moment when violence, like nudity, has become a cliché in films, Buñuel, ever wary of conformity, updates his art by returning to techniques of silent comedy as a fresh means of attack. He does not entirely eliminate violence from his arsenal and includes in this late work perhaps his most brutal sequence. Yet the torture in *Discreet Charm* serves as a reminder in the midst of his amusement of Buñuel's anger at the idle rich—immune from punishment—and at their henchman, the brigadier.

The restraint, balance, and humor of *Discreet Charm* represent not so much a lowering of the heat of Buñuel's rage as a change of tactics. If violence has become an accepted means of film protest, it cannot, for a surrealist filmmaker, be of use any longer. So Buñuel, now in his seventies and having been joined by younger directors in protest, has sought a fresh approach. Buñuel often said he made films for his friends. *Discreet Charm,* however, is not a film made for his friends only, nor a collection of inside jokes and erudite gags,

Buñuel handles violence with elegant detachment: (above) a murderous "working bishop" (Julien Bertheau) chats with the fashionable Sénéchals (Jean-Piere Cassel and Stephane Audran); (below) a fantasy dinner-party ends in fantasy death for the discreet bourgeoisie.

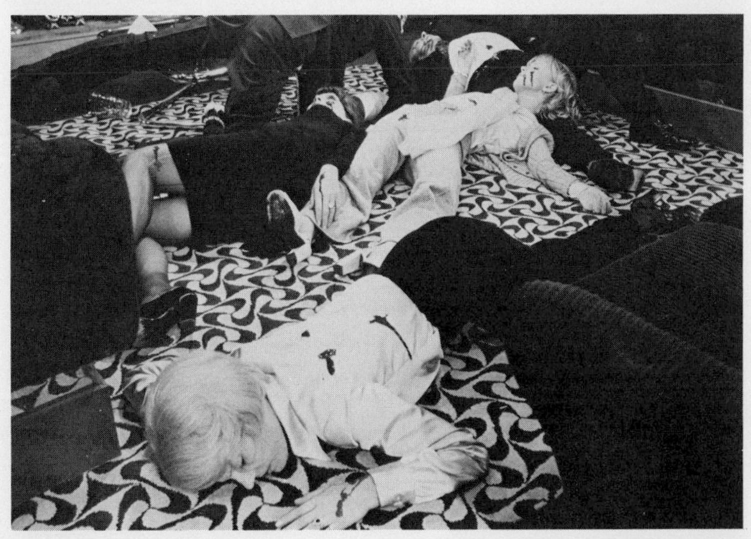

like *L'Age d'or*. Almost subdued by today's standards, it reaches out to a wider audience to welcome the very object of its attack, the bourgeoisie. So Buñuel's light may not have dimmed in *Discreet Charm*, but only enlarged its beam.

The Phantom of Liberty (Le Fantôme de la liberté) (1974)

André Breton and his friends, who would leave one movie for another as soon as they began to understand the narrative, would have been pleased with *Phantom of Liberty*. With no trace of narrative, plot, protagonists, or even a fixed set of characters, *Phantom* is Buñuel's freest and most surreal film since *L'Age d'or*. Vincent Canby is correct when he asserts that "there is no single correct way to read" *Phantom*. Having so stated, however, Canby proceeds to eliminate a promising interpretation: "I'm not sure the film has much to do with ideas about freedom."[26] Yet Buñuel's preoccupation with freedom is evident not only in the film's title and form but also in one of its only vestiges of continuity, the cry of "Vivan las caenas" ("Long live the chains"), which opens *Phantom* and echoes in the final scene like a refrain.

Phantom begins with a depiction of the ultimate deprival of liberty, a firing squad. The victims include a priest (played by Buñuel), an injured official, and a young woman, who are lined up against a wall. To visualize the firing squad Buñuel draws upon the heritage of Spanish painting, the famous *Executions of the Third of May* by Goya. The painting serves as a point of departure from which Buñuel recalls events based on the Napoleonic invasion of Spain in 1808. Spanish peasants, horrified by what they and the Spanish church considered to be armies spreading the heresies of the French revolution, are said to have shouted "Abajo con la libertad" (Down with liberty") when Napoleon's troops marched into Spain. Faithful to their own corrupt monarch, the Spanish populace preferred Spanish rule to an alien government that promised Liberty, Equality, and Fraternity. For Buñuel, the cry of "Abajo con la libertad" is historical proof that, when offered a choice between freedom and servitude, most human beings are more likely to choose enslavement than that which makes them free. The succeeding episodes of *Phantom* depict circumstances and obsessions that constrict behavior or limit human freedom.

The semidocumentary prologue that Buñuel often uses to introduce his films provides here a period setting which is sustained in the next sequence, the dramatization of a tale entitled "El beso" by Spain's best Romantic poet and prose stylist, Gustavo Adolfo Bécquer. Buñuel stresses humor, mystery, and morbid passion in the story of a young officer in Napoleon's army who, inebriated, kisses the statue adorning a woman's tomb. When he leans over the statue, however, the arm of the statue of her husband, kneeling beside his wife, strikes the young officer on the head, knocking him unconscious. Bécquer's tale ends with the fateful kiss, but Buñuel's imagination runs on. So infuriated is the young captain that he vows to have the woman or to cut off his tongue and eat it. Like Francisco of *El* and Archibaldo, the captain is now entirely possessed by desire and rage. He decides to open the tomb of the lovely but long-dead Elvira.

As the slab is lifted from the sarcophagus, Buñuel switches in time from the nineteenth to the twentieth century, from the shadows of the grave in the floor of a Toledo church to a Parisian garden where two maids are reading Bécquer's story, enraptured. Elvira's corpse, untouched by the ravages of death, was discovered in the tomb, her form draped in "an abominable paraphernalia."[27] One maid, in delightful surrealist confusion, explains the term "paraphernalia" to her friend while their charges, the daughters of two rich upper-class families, are being shown what seem to be pornographic postcards by a suspicious-looking passerby. The jump in time from past to present is thus achieved with a wink and a change in tone from nineteenth-century Romanticism to twentieth-century surrealist humor.

Buñuel, master of the jump-cut and unexpected juxtapositions, is careful throughout most of *Phantom* to smooth transitions between episodes even though they may have no logical connection. Thus the viewer, with the illusion of continuity, does not become bored but waits to gather narrative threads. These do not appear, but are instead replaced by variations upon Buñuel's favorite themes. The first of these, treated most strongly in *Exterminating Angel,* is an attack on conformity. Rigid social attitudes lead us to reject what may be useful solutions to problems, as in the case of Henri Foucauld, a bourgeois husband suffering a case of the blahs. He can't sleep at night and his wife, Hélène, complains of his lack of interest: "Yesterday I passed you in the street and looked at you and you didn't even recognize me" (script, p. 29).

When the Foucaulds' daughter comes merrily into the room and hands her mother some cards that "a nice man" gave her, the two parents react like the good bourgeoisie they are. They chastise the maid for allowing the little girl to take gifts from strangers, but, when the maid leaves, the couple pores over the cards with great interest. For the first time, Henri begins to show affection to his wife. "As if the postcards aroused them" (script, p. 31), Henri and Hélène kiss, allowing the postcards to fall to the ground. The viewer sees that they are not pornographic at all, but only ordinary tourist scenes of familiar Parisian landmarks—the Eiffel Tower, the Arch of Triumph, the Madeleine. These hallowed monuments may be obscenities for Buñuel, but this gag has, as most of Buñuel's gags, serious implications that suggest the hypocrisy of bourgeois attitudes. Righteous indignation of upstanding citizens toward "obscenity" often masks their own vicarious pleasure. While privately enjoying sexual arousal from salacious pictures, the Foucalds steadfastly and publicly maintain their indignant opposition to pornography. They dismiss the innocent maid in a display of their loyalty to arbitrarily defined codes of so-called respectability.

That the Foucaulds hide their spontaneous reaction to the censored postcards signals their lack of freedom to express their feelings openly. They are bound by social rules that determine their behavior. Two of the central episodes of *Phantom* stress the whimsical nature of social dictates and the extent to which they rule our daily lives and perceptions.

Buñuel's anthropological view of social customs is expressed in a lecture delivered to a group of disinterested police trainees by a timid professor. The topic of discussion is the relativity of social laws and customs. The professor informs his class that laws serve to maintain order and vary in different cultures. Citing Margaret Mead, he explains that, for example, polygamy is the rule in some countries, while being prohibited in our own. But the beleaguered professor's words are repeatedly interrupted by students arriving late, leaving early for target practice, and by announcements of various catastrophes that require the students' immediate departure.

If the lesson on the relativity of social customs falls on deaf ears, the professor's next example, an illustration of the lesson, is more vivid. The scene unfolds as the professor describes a social gathering which he and his wife attend. Arriving at a friend's house for dinner, the professor and his wife are welcomed into a normal, very polite gathering. But something is awry. The guests are seated around the dining table not on chairs, but on toilet seats. The table is not set with eating utensils but with magazines and ashtrays. Conversation revolves around world problems such as pollution and overpopulation. When the guests excuse themselves, it is to retire to a small back room where they eat quickly and perfunctorily, as if carrying out a task, which, although unimportant, requires privacy. By reversing the manner in which people eat and excrete, Buñuel highlights the illogic of social codes and our complete subjugation to them.

The master manipulator of both personal and social freedom is, of course, the Catholic Church, which is in *Phantom* as meddlesome and capricious as in most of Buñuel's films. When a young nurse complains to some priests that her St. Christopher medal no longer protects her, the priests explain why. Since the church has become stricter about granting sainthood, it is reviewing the status of personages so honored in the past. Some, such as St. Christopher and perhaps St. Teresa, are being deprived of sainthood, while others, such as Savonarola, are being considered as possible candidates. The nurse is horrified that figures as popular and as long a part of Catholic history as these should now be removed, but the priests explain patiently that these arbitrary reversals merely serve to reaffirm the faith.

The Catholic Church is thus seen as an institution which, like some governments, suddenly retires leaders it no longer considers useful and expects its followers' acquiescence. Other institutions also supposedly dedicated to alleviating suffering actually work to increase it. Among these are the police, one of Buñuel's perennial targets, and a new threat, physicians. When another good bourgeois husband, Legendre, goes to his doctor to hear the results of his medical exam, he is confronted by an arrogant, evasive professional who prefers to joke and discuss personal matters rather than his patient's exam. Legendre persists with repeated inquiries, to which the doctor finally responds that he would like to do a liver operation on his patient tomorrow. The prospect of imminent surgery makes Legendre apprehensive and he timidly asks, "What do I have?" "Whatever you say," replies the doctor, "but I would like to see first." Legendre insists that he can stand the truth, to which the doctor admits cryptically, "You have a neoplasm." When asked what this is, the doctor reports blithely, "A proliferation of the cells, or, if you prefer, cancer" (script, p. 93).

This agonizing inquiry and its disastrous outcome seem designed for maximum emotional torment rather than to transmit information. The police and teachers on whom the Legendres rely to locate their missing daughter, Aliette, use similar circuitous procedures. The little girl's teachers report her absence to her parents, who rush to the school. But when the class roll is called, Aliette answers, "Present." "Mama, I'm here," she calls out (script, p. 99). But to no avail. Neither her teacher nor her mother are listening. "Go to your seat," instructs her mother. Aliette soon leaves school accompanied by her irate parents, who go to police headquarters to report their daughter's disappearance.

The bourgeois world is clearly a Wonderland where facts are ignored and missing persons answer questions to help expedite the search underway for them. The Legendres, in angry, blind pursuit, report Aliette's absence to the police chief, who turns to the little girl for the necessary information. "Name?" "Aliette." "Race?" "White." "Age?" "Eight and a half." "How tall are you?" (script, p. 103). An assistant enters and requests permission to take Aliette along to help in the search. "No," the chief replies. "It's not worth it. Take a good look so you can recognize her and begin the search immediately" (script, p. 104). The refusal of the middle class to accept reality and its preference instead for what is restrictive, even painful, is illustrated here with understatement and humor.

For the most part, *Phantom* is composed of scenes in which freedom is undermined by social attitudes and institutions. The hypocrisy with which society tries to define obscenity, the caprice with which some activities are censured and others accepted, and the mindlessness of law-enforcement and health-care institutions are enacted with great skill. The overkill attitude of military minds is sketched in a brief encounter between a nurse who is driving down the highway and a tank corps whose commander is out fox-hunting with tanks. Human beings, however, not only devise monumental Wonderlands of absurd institutions to constrict their lives. They are also victims of their desire, often sexual, to control and restrict, which captures their emotions and frequently leads to thoughts of death.

The period sequence which opens *Phantom* hints that the roots of human bondage are timeless and lie not only in the social conflict enacted in the war scene but also in erotic obsessions such as that of the French captain aroused by the statue of the dead Elvira. Desire and death also haunt the mind of Henri Foucauld, who, while his wife sleeps beside him one night, sees, first, a rooster enter the bedroom, cross in front of the bed, and walk out the opposite door as a bell tolls in the distance. Like the cock in the henhouse of *Los olvidados,* this nocturnal rooster signals erotic desire, yet it is followed by the ultimate phantom of liberty, Death, who now enters the bedroom as a woman dressed in black carrying a candle. Upon reaching the bed, she pulls out a pocketwatch and holds it for Foucauld to see. Then, ominously, she puts out her candle, and, like the rooster, exits. Foucauld's final visitor is the ostrich which appears again in the film's final scene. Described in the script as "elegant and proud" (p. 36), the ostrich is, for Marsha Kinder, the perfect embodiment of Buñuel's vision of man."[28] At the very least, the exotic bird with its wide, innocent eyes and a habit of avoiding danger that has come to symbolize futility, brings to mind a certain lack of astuteness with which Buñuel often characterizes the upper-middle class.

In Buñuel's films, erotic desire finds its most poignant yet desperate expression as a last grasp for life by an aging man, as in *Tristana, Viridiana,* and *Diary of a Chambermaid.* In a curious reversal of this pattern in *Phantom,* a young man becomes enamored of his aging aunt. Taking her to a hotel one night, François forces her to undress, promising he will not touch her. But when he learns she is a virgin, his desire becomes more brutal. He tries to rip off the sheet his aunt has pulled up to her chin. When she struggles, François almost smothers her to death with a pillow.

François's passionate frenzy is not without parallels to the earlier episode of Elvira and the French captain. The form of the white-haired woman lying on a bed under a white sheet suggests a cadaver. But, like Elvira's corpse, the aunt's body is that of a beautiful young woman untouched by time. For François, as for the young captain, eroticism as a means to power and control over another leads directly to the grave.

For the police chief passion leads not only to the grave but also to the police station, where he is taken after being arrested for trying to open the tomb of his sister Margueritte, dead for four years. The police chief, having solved the mystery of the missing Aliette, meets with her parents to inform them. But before he has time to discuss the topic, he hurries off abruptly for an appointment. He goes to a bar where he sees a stunning young woman dressed in black. She reminds him so much of his beloved sister that he has a daydream in which he sees Margueritte playing Schumann's *Carnival* for him on the piano. This fond memory, however, borders on the pornographic, for Margueritte is nude. The sight of a naked piano player does not seem to arouse the police chief until, in a shot recalling the view of Tristana's leg under the piano, he stoops to pick up his lighter and views his sister's legs sheathed in black hose. Following this erotic hallucination, the police chief continues chatting with the woman in black until he is again interrupted, this time by the telephone. It is Margueritte. She asks him to meet her at the family tomb so that he may learn "the true mystery of death" (p. 123).

In a scene straight out of *Don Juan,* by the nineteenth-century Spanish writer, Zorrilla, the police chief finds himself that night at the cemetery under a bright, full moon. Like the young French captain, the police chief tries to open the dead woman's grave. Though the nineteenth-century officer pursued his morbid desire without interruption, efficient police agents apprehend this twentieth-century grave-robber when he pries a steel bar into the tomb's top slab.

As the police chief's arrest suggests, erotic frenzy which seeks control over another so strongly that it desires the dead, quickly becomes pathological. Thus it is not only social restraint that limits human freedom. There is a basic, destructive human need to embrace the very force that eliminates freedom and independence. An example is the scene of a sniper whose several acts of murder are carefully filmed. Yet, after being convicted of his crimes, the sniper is released to a crowd which quickly forms in admiration and respect around him.

In one of the most humorous scenes of *Phantom,* a pleasant chap, who wants to celebrate with friends the coincidence that caused their meeting, enjoys being whipped by the seductive Ms. Rosenblum. The sadistic act is performed in the hotel room of a man identified only as the Hatter (tribute to another Wonderland?). The Hatter invites to his room a group of people, including four priests, who are staying in his hotel. Suddenly the attractive Ms. Rosenblum emerges from the bathroom wearing the garb of the sadist—a black leather suit. With the Hatter's encouragement, she applies a whip to the bare bottom protruding from a section cut out of his otherwise normal trousers. When the horrified onlookers get up to leave, the Hatter begs them, "At least let the priests stay" (script, p. 69). This remark points to the connecting link between sexual and religious flagellation. Erotic punishment, like other kinds of penitence, provides pleasure for guilt-ridden minds.

While many people believe themselves to be autonomous, Buñuel finds that freedom is a responsibility most go to considerable lengths to avoid. We usually prefer instead to be dominated by institutions, public opinion, or our own obsessions. The consequences of submission are conveyed in the final chilling scene of *Phantom,* in which animals in a zoo rebel. The analogy between animals and humans, ancient in the tradition of fables, is a favorite of Buñuel. The cat pounces on a rat, foreshadowing Jorge's move toward Ramona in *Viridiana;* a mangy dog trots through the frames picturing Jaibo's death in *Los olvidados;* sheep in *Exterminating Angel* follow each other into a church, mimicking the earlier action of the elegant bourgeoisie. In *Phantom,* heads of small animals are seen decorating a hotel wall, the dried, grotesque trophies of a predatory culture. Finally, a society which tries to imprison human instincts is symbolized as a zoo from which animals try in vain to escape.

Parallels between the zoo revolt and the opening war scene are numerous and direct. Among the sounds of warfare are heard chains dragging on the ground and the familiar shouts of "Vivan las caenas!" (script, p. 134). The similarities of these two strategic scenes and their repeated cries of "Down with Liberty" make all the more puzzling Pauline Kael's understanding of freedom in *Phantom* as "in the sense of chance."[29] Buñuel himself engineered the sound effects for *Phantom.* The final frames, punctuated by explosions and cries of "Long live the chains," build toward the inescapable conclusion that the human struggle which counts is against social and political oppression. And, in *Phantom,* the struggle is too late.

The fear and disorientation of the ostrich passing in front of the camera are silent and desperate. Buñuel's vision of his time is a cinematic version of Goya's *Third of May* in which the victims are animals whose lives, like those of the Spanish populace, have not prepared them for freedom.

There is much in *Phantom* of Buñuel's earlier works. Already mentioned is his fondness for animals, prominent in *Phantom.* Suggestions of necrophilia, as in *Viridiana,* and erotic sadism, as in *Belle de jour,* still represent for Buñuel the strange human desire for total control over another human being. The device of interruption, developed in *Discreet Charm,* is used in the same way in *Phantom* to trigger a gag with serious implications.

Yet, for all its familiar echoes, *Phantom* offers fresh examples of the vitality of Buñuel's art. The rebellion in the zoo, with its agonizing soundtrack of nonverbal roars and shrieks, is one of cinema's most horrifying images of powerlessness and frustration. The absence of love in *Phantom* again underscores lack of freedom. Buñuel's men, erotically aroused by aging and dead women, are prisoners of sadistic obsessions. By pointing to how often cruelty and desire look alike, Buñuel reminds us that love is based on equality and freedom, both of which are almost entirely absent from *Phantom.*

Finally, Buñuel attempts in *Phantom* the ambitious task of presenting the struggle for freedom on two levels at once, implying that social and psychological freedom are inextricably meshed. He appears to conclude, as Erich Fromm has cautioned, that "we not only have to preserve and increase traditional freedom, but . . . gain a new kind of freedom, one which enables us to realize our own individual self. . . ."[30] The alternatives to freedom, as Buñuel assures us in *Phantom,* are social totalitarianism on the one hand, and pathological behavior on the other. Like an ancient fabulist, Buñuel chooses the ostrich to suggest a society unprepared to cope with the demands of freedom.

That Obscure Object of Desire *(Cet obscur objet du désir)* (1977)

Buñuel approaches his fiftieth year of filmmaking by treating that last, most firmly entrenched bastion of unliberated minds, male-female sex roles. This topic and its related themes of exploitation, misogyny, and sexual sado-masochism are some of Buñuel's lifelong preoccupations. Female subservience appears to him as the touchstone of a repressive culture as early as *L'Age d'or*, in which the Duke of Blangis is revealed to be Jesus, the gentle orgiast. Buñuel's depiction of the role of the Church in the suppression of women in particular and of sexuality in general culminates in this last delightful but ferocious farce, based on Pierre Louÿs's short story "The Lady and the Clown." Buñuel has converted this story into a twentieth-century morality tale in which sexual mores are seen as a curious, rather antique form of terrorism.

The structure of *Desire* is much like that of *Discreet Charm*—a series of vignettes strung together by a leitmotif. In *Discreet Charm*, this motif consists of a view of the six characters strolling down a deserted highway. In *Desire*, narrative fragments are joined by another travel motif, that of a train carrying the narrator, who tells his story to his traveling companions. Sharing his train compartment are a typical group of bourgeois characters including a lady, her young daughter, a magistrate, and a psychiatrist. It is, perhaps, no coincidence that the psychiatrist is a dwarf, who, when the lady's daughter stands to help him lift his suitcase, insists irritably that he doesn't need any help.

The narrator, portrayed to perfection by the familiar Fernando Rey, is Mathew Fabert, an aging Don Juan much like Don Lope, whom Rey played in *Tristana*. He narrates his story by way of explanation to his travel companions, who are aghast when they see him toss a bucket of water on a young woman who, begging him not to leave, tries to board the train. We later learn that the young woman was the object of Mathew's fondest desire, Conchita.

The explanatory flashback discloses that Conchita is a servant at whom he makes a pass in his boudoir. Echoing Don Lope, who assured Tristana that she was not a servant, Mathew now informs Conchita that he is not going to treat her like a maid. The idea of women in servile roles, however, still pleases him, for he looks forward the next morning to being served breakfast by Conchita. To his surprise and disgust, he discovers that she has quit her job and left.

Conchita is played by two actresses whose opposite types suggest that Conchita is both seductive, as the earthy Angela Molina plays the role, as well as glacial and aloof, as portrayed by the more Nordic-looking Carole Bouquet. The idea of two actresses for the leading role was apparently accidental, for Maria Schneider was to have played Conchita before she walked out in a disagreement. The use of two actresses, however, serves an important function. The role of the perverse woman is universalized by creating the impression that, whatever their face or temperament, females are deceptive, wily, and potentially dangerous. The opposing types of beauty implicate all women in an infinite variation of evil in feminine guise.

Such misogynistic attitudes are expressed throughout the film from its earliest scenes. The aging Don Juan wastes no time in tracking down his prey, and it is when he finds Conchita at home and meets her mother that negative allusions toward women begin to be a kind of counterpoint to the revelation of Conchita's character.

Conchita's mother complains of the poverty she and her daughter endured since her husband's death—he committed suicide. Mathew immediately hands the widow money, which she readily accepts, promising to repay him as soon as possible. She leaves, as if to confirm his right to be alone with his newly purchased toy. Considering this handout the first installment on the purchase of Conchita's body, Mathew turns to the young woman and strokes her leg. Conchita, who drapes herself seductively in a chair, contradicts her body language by uttering puritan clichés. While she feeds him candy, she insists that she is not "that kind of girl." On later visits, he makes passes which she protests by insisting that he kisses her without love. As she offers to give him a list of names of girls who will yield to his demands, her mother enters with complaints of poverty and hardship. Conchita tells Mathew that she is a virgin, to which her mother adds, "More women are led astray by other women than by men." This curious and unprovoked censure is announced with the same hostile attitude with which Mathew's butler, Martin, later observes that he has a friend who calls women "sacks of excrement." Mathew, in surprised amusement, replies, "What a thing to say."

Mathew's second installment on the attempted purchase of Conchita comes once again as an offer to her mother. The widow is, appropriately, coming out of church when Martin requests her presence at his employer's home. Mathew begins by confessing his love for Conchita, to which the mother inquires, "You mean you want to marry her?" On the soundtrack a snap is heard. "No," Mathew admits, "Not right now, but I need your help." Martin crosses the room, announcing that he must retrieve a mouse that was just caught in a trap. Recalling the cat pouncing on a rat symbolizing Jorge's conquest of Ramona in *Viridiana*, the mention of marriage by the widow is accompanied by the sound of a trap snapping on a mouse (a device earlier used by Erich von Stroheim in *Greed*). Later Mathew reaffirms this view of marriage as a trap when he confesses to his cousin that he likes to have Conchita near him, but that "if I marry, I'll be completely helpless."

Thus the archaic sexual behavior prescribed for males and females in Christian culture is revealed as constrictive and rigid. In a patriarchal society in which sex has been accepted only for the purpose of procreation, sexuality must be redeemed and refined as love before it may be expressed. Neither males nor females are free to express their sexuality as such. Just as Conchita protests that she must be loved, Mathew, too, admits that he must love his women. Virginity, that cult of purity by which Christianity denies women control of their bodies, remains as a valuable asset to male pride. The French reviewer Alain Masson notes the "gourmandise" with which Mathew kisses Conchita's hand when he learns she is still a virgin.[31]

Virginity is not the only remnant of sexual attitudes in *Desire* that originates from the notion of women as property. Mathew's efforts to buy Conchita increase in generosity from payoffs and handouts to her mother, to the decorating of a room where she as concubine may stay in his house, to a house of her own that he finally buys in Seville. Each increment in the purchase of her body is met by Conchita with corresponding increases in anger, spite, and hatred. Clearly, the manipulation of sexual behavior by economic inducement is seen as unsatisfying, risky, and counterproductive.

Sexual behavior in Christian culture is presented as not only archaic and demeaning, but is also found to be violent and destructive. Conchita's denial of Mathew, at first endured with restraint, patience, and even tears from the tortured man, becomes increasingly flagrant and is met with augmented aggression. She insists that if she gives in, he will no longer want her; yet she torments him by getting into bed wearing an incredible pair of canvas underpants whose infinite tiny knots mock his frustrated efforts to remove them forcefully. The cut back to the astounded traveling companions reveals them to be entirely sympathetic to the aging suitor's despair.

Mathew's obsession to possess Conchita becomes almost pathological in the face of her steadfast refusal. When she asks him why, when he has her to caress, he must possess her sexually, Mathew falls back on the cultural cliché, "Because it's normal." Yet such behavior, accepted by society, is clearly deranged. For Mathew, who represents the average Western male, sexuality has declined into mere genital contact. He is unable to find pleasure in, or indeed think about, any other aspect of Conchita. It is, as David L. Overby points out, that, having " 'decided' to desire her, he probably doesn't see her at all."[32] The female has been converted by male fixation on genital primacy into an object, depersonalized, and dehumanized.

It is this attitude of human beings as objects that relates the theme of misogyny to wider social violence. Just as *Discreet Charm* was punctuated throughout by interruptions of the elegant bourgeois dinners, the theme of terrorism provides a kind of fugal counterpoint to the development of the love affair in *Desire*. In the opening segments of the film a banker's car explodes, blowing apart its occupant and felling those nearby. Later, Mathew is strolling in a park when two young thieves rob him of his money. One of the thieves turns out to be Morenito, Conchita's young lover. It is no coincidence that Conchita herself is implicated in the robbery, for social behavior, in Buñuel's view, is governed by the same morality as sexual behavior. If exploitation is found to be successful in one transaction, it will be applied to others, including sexual behavior. The manipulation of exploitation for sexual purposes is directly suggested when Conchita returns Mathew's billfold to him and he gives her back the money.

References to terrorism continue to tie together the fabric of the film. Mathew's cousin, a judge, is currently presiding over a trial of some terrorists. On the way to his country villa outside Paris, Mathew finds that city lights have been extinguished in a terrorist attack on a power plant. The integration of terror with sexual intimacy unavoidably establishes a relationship between social violence and sex. Conchita kisses Mathew as she would her father and informs him, "You wouldn't love me if I gave in." This comment wounds Mathew. Outside, sounds of shooting interrupt their rendezvous, while the camera focuses on a body lying on the ground below. Conchita flees and finds Morenito waiting for her. They slip into an adjoining room but are both ordered out when Mathew discovers them embracing.

Sexual violence builds as terrorist activity increases. With the collusion of his cousin, Mathew gets an expulsion order served on Conchita and her mother which forces them to vacate their apartment in twenty-four hours. Conchita's flaunting of her sexual power over the old man escalates after her eviction. Mathew discovers to his horror that Conchita, back in Seville, dances nude flamenco for male tourists. He chases her surprised male audience out, provoking Conchita to fury at his display of possessive force. Demanding independence, she fumes, echoing Tristana, "You're not my father and you're not my lover. I'm mine." Like Tristana, Conchita takes terrible revenge for his attempt to exploit her body. When, in an effort to secure her affection, Mathew buys her a house, she takes possession of it by locking him outside the wrought-iron gate and making love with Morenito in the patio while the rich, frustrated, and miserable old man looks on. Destroyed, Mathew turns away and drives down a street only to be stopped at the scene of a robbery, where his driver is hauled out and beaten. Clearly the sadistic Conchita has beaten the male ego as severely as the thug beats the unsuspecting chauffeur.

Just as social disorder breeds violence, a disordered sexual code breeds sexual exploitation, reprisal, and revenge between male and female. The sexual servitude of females in the male-dominated Christian social hierarchy inevitably calls forth the kind of sexual retribution seen in Conchita's spiteful display of her sexual favors to punish Mathew. That Mathew, given the chance, will retaliate, is unavoidable. Conchita, now like a terrorist herself, pays a call on Mathew the next day to "see how you'd died." Unsurprisingly, it is her time to receive a beating much like those the robbers administer to their victim in the streets. While her nose bleeds she assures her assailant that she is still a virgin, a flagrant, hilarious reminder of the falsity of the antique system by which a female's moral integrity is determined by the state of her genitals. The hypocrisy of the cult of virginity is again revealed in all its emptiness in this scene in which the female must rely upon it as the last means of protection while the male gives her the beating of her life. Back in the train compartment, bourgeois attitudes toward these empty, hypocritical sexual notions are still intact. "You see why I wanted to kill her," explains Mathew to his sympathetic companions, who reply in chorus, "But of course."

How did sexual morality become so repressive and restrictive that free expression of sexual desire is denied males as well as females? Buñuel finds the repressive organization of sexuality deeply rooted in Christian morality and upheld by centuries of tradition. This tradition is suggested by Conchita's mother, who defends misogynistic attitudes as staunchly as any male, much like the frail little lady in *The River and Death* who upholds machismo by reprimanding her son for not wearing his gun in his workshop.

That Christianity distorts and manipulates sexuality for its own purposes is clear in the final scene, when Conchita and Mathew walk chatting together along some famous Paris streets. They pass into a mall where the latest terrorist incident is announced over public radio speakers. A group calling itself the "Revolutionary Army of the Infant Jesus" has attacked a victim who now lingers near death. "His brain is dead," the loudspeaker informs us in the last gag of the film, an analogy between the Christian sexual code and its victim, the bourgeois mind. So unwilling or unable to deal sanely with sexuality that its brain seems dead, bourgeois society remains the victim of almost tribal sexual brutality. The camera closes in on a woman mending lace on a bloody sheet in a linen-shop window, suggesting the tenacity with which the ancient violence of male-female sex roles is kept alive. Like a bloodstained family heirloom, the idea of human beings as sexual objects is tenderly refurbished century after century. That Buñuel finds bourgeois sexual repression to be destructive is once again affirmed in the explosion and fire that engulf Mathew and Conchita and end the film. Male as well as female are victims of a society whose sexual politics are as violent as its social politics.

Buñuel's technical mastery of his medium has become so flawless in *Desire* that the most disordered arrangements of time and place cause not a ripple in the flow of ideas the director wishes to convey. Transitions are cued with recognizable techniques, such as the beginning of new segments of action with Mathew strolling beside a lake or through a park. Terrorist violence is intercalated into the film in such a way as to build, as clearly as musical crescendo, the analogy between social, political, and sexual violence. Such technical virtuosity may indeed reveal Buñuel at peace with himself and his medium, as Pauline Kael suggests. But he is not at peace with repression and destruction. Buñuel is not, like Matisse with his cutouts, amusing himself with what Kael deigns as "shallow great art," the musings of an old man.[33]

If *Desire* seems to drag at times, the attack on eroticism defiled by Christianity is as fierce and as consistently central to this film as any Buñuel has ever made. The development of the theme is subtle; the almost fugal complexity of presentation, intriguing. The curious contrast between the antique world of sexual attitudes and their contemporary setting, replete with terrorist outbreaks, is characteristic of Buñuel's art. That an artist should be capable of delivering satiric barbs that delight and, at the same time, provoke his audience is a considerable achievement at any age. Buñuel continues to do just this, as he has for fifty years.

6

The Filmmaker as Moralist

THE DIVISION of Buñuel's masterworks into two groups—character studies and social satires—is arbitrary but can illuminate some important features of his art. It reveals that Buñuel evolves from preoccupation in the 1960s with a series of characters—Viridiana, Simon, Belle de Jour—to a wider satiric view in the 1970s, during which he made only one character study, *Tristana*. Since then, Buñuel has concentrated upon the bourgeoisie as a social class rather than representing it by an individual. Even in his last film, the stress upon the individual is diffused by use of two actresses to portray one role. Thus Buñuel can be seen developing away from the creation of characters to the larger canvas of social panorama.

Evaluation of Buñuel's art will depend, to a large extent, on which of his films best endure the passage of time and changes in cinema. Assessment is complicated by reviewers and critics who have for years proclaimed his latest film, whatever it might be, his "best." So far, critical esteem appears to favor those films which focus upon a central character. Buñuel dissects society best when it looms as a matrix from which springs a personification of bizarre behavior tolerated, or demanded, by its codes. The later satires, however, while depriving the viewer of the pleasure of identifying with a central character, continue to amaze by their technical brilliance and the ease with which Buñuel controls his craft.

The originality of Buñuel's contribution has been to translate one of the richest artistic languages of his, or any other time, surrealism, into film language and thus to make of film a compelling moral force. In the era of discovery, when filmmakers were enthralled with the technical capacity of cinema, Buñuel never lost sight of the conception of film as a social instrument as well as a visual toy. He owes his

The Passion of Viridiana—the high point of Buñuel's fusion of art with moral vision in his criticism of society and religion (Silvia Pinal as Viridiana).

determination to disturb and provoke, rather than to merely display, to surrealism.

Sustaining his early achievement over fifty years by making it more accessible to a wider public, Buñuel continually updates his vision of a society paralyzed by worn-out formulae. Like a kaliedoscope, his art renders his few basic themes in infinite variations. His visual probe into the obsessions of the human mind and their social consequences is as thorough as any inquiry into society today. It may be that, for the first time, one of the great moralists of the century happens to be a filmmaker.

Notes and References

Chapter One

1. José Francisco Aranda, *Luis Buñuel: A Critical Biography* (New York, 1975), p. 13. Further references to this edition are followed by page numbers throughout the text.
2. Manuel Alcalá, *Buñuel (Cine e ideología)* (Madrid, 1973), p. 35.
3. Federico García Lorca, *Obras completas* (Madrid, 1963), p. 17. All translations mine.
4. C. B. Morris, *Surrealism and Spain, 1920–1936* (Cambridge, 1972), p. 229.
5. *La arboleda perdida* (Buenos Aires, 1959), p. 285.
6. "Film-arte film-antiartístico," in Ramón Buckley, ed., *Los vanguardistas españoles (1925–1935)* (Madrid, 1973), pp. 228–29.
7. Elena Poniatowska, "Buñuel," *Revista de la Universidad de Mexico* (January 1961), p. 16.
8. *Ibid.*, p. 14.
9. "Una noche en el 'Studio de Ursulines,' " in Ramón Buckley, ed., *Los vanguardistas españoles (1925–1935),* pp. 222–23.
10. "Experimental Film in France," in Roger Manvell, ed., *Experiment in the Film* (New York, 1970), p. 99.
11. Frank Stauffacher, ed., *Art in Cinema* (San Francisco, 1947), p. 29.
12. *Manifestes du surréalisme* (Paris, 1973), p. 24.
13. *Ibid.*, pp. 76, 95.
14. *Le Surréalisme et le cinéma* (Paris, 1963), p. 208.
15. Harry M. Geduld, *Filmmakers on Filmmaking* (Bloomington, Indiana, 1967), p. 281.
16. *Manifestes du surréalisme,* p. 76.
17. *Un Chien andalou* and *L'Age d'or* tr. Marianne Alexandre (New York, 1968), p. 10.
18. Jacques Brunius, "Experimental Film in France," in Roger Manvell, ed., *Experiments in the Film* (London, 1970), p. 94.
19. "Prólogo," in Luis Buñuel, *Viridiana* tr. José de la Colina (Mexico, 1966), pp. 14–15.

Chapter Two

1. "Experimental Film in France," in Manvell, ed., *Experiment in the Film,* p. 66.
2. *The Unquiet Grave* (New York, 1945), p. 125.
3. *The Cinema of Luis Buñuel,* tr. Peter Graham (New York, 1973), p. 10.
4. Carlos Rebolledo, *Buñuel* (Paris, 1964), p. 10.
5. Brunius, "Experimental Film in France," p. 100.
6. *Luis Buñuel* (Berkeley, 1968), p. 22.
7. *Surrealism and Film* (Ann Arbor, Michigan, 1971), p. 85.
8. Stauffacher, ed., *Art in Cinema,* p. 30.
9. José Francisco Aranda, "Surrealismo español en el cine," *Insula,* 29 (December 1974), p. 46.
10. *Luis Buñuel,* p. 24.
11. *Surréalisme et sexualité* (Paris, 1971), p. 349.
12. "Symbolisme au second degré: *Un Chien andalou,*" *Etudes cinematographiques,* 22–23 (1963), p. 151.
13. *Surrealism and Film,* p. 85.
14. Renaud, "Symbolisme au second degré: *Un Chien andalou,*" *Etudes cinématographiques,* 22–23 (1963), p. 149.
15. "Pauvreté et richesse du style de Buñuel," *Etudes cinématographiques,* 20–21 (1962), p. 128.
16. *L'Avant-Scène du cinéma,* 27–28 (1963), p. 10.
17. "Manifeste des surréalistes à propos de *L'Age d'or,*" *Ibid.,* p. 27.
18. *Le Surréalisme au cinéma* (Paris, 1963), p. 211.
19. *L'Age d'or and Un Chien andalou,* tr. Marianne Alexandre (New York, 1968), p. 16. Further references to this edition are followed by the designation "script" and page numbers in the text.
20. *Art and Pornography* (New York, 1969), p. 256.
21. Tr. Guy Wernham (New York, 1946), p. 145.
22. *Le Surréalisme au cinéma,* p. 211.
23. Poniatowska, "Buñuel," p. 19.
24. Brunius, "Experimental Film in France," p. 103.
25. "A la recherche de Luis Buñuel," *Cahiers du Cinéma* No. 7 (1951), 20.
26. Voted by judges gathering at the International Film Festival, Mannheim, Germany, 1952.
27. Luis Buñuel, *Las Hurdes (Tierra sin pan)* in *Nuestro cine* 36 (December 1964), 11. Further references to this edition are followed by the designation "script" and page numbers in the text.
28. André Bazin. *Le Cinéma de la cruauté: de Buñuel à Hitchcock* (Paris, 1975), p. 105.
29. *L'Ecran merveilleux: Le rêve et le fantastique dans le cinéma français* (Paris, 1959), p. 110.

30. "Une fonction de constat; Notes sur l'oeuvre de Buñuel," *Cahiers du Cinéma* No. 7 (1951), p. 7.
31. Poniatowska, "Buñuel" pp. 19–20.
32. Bazin, p. 106.
33. Randall Conrad, "The Minister of the Interior is on the Telephone: The Early Films of Luis Buñuel," *Cineaste*, 7, 3(Fall 1976), pp. 2–14.
34. Carlos Fuentes, "Spain, Catholicism, Surrealism, and Anarchism: The Discreet Charm of Luis Buñuel," *New York Times Magazine*, March 11, 1973, p. 87.
35. Bazin, p. 107.
36. *Ibid.*
37. J. Cobos and G. S. de Erice, "Entretien avec Luis Buñuel," *Cahiers du Cinéma* No. 191 (June 1967), 18.

Chapter Three

1. Bazin, p. 66.
2. "Luis Buñuel: The Macabre Master of Movie-Making," *Show*, 3 (November 1963), p. 135.
3. Bazin, p. 108.
4. Jean Bastaire, "Une Chronique buñuelienne: *Subida al cielo*," *Etudes cinématographiques*, 22–23 (1963), p. 239.
5. *Cahiers du Cinéma* 4 (March 1966), pp. 19–25.
6. *Jeune Cinéma* 12 (February 1966) pp. 3–7.
7. *Luis Buñuel* (Berkeley, 1968), p. 82.
8. "Mosk," [Review of *The Young One*], *Filmfacts*, 4 (1961), p. 19.
9. *Il cinema di Luis Buñuel* (Palermo, 1973), p. 128.
10. Ado Kyrou, *Luis Buñuel* (Paris, 1962), p. 57, and Freddy Buache, *The Cinema of Luis Buñuel* (New York, 1970), p. 115.
11. Buache, p. 113.
12. Luis Buñuel, *The Exterminating Angel, Nazarín and Los olvidados*, tr. Nicholas Fry (New York, 1972), p. 217. Further references to this edition are indicated by the designation "script" and page numbers in the text.
13. "Luis Buñuel's *Los olvidados*," *Quarterly of Film, Radio, TV*, 7 (Summer 1953), p. 397.
14. *Qu'est ce que c'est le cinéma*, 3 (Paris, 1961), p. 26.
15. "Poesía y cine," *Nuestro cine*, 66 (October 1967), pp. 20–22.
16. Bazin, *Le Cinéma de la cruauté: de Buñuel à Hitchcock*, p. 109.
17. Claude Gauteur, "Humour et érotisme dans *Susana la perverse*," *Etudes cinématographiques*, 22–23 (1963), p. 176.
18. Jean-Jacques Brochier, ed., *Dictionnaire du cinéma* (Paris, 1966), p. 144.
19. *Manifestes du surréalisme* (Paris, 1973), p. 25.
20. "Retour aux sources: *Cumbres borrascosas* ou *Abismos de passion*," *Etudes cinématographiques*, 22–23 (1963), p. 245.

21. For a discussion of this Samuel Goldwyn production of *Wuthering Heights*, see Foster Hirsch, *Laurence Olivier* (Boston, Twayne, 1979).
22. "La splendeur du mélodrame: *El Bruto*," *Etudes cinématographiques*, 22–23 (1963), p. 241.
23. Emilio García Riera, "The Eternal Rebellion of Luis Buñuel," *Film Culture*, 21 (Summer 1960), p. 49.
24. Buache, p. 66.
25. *The Literature of the Spanish People* (New York, 1957), p. 288.
26. Claude Beylie, "*El* ou le héros buñuélien," *Etudes cinématographiques*, 22–23 (1963), p. 186. Ado Kyrou, *Luis Buñuel* (Paris, 1962), p. 46.
27. *Surrealism and Film*, p. 151.
28. "Les Obsessions d'Archibaldo de la Cruz," *Etudes cinématographiques*, 22–23 (1963), p. 191.
29. "Le Chiffre deux," *Cahiers du Cinéma* No. 11 (November 1956), p. 52.
30. *Manifeste du surréalisme* (Paris, 1973), p. 76.
31. "Le Chiffre deux," p. 52.
32. Daniel Aubrey and J. M. Lacor, "Luis Buñuel," *Film Quarterly*, 12 (Winter 1958), p. 8.
33. *Luis Buñuel* (Paris, 1962), p. 52.
34. *Confessions of a Cultist: On the Cinema, 1955–1969* (New York, 1970), p. 57.

Chapter Four

1. Luis Buñuel, *The Exterminating Angel, Nazarín,* and *Los Olvidados*, tr. Nicholas Fry (New York, 1972), p. 123. Further references to this edition are indicated by the designation "script" and page numbers in the text.
2. *Filmfacts* 11 (September 1968), p. 249.
3. *José Antonio Bardem*, UNAM, Dirección General de difusión cultural, Mexico, 1962), p. 15.
4. Kyrou, p. 56; Octavio Paz, "Nazarín," *Film Culture*, 21 (Summer 1960), p. 62; and Emilio García Riera, "The Eternal Rebellion of Luis Buñuel," *Film Culture*, 21 (Summer 1960), p. 58.
5. "Un desespoir actif," *Cahiers du Cinéma*, No. 2 (January 1961), p. 48.
6. Geoffrey Nowell-Smith, "Nazarín," *Sight and Sound*, 32 (Autumn 1963), pp. 194–95.
7. J. F. Aranda, "La passion selon Buñuel," *Cahiers du Cinéma*, No. 93 (March 1959), p. 28.
8. Bernard Dort, "Viridiana: Une autre Sainte Jeanne?" *Etudes cinématographiques*, 22–23 (1963), pp. 210–15.
9. In an interview with Yvonne Baby, *Le Monde*, June 1, 1961, p. 12.
10. Luis Buñuel, *Three Screenplays*: *Viridiana*, *The Exterminating*

Angel, Simon of the Desert (New York, 1969), p. 97. Further references to this edition are indicated by the designation "script" and page numbers in the text.

11. "Buñuel et l'antiphrase," *Etudes cinématographiques*, 20–21 (1962), p. 94.

12. Aranda, p. 205. Also see Dort, "Viridiana: Une autre Sainte Jeanne?" p. 215; Andrew Pierre Uytterhoeven, "*Viridiana*, Un film révolutionnaire," *Etudes cinématographiques*, 22–23 (1963), p. 222.

13. Jon Katz, "Interview with José Luis Font," *Vision*, 1, 2 (Summer 1962), p. 42.

14. Frederic J. Hoffman, "*Viridiana*," in Arthur Lenning, ed., *Classics of the Film* (Madison, Wisconsin, 1965), p. 195.

15. See Aranda for a full account of the *Viridiana* scandal.

16. *New Republic*, April 9, 1962, p. 25; *Luis Buñuel* (Berkeley, 1968), p. 124.

17. Dort, "Une autre Sainte Jeanne?" p. 214.

18. "*Viridiana*: Satanisme et santé de Buñuel," *Etudes cinématographiques*, 22–23 (1963), p. 208.

19. "La vie privée des fascistes," *Positif*, 60 (April–May 1969), pp. 69–71.

20. Luis Buñuel, *Le Journal d'une femme de chambre* (Paris, 1971), p. 15. Further references to this edition are indicated in my text with the designation "script" and page numbers.

21. *Six European Directors* (Baltimore, Maryland, 1974), p. 131.

22. *What Do You Say after You Say Hello?* (New York, 1973), p. 268.

23. *Il cinema di Luis Buñuel* (Palermo, 1973), p. 152.

24. Peter P. Schillaci, "Luis Buñuel and the Death of God," in James Wall, ed., *Three European Directors* (Grand Rapids, Michigan, 1973), p. 145.

25. "The Two Chambermaids," *Sight and Sound*, 33 (Autumn 1964), p. 177.

26. *Ibid.* p. 178.

27. Jacques Goimard, "Quelques reflexions sur Buñuel et le christianisme," *Positif*, 108 (September 1969), pp. 1–11. Goimard insists that Simon is "not an outcast, not even a voluntary one, but an olympic champion of asceticism." The film script, however, identifies Simon as a hermit, one who voluntarily withdraws from human society.

28. "Luis Buñuel and the Death of God," in James M. Wall, ed., *Three European Directors* (Grand Rapids, Michigan, 1973), p. 148.

29. "*Simon of the Desert*," *New York Times*, February 12, 1969, p. 9.

30. "*Simon of the Desert*," *Film Quarterly*, 19 (Winter 1965–1966), p. 48.

31. *New Yorker*, February 15, 1969, p. 115.

32. *Nuestro cine*, 45 (1965), p. 16.

33. Educational Television interview, July 2, 1962.

34. *Manifestes du surréalisme* (Paris, 1973), pp. 23–24.

35. Durgnat, *Luis Buñuel*, p. 145; John Simon, *Movies Into Film: Film Criticism, 1967–1970* (New York, 1971), p. 139; Buache, p. 166.

36. *Focus on the Horror Film*, Roy Huss, and T. J. Ross, eds., (Englewood Cliffs, N.J., 1972), p. 156n.

37. *Surrealism and Film* (Ann Arbor, Michigan, 1971), p. 139.

38. Berne, *What Do You Say after You Say Hello?*, p. 213.

39. *Man and His Symbols* (New York, 1974), pp. 128–33.

40. Luis Buñuel, *Belle de jour*, tr. Robert Adkinson (New York, 1971), p. 76. Further references to this edition are followed by the designation "script" and page numbers in the text.

41. Julius E. Heuscher, *A Psychiatric Study of Myths and Fairy Tales: Their Origin, Meaning and Usefulness* (Springfield, Illinois, 1974), pp. 213–14.

42. Jean-André Fieschi, "La fin ouverte," *Cahiers du Cinéma*, 191 (June 1967), p. 22.

43. Kernan, Margot S. Review of *Belle de jour* in *Film Quarterly*, 22 (Fall 1969), p. 39.

44. Heuscher, p. 213.

45. *Manifestes du surréalisme*, pp. 21–22.

46. Elliot Stein, Review of *Belle de jour* in *Sight and Sound*, 36 (Autumn, 1967), p. 173.

47. "La Tristana de don Luis," in Luis Buñuel, *Tristana* (Barcelona, 1971), p. 12. Further references to this edition are followed by the designation "script" and page numbers in the text.

48. *La arboleda perdida* (Buenos Aires, 1959), p. 220.

49. *Il cinema di Luis Buñuel* (Palermo, 1973), p. 178.

50. *Tristana*, tr. R. Selden Rose (Peterborough, New Hampshire, 1961), p. 19.

51. *Six European Directors* (Baltimore, Maryland, 1974), p. 129.

52. "Le curé de la guillotine," *Cahiers du Cinema*, 223 (August-September 1970), p. 5.

53. "*Tristana*", *Sight and Sound*, 40 (Spring 1971), p. 103.

54. Robert Benayoun, "Trois tempéraments à leur parfaite extrémité (Antonioni, Buñuel, Kazan)," *Positif*, 117 (June 1970), p. 8.

55. "Buñuel's Obsessed Camera: Tristana Dismembered," *Diacritics*, (Spring 1972), p. 56.

Chapter Five

1. Richard Schickel, *Second Sight: Notes on Some Movies: 1965–1970* (New York, 1972), p. 137.

2. Michel Estève, "*L'Ange exterminateur:* Le *Huit Clos* de la condition humaine," *Etudes cinématographiques*, 22–23 (1963), 223–32.

3. Carl Jung, *Man and His Symbols* (New York, 1964), pp. 173–74.

4. *Luis Buñuel* (Paris, 1962), p. 25.

5. *Saint Cinema: Writings on the Film: 1929–1970* (New York, 1973), p. 213.
6. "The Evolution of an Anarchist," in James M. Wall, ed., *Three European Directors* (Grand Rapids, Michigan, 1973), p. 144.
7. *Luis Buñuel* (Berkeley, 1968), p. 126.
8. *The Lonely Crowd* (New Haven, Connecticut, 1950), p. 242.
9. Alain Girard, "Le Chemin de St. Jacques de Compostelle vu par Luis Buñuel," *Revue de Cinéma International* (May 1969), pp. 31–33.
10. Manuel Alcalá, *Luis Buñuel (Cine e ideología)* Madrid, 1973), p. 55. Raymond Durgnat, "Phantom of Liberty," *Film Culture*, 2 (July 1974), p. 40.
11. Vincent Canby, "*The Milky Way*," *New York Times*, January 27, 1970, p. 47.
12. Luis Buñuel, "*La Voie lactée*," *L'Avant-Scène du cinéma*, 94–95 (July-September 1969), p. 2. Further references to this edition are followed by the designation "script" and page numbers in the text.
13. "Phantom of Liberty," *Film Culture*, 2 (July 1974), p. 37; *Time*, November 28, 1969, p. 103.
14. Giorgio Tinazzi, *Il cinema di Luis Buñuel* (Palermo, 1973), p. 170.
15. *Deeper into Movies* (New York, 1973), p. 128.
16. *New York Times*, January 27, 1970, p. 47.
17. Pierre Billard, *Express*, March 17, 1969, n.p.; Vincent Canby, *New York Times*, January 27, 1970, p. 47.
18. Tinazzi, *Il cinema di Luis Buñuel*, p. 165.
19. *L'Avant-Scène du cinéma*, 94–95 (July-September 1969), p. 9.
20. Roxane Saint-Jean, "Encadenado en la libertad," in Luis Buñuel, *El fantasma de la libertad* (Barcelona, 1974), pp. 11–12.
21. Steven Kovacs, "*The Discreet Charm of the Bourgeoisie*," *Film Quarterly*, 26 (Winter 1972), p. 17.
22. *Filmfacts*, 15, 18 (1972), p. 418.
23. Jay Cocks, *Time*, November 6, 1972, p. 87; Gary Arnold, *Washington Post*; Pauline Kael, *New Yorker Magazine*, November 11, 1972, p. 153–158.
24. Paul D. Zimmerman, "Fool's Paradise," *Newsweek*, November 6, 1972, p. 122.
25. "Interruption as Style: Buñuel's *Le Charme discret de la bourgeoisie*," *Sight and Sound*, 42 (Winter 1972), pp. 2–3.
26. *New York Times*, October 14, 1974, p. 39.
27. Luis Buñuel, *El fantasma de la libertad* (Barcelona, 1974), p. 24. Further references to this edition are followed by the designation "script" and page numbers in the text.
28. "The Tyranny of Convention of Phantom of Liberty," *Film Quarterly*, 28 (Summer 1975), p. 22.
29. *Reeling* (New York, 1976), p. 482.

30. *Escape from Freedom* (New York, 1941), p. 106.
31. "Le plaire de la confusion," *Positif*, 198 (October 1977), p. 7.
32. "*Cet obscur objet du désir*," *Sight and Sound*, 47 (Winter 1977–78), pp. 7–8.
33. *New Yorker*, December 19, 1977, p. 128.

Selected Bibliography

1. Books

ALCALÁ, MANUEL. *Buñuel (Cine e ideología).* Madrid: Cuadernos para el diálogo, 1973. An admirable effort by a Spanish priest to present the values of Buñuel's films to his Catholic countrymen [in Spanish].

ARANDA, JOSÉ FRANCISCO. *Luis Buñuel: A Critical Biography*, tr. David Robinson. New York: Da Capo Press, 1975. The most informative, although unscholarly, full-length study, translated from the Spanish.

BUACHE, FREDDY. *The Cinema of Luis Buñuel,* tr. Peter Graham. New York: A. S. Barnes & Co., 1973. Useful introduction to the career and works, translated from the French.

CESARMAN, FERNANDO. *El ojo de Buñuel.* Barcelona: Editorial Anagrama, 1976. A prologue by Carlos Fuentes introduces this discussion of the films from a Mexican psychoanalyst's perspective [in Spanish].

DURGNAT, RAYMOND. *Luis Buñuel.* Berkeley: University of California Press, 1968. A thorough critical interpretation from a Marxist view.

KYROU, ADO. *Luis Buñuel.* Paris: Editions Seghers, 1962. An informative analysis which includes an anthology of surrealist texts and critical reviews [in French].

2. Parts of Books

BAZIN, ANDRÉ. *Le cinèma de la cruauté: de Buñuel à Hitchcock.* Paris: Flammarion, 1975, pp. 66–119. Reprints an interview, in French, with the author and Jacques Doniol-Valcroze, in which Buñuel discusses his Mexican career.

BUÑUEL, LUIS. In *Films: The Filmmaker and the Audience*, ed. Robert Hughes. New York: Grove Press, 1959. Excerpt from a statement of the director's view of filmmaking.

———. "Statement," in *Film Makers on Film Making*, ed. Harry M. Geduld. Bloomington, Indiana: Indiana University Press, 1967. The director comments further on his philosophy of filmmaking.

CASTY, ALAN. *Development of the Film.* New York: Harcourt, Brace,

Jovanovich, Inc., 1973, pp. 306–25. Cogent remarks on the director's film style.

HARCOURT, PETER. *Six European Directors*. Baltimore, Maryland: Penguin Books, 1974, pp. 102–134. Stresses the surrealist and Spanish heritage of Buñuel's art.

KYROU, ADO. *Le Surréalisme au cinèma*. Paris, Le Terrain Vague, 1963, pp. 207–68. Essential for understanding of the director's early films, this chapter also includes an analysis of the later works, including *Viridiana*.

MATTHEWS, J. H. *Surrealism and Film*. Ann Arbor, Michigan: University of Michigan Press, 1971, pp. 138–74. A distinguished scholar of surrealism discusses Buñuel's entry into commercial film.

MELLEN, JOAN. *Women and Sexuality in the New Film*. New York: Dell, 1973, pp. 176–83. The author studies the effects of dependence in *Tristana*.

PAZ, OCTAVIO. *Alternating Current*, tr. Helen R. Lane. New York: Viking Press, 1973, pp. 104–10. This brief essay makes clear why Buñuel disappoints many dedicated to leftist politics, who hoped for more straightforward political art from him.

PECHTER, WILLIAM S. *Twenty-four Times a Second: Films and Film-makers*. New York: Harper & Row, 1971, pp. 215–25. The critic contrasts Buñuel's technical ease with his bitter social attack.

SARRIS, ANDREW. *Confessions of a Cultist: On the Cinema 1955–1969*. New York: Simon and Schuster, 1970, pp. 53–60. The American film critic with the most insight into Buñuel's art comments on his career, especially on *Viridiana*.

SCHILLACI, PETER P. "Luis Buñuel and the Death of God," in *Three European Directors*, ed. James M. Wall. Grand Rapids, Michigan: William B. Eerdmans, 1973, pp. 111–212. This view of Buñuel's life and work stresses some positive values of the director's "eccentric atheism."

TAYLOR, JOHN RUSSELL. *Cinema Eye, Cinema Ear: Some Key Film-makers of the Sixties*. New York: Hill and Wang, 1964, pp. 82–114. A summary of the life and films up to *Exterminating Angel*.

3. Articles

CONRAD, RANDALL. "The Minister of the Interior is on the Telephone: The Early Films of Luis Buñuel," *Cineaste* 7, iii (1976), 3–14. A detailed and lively discussion including stills from *Spain, 1937*.

———. "A Magnificent and Dangerous Weapon: The Politics of Luis Buñuel's Later Films," *Cineaste* 8, iv (1976), 10–18, 51. A summary of the films from the Mexican period through *Phantom of Liberty* in which the author observes the contradiction between Buñuel's materialism and his subjective world which frequently baffles critics.

FUENTES, CARLOS. "Spain, Catholicism, Surrealism and Anarchism: The

Discreet Charm of Luis Buñuel," *New York Times Magazine*, March 11, 1973, pp. 27–29. A personal view of the director by one of his close friends, the famous Mexican novelist.

———. "Luis Buñuel: The Macabre Master of Movie-Making," *Show*, November 1963, pp. 8, 134, 135.

GARCÍA ABRINES, LUIS. "Rebirth of Buñuel, *Yale French Studies* 17 (Summer 1956) 54–66. A discussion of the Mexican films.

GARCÍA RIERA, EMILIO. "The Eternal Rebellion of Luis Buñuel," *Film Culture* 21 (Summer 1960), 42–60. Interesting details of the early career and Mexican period.

GROSSVOGEL, DAVID I. "Buñuel's Obsessed Camera: Tristana Dismembered," *Diacritics* 2 (Spring 1972), 51–56. Pointing out how Buñuel converts ideas into images, this article concerns matters of wider range and interest than the single film which is its primary focus.

MILNE, TOM. "The Mexican Buñuel," *Sight and Sound* 35 (Winter 1965–66), 36–39. A good introductory summary.

PONIATOWSKA, ELENA. "Buñuel," *Revista de la Universidad de Mexico* (January 1961), 14–21. One of the director's more informative and candid interviews.

Filmography

AN ANDALUSIAN DOG (UN CHIEN ANDALOU), 1928

Producer:	Luis Buñuel
Screenplay:	Buñuel and Salvador Dali
Cinematographer:	Albert Dubergen
Set Decoration:	Pierre Schilzneck
Music:	Beethoven, Wagner *(Tristan and Isolde)*
Cast:	Simone Mareuil, Pierre Batcheff, Jaime Miravilles, Luis Buñuel, Salvador Dali
Running time:	17 minutes
Premiere:	Paris, February 1928
16mm. rental:	Em Gee Film Laboratory; Museum of Modern Art and others. 16mm. sale: Reel Images

THE GOLDEN AGE (L'AGE D'OR), 1930

Producer:	Viscount Charles Noailles
Assistant Director:	Jacques Brunius
Screenplay:	Buñuel and Salvador Dali
Cinematographer:	Albert Dubergen
Set Decoration:	Pierre Schilzneck
Music:	Wagner, Mendelssohn, Beethoven, Debussy; George van Parys.
Cast:	Gaston Modot, Lya Lys, Max Ernst, Pierre Prévert, José Antigas, Caridad de Laberdesque, Liorens Artigas, Lionel Salem, Madame Noizet, Duhange, Ibáñez
Running time:	63 minutes
Premiere:	Paris, 1930
16mm. rental:	Em Gee Film Laboratory

LAS HURDES: LAND WITHOUT BREAD (LAS HURDES: TIERRA SIN PAN), 1932

Producer:	Ramón Acín
Assistant Directors:	Pierre Unik, Rafael Sánchez Ventura

Screenplay: Luis Buñuel
Cinematographer: Eli Lotar
Music: Brahms (Fourth Symphony)
Editor: Luis Buñuel
Running time: 27 minutes
Premiere: Madrid, 1933
16mm. rental: Museum of Modern Art, New York
16mm. Sale: Thunderbird Films

THE GREAT CASINO (EL GRAN CASINO) (Filmadora Anahuac, 1947)
Producer: Oscar Dancigers
Assistant Director: Moisés Delgado
Screenplay: Mauricio Magdaleno, Edmundo Báez, from a story by Michel Weber
Cinematographer: Jack Draper
Art Director: Javier Torres Torija
Music: Manuel Esperón
Sound: Javier Mateos
Editor: Gloria Schoemann
Cast: Libertad Lamarque, Jorge Negrete, Mercedes Barba, Agustín Isunza, Julio Villarreal, Charles Rooner, José Baviera, Francisco Jambrina, Alfonso Bedoya, Bertha Lear
Running time: 85 minutes
Premiere: Mexico, June 12, 1947

THE GREAT MADCAP (EL GRAN CALAVERA) (Ultramar Films, S. A., 1949)
Producer: Oscar Dancigers
Assistant Director: Mario Llorca
Screenplay: Raquel Rojas and Luis Alcoriza, from a comedy by Adolfo Torrado
Cinematographer: Ezequiel Carrasco
Set Decoration: Luis Moya and Dario Cabanas
Music: Manuel Esperón
Sound: Eduardo Arjona
Cast: Fernando Soler, Rosario Granados, Rubén Rojo, Andrés Soler, Maruja Crufell, Gustavo Rojo, Luis Alcoriza
Running time: 90 minutes
16mm. rental: MacMillan/Audio Brandon

THE YOUNG AND DAMNED (LOS OLVIDADOS—also known in English as **THE FORGOTTEN ONES**) S. A., 1950)

Producer:	Oscar Dancigers
Assistant Director:	Ignacio Villarreal
Screenplay:	Luis Buñuel and Luis Alcoriza
Cinematographer:	Gabriel Figueroa
Art Director:	Edward Fitzgerald
Music:	Rodolfo Hahfter
Sound:	José B. Carles
Editor:	Carlos Savage
Cast:	Alfonso Mejía, Roberto Cobo, Estela Inda, Efraín Arauz, Mario Ramírez, Alma Delia Fuentes, Francisco Jambrina, Javier Amezcua, Miguel Inclán
Running time:	88 minutes
Premiere:	November 9, 1950
16mm. rental:	MacMillan/Audio Brandon

International Critics' Prize, Cannes Film Festival, 1951

SUSANA (Internacional Cinematográfica, 1951)

Producer:	Sergio Kogan
Assistant Director:	Ignacio Villarreal
Screenplay:	Jaime Salvador, from a novel by Manuel Reachi
Cinematographer:	José Ortíz Ramos
Art Director:	Gunther Gerzso
Music:	Raul Lavista
Sound:	Nicolás de la Rosa
Editor:	Jorge Bustos
Cast:	Rosita Quintana, Fernando Soler, Victor Manuel Mendoza, Matilde Palou, María Gentil Arcos, Luis López Somoza
Running time:	82 minutes
Premiere:	April 11, 1951

DAUGHTER OF DECEIT (LA HIJA DEL ENGAÑO) (Ultramar Films, S. A., 1951)

Producer:	Oscar Dancigers
Assistant Director:	Mario Llorca
Screenplay:	Raquel Rojas and Luis Alcoriza, from "Don Quíntin el amargao" by Carlos Arniches
Cinematographer:	José Ortiz Ramos

Art Director: Edward Fitzgerald
Music: Manuel Esperón
Sound: Eduardo Arjona
Cast: Fernando Soler, Alicia Caro, Rubén Rojo, Nacho Contra, Fernando Soto, Lily Aclemar
Running time: 80 minutes
Premiere: August 29, 1951
16mm. rental: MacMillan/Audio Brandon

MEXICAN BUSRIDE (**SUBIDA AL CIELO**) (Producciones Usla, 1952)
Producer: Manuel Altolaguirre
Assistant Director: Jorge López Portillo
Screenplay: Luis Buñuel, Juan de la Cabada, Manuel Altolaguirre, from a story by Altolaguirre and Manuel Reachi
Cinematographer: Alex Phillips
Art Directors: Edward Fitzgerald, José Rodríguez Granada
Music: Gustavo Pittaluga
Sound: Eduardo Arjona
Editor: Rafael Portillo
Cast: Lilia Prado, Carmelita González, Esteban Márquez, Manuel Dondé, Roberto Cobo, Luis Acevez Castañeda
Running time: 85 minutes
Premiere: Mexico, June 26, 1952
16mm. rental: Contemporary Films/McGraw-Hill

A WOMAN WITHOUT LOVE (**UNA MUJER SIN AMOR**) (Internacional Cinematográfica, S. A., 1952)
Producers: Oscar Dancigers and Sergio Kogan
Assistant Director: Mario Llorca
Screenplay: Jaime Salvador, from Guy de Maupassant's *Pierre et Jean*
Cinematographer: Raúl Martínez Solares
Art Director: Gunther Gerzso
Music: Raúl Lavista
Sound: Rodolfo Benítez
Editor: Jorge Bustos
Cast: Julio Villarreal, Rosario Granados, Tito Junco, Xavier Loyá, Joaquín Cordero, Jaime Colpe, Elda Peralta, Miguel Manzano, Eva Calvo

Running time: 90 minutes
Premiere: Mexico, July 31, 1952

ROBINSON CRUSOE (Ultramar Films, S. A., 1952)
Producer: Oscar Dancigers and Henry F. Ehrlich
Assistant Director: Ignacio Villarreal
Screenplay: Luis Buñuel and Philip Roll, from Daniel Defoe's novel
Cinematographer: Alex Philips
Music: Anthony Collins
Sound: Javier Mateos
Editor: Carlos Savage
Cast: Dan O'Herlihy (Crusoe) Jaime Fernández
Running time: (Friday), Felipe de Alba
Premiere: 100 minutes
16mm. rental: Mexico, June 30, 1955
Filmed in Pathé Color MacMillan/Audio Brandon

ILLUSION TRAVELS BY STREETCAR (LA ILUSIÓN VIAJA EN TRANVIA (Clasa Films Mundiales, 1953)
Producer: Armando Orive Alba
Assistant Director: Ignacio Villarreal
Screenplay: Mauricio de la Serna, José Revueltas, from a story by Mauricio de la Serna
Cinematographer: Raúl Martínez Solares
Art Director: Edward Fitzgerald
Music: Luis Hernández Bretón
Sound: José D. Pérez
Editor: Jorge Bustos
Cast: Lilia Prado, Carlos Navarro, Domingo Soler, Fernando Soto, Augustín Isunza
Running time: 90 minutes
Premiere: Mexico, June 18, 1954
16mm. rental: MacMillan/Audio Brandon

THE BRUTE (EL BRUTO) (Internacional Cinematográfica, S. A., 1953)
Producer: Oscar Dancigers
Assistant Director: Ignacio Villarreal
Screenplay: Luis Buñuel and Luis Alcoriza
Cinematographer: Augustín Jiménez
Art Director: Gunther Gerzso
Music: Raúl Lavista

Sound: Javier Mateos
Editor: Jorge Bustos
Cast: Pedro Armendáriz, Katy Jurado, Rosita Arenas, Andrés Soler
Running time: 83 minutes
Premiere: Mexico, February 5, 1953

HE (**ÉL**—also known in English as **THIS STRANGE PASSION**) (Nacional Films, 1953)
Producer: Oscar Dancigers
Assistant Director: Ignacio Villarreal
Screenplay: Luis Buñuel and Luis Alcoriza, from the novel *Pensamientos* by Mercedes Pinto
Cinematographer: Gabriel Figueroa
Art Director: Edward Fitzgerald
Music: Luis Hernández Bretón
Sound: José D. Pérez
Editor: Carlos Savage
Cast: Arturo de Córdova, Delia Garcés, Luis Beristain, Aurora Walker, Carlos Martínez Baena, Fernándo Casanova, Manuel Dondé, Rafael Banquells
Running time: 80 minutes
Premiere: Mexico, July 9, 1953
16mm. rental: MacMillan/Audio Brandon

WUTHERING HEIGHTS (**ABISMOS DE PASIÓN**) (Tepeyac Producciones, S. A., 1954)
Producers: Oscar Dancigers, Abelardo Rodríguez
Assistant Director: Ignacio Villarreal
Screenplay: Luis Buñuel, Arduino Maiuri, Julio Alejandro de Castro, from Emily Brontë's novel
Cinematographer: Agustín Jiménez
Art Director: Edward Fitzgerald
Music: Wagner ("Tristan and Isolde"), adapted by Raúl Lavista
Sound: Eduardo Arjona
Editor: Carlos Savage
Cast: Irasema Dilian, Jorge Mistral, Lilia Prado, Ernesto Alonso, Luis Aceves Castañeda, Francisco Reiguera
Running time: 90 minutes
Premiere: Mexico, July 3, 1954

THE STORY OF A CRIME: THE CRIMINAL LIFE OF ARCHIBALDO DE LA CRUZ (ENSAYO DE UN CRIMEN: LA VIDA CRIMINAL DE ARCHIBALDO DE LA CRUZ) (Alianza Cinematográfica, S. A., 1955)

Producer:	Alfonso Patiño Gómez
Assistant Director:	Luis Abadie
Screenplay:	Luis Buñuel and Eduardo Ugarte, from the story by Rodolfo Usigli
Cinematographer:	Augustín Jiménez
Art Director:	Jesus Bracho
Music:	Jorge Pérez Herrera
Sound:	Rodolfo Benítez
Cast:	Ernesto Alonso, Miroslava Stern, Rita Macedo, Ariadna Welter
Running time:	91 minutes
Premiere:	Mexico, April 3, 1955
16mm. rental:	MacMillan/Audio Brandon

THE RIVER AND DEATH (EL RIO Y LA MUERTE) Clasa Films Mundiales, S. A., 1955)

Producer:	Armando Orive Alba
Assistant Director:	Ignacio Villarreal
Screenplay:	Luis Buñuel and Luis Alcoriza, from Miguel Alvarez Acosta's novel *Muro blanco sobre roca negra*
Cinematographer:	Raul Martínez Solares
Art Directors:	Edward Fitzgerald, Gunther Gerzso
Music:	Raul Lavista
Sound:	José D. Pérez
Editor:	Jorge Bustos
Cast:	Columba Dominguez, Miguel Torruco, Joaquín Cordero, Jaime Fernández
Running time:	90 minutes
Premiere:	February 28, 1955
16mm. rental:	MacMillan/Audio Brandon

DEATH IN THIS GARDEN (LA MORT EN CE JARDIN) (Dismage, [Paris]/Producciones Tepeyac [Mexico], 1956)

Producers:	Oscar Dancigers, David Mage
Screenplay:	Luis Buñuel, Luis Alcoriza and Raymond Queneau, from the story by Raymond Queneau
Cinematographer:	Jorge Stahl (filmed in Eastmancolor)
Art Director:	Edward Fitzgerald

Music:	Paul Misraki
Sound:	José D. Pérez
Editor:	Marquerite Renoir
Cast:	Simone Signoret, Georges Marchal, Michel Piccoli, Michel Girardou, Charles Vanel, Tito Juneo, Luis Aceves Castañeda
Running time:	110 minutes
Premiere:	Paris, September 21, 1956
16mm. rental:	MacMillan/Audio Brandon

ITS NAME IS DAWN (CELA S'APPELLE L'AURORE) (Film Marceau [France], Laetitia Films, Insignia Films[Italy], 1956)

Producer:	André Cultet
Assistant Directors:	Marcel Camus, Jacque Deray
Screenplay:	Luis Buñuel and Jean Ferry from Emmanuel Robles' novel
Cinematographer:	Robert Lefebvre
Art Director:	Max Douy
Music:	Joseph Kosma
Sound:	Antoine Petitjean
Editor:	Marguerite Renoir
Cast:	Georges Marchal, Lucia Bosé, Gianni Esposito, Julien Berthau, Nelly Borgeaud, Jean-Jacques Delbo, Robert LeFort, Brigitte Elloy, Henri Nassiet, Gaston Modot, Pascal Mazotti, Simone Paris
Running time:	102 minutes
Premiere:	Paris, May 9, 1956
16mm. rental:	MacMillan/Audio Brandon

NAZARÍN (Producciones Barbachano Ponce, 1959)

Producer:	Federico Amerigao
Assistant Director:	Ignacio Villarreal
Screenplay:	Luis Buñuel and Julio Alejandro, from the novel by Benítez Pérez Galdós
Cinematographer:	Gabriel Figueroa
Art Director:	Edward Fitzgerald
Costumes:	Georgette Somohano
Music:	"Drums of Calanda"
Sound:	José Pérez
Sound Effects:	Abraham Cruz
Editor:	Carlos Savage
Cast:	Francisco Rabal, Marga López, Rita

	Macedo, Ignacio López Tarso, Ofelia Guilmain, Luis Aceves Castañeda, Noé Murayama, Rosenda Monteros
Running time:	94 minutes
Premiere:	Mexico, June 4, 1959
16mm. rental:	MacMillan/Audio Brandon

FEVER MOUNTS ON EL PAO (LA FIEVRE MONTE À EL PAO) (Groupe des Quatre [Paris], Cinematográfica Filmes, S. A. [Mexico], 1960)

Producer:	Raymond Broderie
Assistant Director:	Ignacio Villarreal
Screenplay:	Luis Buñuel, Luis Alcoriza, Louis Sapin, Charles Dorat, from the novel by Henri Castillou
Cinematographer:	Gabriel Figueroa
Art Director:	Jorge Fernández
Music:	Paul Misraki
Sound:	William Robert Sivel
Editor:	James Cuenet, Rafael López Ceballos
Cast:	Gérard Philipe, María Féliz, Jean Servais, Miguel Angel Ferriz, Raúl Dantés, Domingo Soler, Víctor Junco, Roberto Cañedo
Running time:	97 minutes
Premiere:	Mexico, October 20, 1960
16mm. rental:	Azteca Films

THE YOUNG ONE (LA JOVEN) (Producciones Olmec, 1960)

Producer:	George Werker
Assistant Directors:	Ignacio Villarreal, Juan-Luis Buñuel
Screenplay:	Luis Buñuel and H. B. Addis, from the short story, "Travellin' Man" by Peter Matthiessen.
Cinematographer:	Gabriel Figueroa
Art Director:	Jesús Bracho
Music:	Jesús Zarzoza, Leon Bibb
Sound:	José B. Carlos
Editor:	Carlos Savage
Cast:	Zachary Scott, Kay Meersman, Bernie Hamilton, Crahan Deutou, Claudio Brooke
Running time:	95 minutes

Premiere: London, November 1960
16mm. rental: MacMillan/Audio Brandon

VIRIDIANA (Uninci Films 59, 1961)
Producer: Gustavo Alatriste
Assistant Directors: Juan-Luis Buñuel, J. Pujol
Screenplay: Luis Buñuel and Julio Alejandro
Cinematographer: José F. Aguayo
Art Director: Francisco Canet
Music: Handel and Mozart, arranged by Gustavo Pittaluga
Editor: Pedro del Rey
Cast: Silvia Pinal (Viridiana), Francisco Rabal (Jorge), Fernando Rey (Don Jaime), Margarita Lozano (Ramona), Victoria Zinny (Lucia), Teresa Rabal (Rita)
Running time: 90 minutes
Premiere: Cannes, France, May 17, 1961 (Cowinner, Grand Prize, Cannes Film Festival)
16mm. rental: MacMillan/Audio Brandon

THE EXTERMINATING ANGEL (EL ANGEL EXTERMINADOR) (Uninci Films 59, 1962)
Producer: Gustavo Alatriste
Assistant Director: Ignacio Villarreal
Screenplay: Luis Buñuel and Luis Alcoriza, from José Bergamín's unfinished play
Cinematographer: Gabriel Figueroa
Art Director: Jesús Bracho
Costumes: Georgette Somonhano
Music: Raúl Lavista, Scarlatti, Paradisi
Sound: José B. Carles
Editor: Carlos Savage
Cast: Silvia Pinal, Enrique Rabal, Jacqueline Audere, José Baviera, Augusto Benedico, Luis Beristain, Antonio Bravo, Claudio Brooke, César del Campo, Rosa Elena Durgel, Lucy Gallardo, Enrique García Alvarez, Ofelia Guilmain, Nadia Haro Oliva, Tito Junco, Xavier Loya, Patricia Moran, Bertha Moss, Ofelia Montesco, Angel Merino, Patricia de Morelos
Running time: 95 minutes

Premiere:	Mexico, May 8, 1962
16mm. rental:	MacMillan/Audio Brandon

DIARY OF A CHAMBERMAID (**LE JOURNAL D'UNE FEMME DE CHAMBRE**) (Speva Films—Cine Alliances Filmsonor [Paris] and Dear Film Produzione [Rome], 1964)

Producers:	Serge Silberman and Michel Safra
Assistant Directors:	Pierre Lary, Jean-Luis Buñuel
Screenplay:	Luis Buñuel and Jean-Claude Carrière, from the novel by Octave Mirbeau
Cinematographer:	Adolphe Charlet
Set Decoration:	Georges Wakhevitch
Costumes:	Jacqueline Moreau
Sound:	Antoin Petitjean
Editor:	Louisette Hautecoeur
Cast:	Jeanne Moreau, Georges Géret, Michel Piccoli, Françoise Lugagne, Jean Ozenne, Daniel Ivernel, Gilberte Geniat, Bernard Musson, Jean-Claude Carrière, Muni, Claude Jaeger, Dominique Sauvage
Running time:	98 minutes
Premiere:	Paris, March 4, 1964
16mm. rental:	Films, Inc.

SIMON OF THE DESERT (**SIMÓN DEL DESIERTO**), 1965

Producer:	Gustavo Alatriste
Screenplay:	Luis Buñuel and Julio Alejandro
Cinematographer:	Gabriel Figueroa
Music:	Raúl Lavista: "Drums of Calanda"
Sound:	James L. Fields
Editor:	Carlos Savage
Cast:	Silvia Pinal, Claudio Brooke, Hortensia Santovana, Jesús Fernández, Enrique del Castillo, Enrique Alvarez Félix, Luis Aceves Castañeda, Francisco Regueira, Antonio Bravo
Running time:	42 minutes
16mm. rental:	MacMillian/Audio Brandon

BELLE DE JOUR (Paris Film Production, Five Film [Rome], 1967)

Assistant Directors:	Pierre Lary, Jacques Fraenkel
Screenplay:	Luis Buñuel and Jean-Claude Carrière from Joseph Kessel's novel

Cinematographer: Sacha Vierney
Art Director: Robert Clavel
Set Decoration: Maurice Barnathan
Costumes: Hélène Nourry
Sound: René Longuet
Editor: Louisette Hautecoeur
Cast: Catherine Deneuve (Severine Sevigny), Jean Sorel (Pierre Sevigny), Geneviève Page (Mme. Anais), Michel Piccoli (Henri Husson), Francisco Rabal (Hyppolite), Macha Meril (Renée), Pierre Clementi (Marcel)
Running time: 100 minutes
Premiere: Paris, May 24, 1967
16mm. rental: Hurlock Cine World

THE MILKY WAY (LA VOIE LACTÉE) (Greenwich Films [Paris], Medusa [Rome], 1969)

Producer: Serge Silberman
Assistant Directors: Pierre Lary, Patrick Saglio
Screenplay: Luis Buñuel and Jean-Claude Carrière
Cinematographer: Christian Matras
Art Director: Pierre Guffroy
Costumes: Jacqueline Goyot
Music: Luis Buñuel
Sound: Jacques Gallois
Editor: Louisette Hautecoeur
Cast: Paul Frankeur, Laurent Terzieff, Delphine Seyrig, Edith Scob, Bernard Verley, François Maistre, Claude Cerval, Georges Marchal, Jean Piat, Jean-Claude Carrière, Julien Guiomar, Marcel Pérès, Michel Piccoli, Alain Cuny, Pierre Clementi, Michel Etcheverry, Julian Berthau, Claudio Brooke
Running time: 98 minutes
Premiere: Paris, March 15, 1969
16mm. rental: Warner Bros, Non-Theatrical Division.

TRISTANA (Epoca Film/Talia Film [Madrid], 1970)

Producer: Robert Dorfmann
Assistant Directors: Pierre Lary, José Puyel
Screenplay: Luis Buñuel and Julio Alejandro, from the novel by Benítez Pérez Galdós

Cinematographer: José F. Aguayo
Set Decoration: Enrique Alarcón
Sound: José Nogueira and Dino Fronzetti
Editor: Pedro del Rey
Cast: Catherine Deneuve, Fernando Rey, Franco Nero, Lola Gaos, Jesús Fernández, Antonio Casas
Running time: 105 minutes
Premiere: France, May 1970
16mm. rental: MacMillan/Audio Brandon

THE DISCREET CHARM OF THE BOURGEOISIE (LE CHARME DISCRET DE LA BOURGEOISIE) (Greenwich Film Production, 1972)

Producer: Serge Silberman
Screenplay: Luis Buñuel and Jean-Claude Carrière
Cinematographer: Edmond Richard (in color)
Art Director: Pierre Guffroy
Editor: Helene Plemiannikov
Cast: Fernando Rey (The Ambassador of Miranda), Jean-Pierre Cassel (M. Senechal), Stéphane Audran (Mme. Senechal), Paul Frankeur (M. Thévenot), Delphine Seyrig (Mme. Thévenot), Bulle Ogier (Florence), Julien Bertheau (Bishop), Claude Pierplui (Colonel), Michel Piccoli (Home Secretary), Muni, Milena Vukotic
Running time: 105 minutes.
Premiere: Paris, September 15, 1972 (shown at New York Film Festival, October 14, 1972)
16mm. rental: Films, Inc.

THE PHANTOM OF LIBERTY (LE FANTÔME DE LA LIBERTÉ) (Greenwich Films, 1974)

Producer: Serge Silberman
Screenplay: Luis Buñuel and Jean-Claude Carrièrre
Cinematographer: Edmond Richard
Set Decoration: Pierre Guffroy
Costumes: Jacqueline Guyot
Sound: Guy Villette
Sound Effects: Luis Buñuel
Editor: Hélène Plemiannikov
Cast: Adriana Asti, Julian Bertheau, Jean-Claude Brialy, Adolfo Celi, Paul Frankeur, Michel Lonsdale, Pierre Maguelon,

	François Maistre, Hélène Perdrière, Michel Piccoli, Claude Pieplu, Jean Rochefort, Bernard Verley, Monica Vitti, Milena Vukotic
Running time:	104 minutes
Premiere:	Paris, September 1974
35 mm. Rental:	Twentieth Century-Fox

THAT OBSCURE OBJECT OF DESIRE (CET OBSCUR OBJET DU DÉSIR) (Greenwich Film Production–Galaxy Films [Paris]–Incine [Madrid], 1977)

Producer:	Serge Silberman
Assistant Directors:	Pierre Lary and Jean-Luis Buñuel
Screenplay:	Luis Buñuel and Jean-Claude Carrière, from Pierre Loüys's *La Femme et le pantin*
Cinematographer:	Edmond Richard
Art Director:	Pierre Guffroy
Sound:	Guy Villette
Editor:	Hélène Plemiannikov
Cast:	Fernando Rey, (Matthias), Carole Bouquet and Angela Molina (Conchita), Julien Bertheau, André Weber, Milena Vukotic, María Asquerino, Ellen Bahl, Valerie Bianco, Augusta Carrière, Jacques Debary, Antonio Duque
Running time:	103 minutes
Premiere:	Paris, 1977

Index

DISCARDED